The Court of Comedy

The Court of Comedy

Aristophanes, Rhetoric, and Democracy in Fifth-Century Athens

Wilfred E. Major

The Ohio State University Press
Columbus

Copyright © 2013 by The Ohio State University.
All rights reserved.

Library of Congress Cataloging-in-Publication Data
Major, Wilfred E., 1967–
The court of comedy : Aristophanes, rhetoric, and democracy in fifth-century Athens / Wilfred E. Major.
p. cm.
Includes bibliographical references and index.
ISBN 978-0-8142-1224-0 (cloth : alk. paper) — ISBN 0-8142-1224-7 (cloth : alk. paper) — ISBN 978-0-8142-9326-3 (cd)
Rhetoric, Ancient—History. 2. Greek drama (Comedy)—History and criticism. 3. Aristophanes—Criticism and interpretation. I. Title.
PA3265.M34 201
882'.01—dc23
            2013001523

Cover design by AuthorSupport.com
Text design by Juliet Williams
Type set in Adobe Garamond Pro

∞ The paper used in this publication meets the minimum requirements of the American National Standard for Information Sciences—Permanence of Paper for Printed Library Materials. ANSI Z39.48–1992.

9 8 7 6 5 4 3 2 1

Contents

List of Abbreviations		vi
Acknowledgments		vii
Introduction		1
Chapter 1	Sicilian Pioneers of Comedy and Rhetoric and Their Transmission to Athens	23
Chapter 2	Old Comedy and Proto-Rhetoric in Athens before 425 B.C.E: The Age of Pericles	36
Chapter 3	The Young Comic Playwrights Attack, 425–421 B.C.E.	51
Chapter 4	The Years of Confidence, 421–414 B.C.E.	115
Chapter 5	Crawling from the Wreckage, 411 B.C.E.	133
Chapter 6	Tongues, *Frogs*, and the Last Stand	146
Epilogue		179
Appendix	Catalog of Terminology, Practitioners, and Institutions Related to Rhetoric in the Remains of Fifth-Century Comedy	185
Bibliography		207
Index locorum		221
General Index		225

Abbreviations

AS   Ludwig Radermacher. *Artium scriptores: Reste der voraristotelischen Rhetorik.* Vienna, 1951.

DK   Hermann Diels and Walther Kranz. *Die Fragmente der Vorsokratiker.* 7th ed. Berlin, 1954.

LGPN   M. J. Osborne and S. G. Byrne. *Lexicon of Greek Personal Names.* Vol 2: Attica. Oxford, 1994.

Olson   S. Douglas Olson. *Broken Laughter: Select Fragments of Greek Comedy.* Oxford, 2007.

PA   Johannes Kirchner. *Prosopographia attica.* 2 vols. Berlin, 1901.

PAA   John S. Traill. *Persons of Ancient Athens.* 21 vols. Toronto, 1994–2012.

PCG   Rudolph Kassel and Colin Austin. *Poetae comici graeci.* 8 vols. Berlin, 1983–2001.

The Greek text of Aristophanes' complete plays follows that of N. G. Wilson (*Aristophanis: Fabulae.* 2 vols. Oxford, 2007), except where noted.

The numbering and text of comic fragments follow that of PCG, except where noted.

Acknowledgments

This book has been so long in gestation, more than half of my life, that even an extensive list of names of individuals who were essential and invaluable to the final product would be woefully inadequate. Therefore, my being so limited and selective in naming a few should not diminish the importance of so many others. First, I want to thank the many scholars and performers of ancient drama, some of whom I have been fortunate enough to perform with, but all of whose expertise and collegiality have inspired the best of this book throughout. Timothy Long, Mathew Christ, and Edward Schiappa guided my dissertation and the long evolution afterwards. Frederick Williams and Tony Earls initially fired my passion for Aristophanes, while Joan O'Brien and Charles Speck broadened my understanding of the classical world. My parents, Virginia B. Major and Wilfred J. Major, each in different ways shaped, inspired, and cultivated my love of learning and devotion to the life of a scholar. Anything in this volume of merit should reflect positively on what I have learned from others, while its deficiencies are mine exclusively. Accordingly, I want to note two valuable volumes: David Sansone's *Greek Drama and the Invention of Rhetoric* and a collected volume edited by C. W. Marshall and George Kovacs, *No Laughing Matter: Studies in Athenian Comedy*. Both arrived on my desk too late in 2012 for me to capitalize on them in my own work. Special mention goes to Jeffrey Carnes for producing an index of a MS loaded with citations of fragments. Finally, at The Ohio State University Press, Eugene O'Connor has been amazingly supportive and Marian Rogers improved the manuscript beyond my hopes.

Introduction

Aristotle is working out the characteristics of the discipline of rhetoric (ῥητορική), when he makes a sharp distinction about those attending a speech: ἀνάγκη δὲ τὸν ἀκροατὴν ἢ θεωρὸν εἶναι ἢ κριτήν, "The listener must be either a spectator or a judge" (*Rhet.* 1.3.2.1358b2–3). He then divides judges into those who judge about the future, as in the Assembly, and those who judge about the past, as jurors in court, but reckons spectators as those who judge merely a speaker's ability. He delves at length into the mechanisms at play in persuading judges, but spectators disappear from his analysis. According to Aristotle, then, spectators play only a superficial role in the Assembly and courts. In using this terminology, knowingly or not, Aristotle shuts down and dismisses what had been a lively debate two generations earlier, a debate about the deliberative process not only in the Assembly and courts, but also in the Athenian democratic Council and in another venue where spectators routinely rendered judgments—the theater.[1]

This debate suffused discussion in a range of genres and public venues for decades, but the year 427 B.C.E. was pivotal. Events of that year proved

---

1. For a broad discussion about the governing and efficacy of Athenian democracy and deliberation, see Ober (2008). For surveys of the discussions about modern "deliberative democracy," see Elster (1998) and Gutmann and Thompson (2004). For these issues applied to Aristophanes, see Zumbrunnen (2012).

seminal for the history of (comic) drama and of rhetoric, but equally for the history of the Greek world, especially for Athens and its ill-fated imperial ambitions. Two ancient historical accounts of the year, separated by time and perspective, differ in some details but agree that fascination with language in performance shaped the way the Athenians forged their political decisions. The earlier account appears in Thucydides, who wrote his history after his exile from Athens, and with a decade or two of hindsight, but he would still have resided in the city in 427.[2] The later version Timaeus of Tauromenium composed in the late fourth or early third century B.C.E., thus with no first-hand experience of the events, but bringing a perspective from his native Sicily, a major player in 427, and being able to reflect on the consequences of the year's events for the political and military history of both Athens and Sicily. He also wrote after Aristotle had composed his *Rhetoric*. Timaeus' interpretation lies behind the account preserved in Diodorus, who wrote his version some two centuries later, in the first century B.C.E., by which time rhetoric was a well-established technical industry central to elite education.

The accounts agree that by the end of 427 B.C.E., the Athenians were engaged in a rare winter military campaign, their first military engagement with Sicilian forces, on the Aeolian islands just north of Sicily. Likewise they agree that the campaign was precipitated earlier that year by the city of Leontini seeking support from the Athenians against the domination of Syracuse. Thucydides ascribes the success of the Leontines' appeal to nascent Athenian imperial ambitions in Sicily (3.86). The account of the embassy in Diodorus agrees with the motive offered by Thucydides but adds that the Leontine embassy succeeded because the famous speaker and intellectual Gorgias was the premiere ambassador.[3] In Diodorus' account, a dazzling oration in favor of the alliance enthralled the Athenians:

οὗτος οὖν καταντήσας εἰς τὰς Ἀθήνας καὶ παραχθεὶς εἰς τὸν δῆμον διελέχθη τοῖς Ἀθηναίοις περὶ τῆς συμμαχίας, καὶ τῷ ξενίζοντι τῆς λέξεως ἐξέπληξε τοὺς Ἀθηναίους ὄντας εὐφυεῖς καὶ φιλολόγους. πρῶτος γὰρ ἐχρήσατο τοῖς τῆς λέξεως σχηματισμοῖς περιττοτέροις καὶ τῇ φιλοτεχνίᾳ διαφέρουσιν, ἀντιθέτοις καὶ ἰσοκώλοις καὶ παρίσοις καὶ ὁμοιοτελεύτοις καί τισιν ἑτέροις τοιούτοις, ἃ τότε μὲν διὰ τὸ ξένον τῆς κατασκευῆς ἀποδοχῆς ἠξιοῦτο, νῦν δὲ περιεργίαν ἔχειν δοκεῖ καὶ φαίνεται καταγέλαστα πλεονάκις καὶ κατακόρως τιθέμενα.

---

2. Ober (1998, 94–104) analyzes Thucydides' presentation of the debate in terms of the tensions between democracy and tyranny.

3. [Plato,] *Hippias Major* 282b also mentions this trip and Gorgias' success. This would be more valuable testimony if Platonic authorship were secure, but, if nothing else, it is likely an early specimen of the perspective that the embassy was a triumph for Gorgias himself.

τέλος δὲ πείσας τοὺς Ἀθηναίους συμμαχῆσαι τοῖς Λεοντίνοις, οὗτος μὲν θαυμασθεὶς ἐν ταῖς Ἀθήναις ἐπὶ τέχνῃ ῥητορικῇ τὴν εἰς Λεοντίνους ἐπάνοδον ἐποιήσατο.

Now when he [Gorgias] came down to Athens and was introduced to the people, he engaged in conversation with the Athenians about the alliance, and by the exotic manner of his speech stunned the Athenians, who are clever and love speeches. For he was the first to use structures of speech that were rather unusual, yet lovingly crafted in their unorthodoxy, such as antitheses, equal and balanced clauses, similar endings, and other such things, all of which at that time were received positively because of the exotic nature of the tricks being delivered, but now come across as precious and silly in their fullness, especially when employed excessively. In the end he persuaded the Athenians of an alliance with the Leontines, and, having made his impact in Athens for his rhetorical skill, made his return to Leontini. (12.53.3–5)[4]

Thucydides does not mention Gorgias in his account of the embassy, but his history of the year does include comment on the Athenian mania for the spectacle of a good orator. Following a revolt at Mytilene, debate ensues in Athens about punishment for the rebels. The Assembly voted to execute the entire male population and enslave the rest, but the next day brought renewed debate about the decision. Thucydides here introduces the original bill's sponsor, Cleon, "the most violent of citizens in other respects and by far the most persuasive with the Demos at the time" (ἐς τὰ ἄλλα βιαιότατος τῶν πολιτῶν τῷ τε δήμῳ παρὰ πολὺ ἐν τῷ τότε πιθανώτατος, 3.36.6).[5] Thucydides has Cleon, in defending his motion, sharply criticize the Athenian fascination with performed speeches:

αἴτιοι δ᾽ ὑμεῖς κακῶς ἀγωνοθετοῦντες, οἵτινες εἰώθατε θεαταὶ μὲν τῶν λόγων γίγνεσθαι, ἀκροαταὶ δὲ τῶν ἔργων, τὰ μὲν μέλλοντα ἔργα ἀπὸ τῶν εὖ εἰπόντων σκοποῦντες ὡς δυνατὰ γίγνεσθαι, τὰ δὲ πεπραγμένα ἤδη, οὐ τὸ δρασθὲν πιστότερον ὄψει λαβόντες ἢ τὸ ἀκουσθέν, ἀπὸ τῶν λόγῳ καλῶς ἐπιτιμησάντων καὶ μετὰ καινό-

---

4. All translations are my own, except where indicated.
5. Throughout this book I leave the Greek word δῆμος untranslated, or more accurately, just transliterated as "Demos." I do this because I want to be clear and consistent about when Greek sources use the term, and because no English word corresponds to the sense of the Demos as both the mass populace and the franchised citizen body of Athens. Greek at this time of course has no orthographic means (such as capitalization) to distinguish a generic instance of the word from a formal, legal designation.

τητος μὲν λόγου ἀπατᾶσθαι ἄριστοι, μετὰ δεδοκιμασμένου δὲ μὴ
ξυνέπεσθαι ἐθέλειν, δοῦλοι ὄντες τῶν αἰεὶ ἀτόπων, ὑπερόπται δὲ
τῶν εἰωθότων, καὶ μάλιστα μὲν αὐτὸς εἰπεῖν ἕκαστος βουλόμενος
δύνασθαι, εἰ δὲ μή, ἀνταγωνιζόμενοι τοῖς τοιαῦτα λέγουσι μὴ ὕστε-
ροι ἀκολουθῆσαι δοκεῖν τῇ γνώμῃ, ὀξέως δέ τι λέγοντος προεπαινέ-
σαι, καὶ προαισθέσθαι τε πρόθυμοι εἶναι τὰ λεγόμενα καὶ προνοῆσαι
βραδεῖς τὰ ἐξ αὐτῶν ἀποβησόμενα, ζητοῦντές τε ἄλλο τι ὡς εἰπεῖν
ἢ ἐν οἷς ζῶμεν, φρονοῦντες δὲ οὐδὲ περὶ τῶν παρόντων ἱκανῶς·
ἁπλῶς τε ἀκοῆς ἡδονῇ ἡσσώμενοι καὶ σοφιστῶν θεαταῖς ἐοικότες
καθημένοις μᾶλλον ἢ περὶ πόλεως βουλευομένοις.

You are to blame for setting up these contests; you are accustomed to being spectators at speeches, mere hearers of deeds. As for deeds to be done, you determine their possibility on the basis of someone's capable speaking, while for what has already been done, you do not consider your sight more reliable than what you have heard, on the basis of someone honoring the past with a pretty speech. Superb at being deceived by the strangeness of an argument, unwilling to agree with a decision even after it has been approved; slaves to the eternally eccentric, despisers of the ordinary, absolutely everyone wants to speak first himself, or if not, to struggle to seem to follow the ideas of those saying all this, to declare praise sooner than someone can say anything, and yet preferring to be eager for what's said while also to be slow about the consequences of it. You seek out something other, so to speak, than the world in which we live; you give insufficient thought to your circumstances. Completely dominated by the pleasure of sound, you resemble seated spectators before performers more than those deliberating about their city. (3.38.4–7)

While there is no doubt that there was a cultural fascination among the Athenians for oratory, these historians differ sharply in tone and context. For Thucydides, the fondness for dynamic public speaking eviscerates the intelligent deliberative process that should guide the city.[6] Writing with at least some perspective of the later consequences of the events of 427, Thucydides tacitly embeds the idea that the stakes are high. Five seasons into war with Sparta, scarcely two years after the death of Pericles, the Athenians are finally experiencing a reprieve from the plague (which will surge again later in the year) and making decisions that will shape their long-term policies in the

---

6. For analysis of Thucydides' models of deliberation and democracy, see Pope (1988), Yunis (1991), Zumbrunnen (2008) and Foster (2010, 119–220). For debate about this passage's relevance to deliberation on the tragic stage, see Hesk (2011, 121–27) and Heath (2011, 167–69).

war and their relations with the rest of the Greek world. While he is narrowly defeated in his appeal to sustain his motion in favor of executing the Mytilenians, Cleon himself will come to dominate Athenian war policy and lead the city all but irrevocably on a path toward more blunt pursuit of empire. The alliance with Leontini will mushroom into the monstrous and disastrous expedition against Sicily a dozen years later, arguably the decisive turn in the entire Peloponnesian War.

For Timaeus and Diodorus, the embassy from Leontini in 427 not only foreshadows the later Athenian expedition to Sicily but also showcases a fellow Sicilian, and historical hindsight allows them some perspective on Gorgias, specifically that he was a pioneer in the techniques of rhetoric, but his style seemed dated and primitive in a world where education and practice in formal rhetoric was highly technical and professionalized. Still, the later account recognizes the impact that Gorgias' unusual methods of speech making must have had on the Athenians and the long-range legacy of the fascination of Athenian audiences, or spectators, for inventive oratory.

Another Athenian, however, also put on a show for those crowds of spectators in 427 and also commented explicitly and forcefully on the issues raised in both historical accounts: the functioning of the Athenian democracy, the policies Athenians should pursue in war and empire building, the role of public oratory in both, the influence of intellectualism via foreigners, and the flowering of unorthodox language. A young Aristophanes made his debut at the Theater of Dionysus with *Banqueters* (frr. 205–55) that same year, prior to both the debate over Mytilene and the embassy from Leontini. The play involved two young men of markedly different character, "a decent one and a butt-fuck," as he would refer to them a decade or so later (ὁ σώφρων τε χὠ καταπύγων, *Clouds* 529).[7] The repugnant youth competes with an older man regarding language usage. In one fragment, the adolescent challenges his elder on the meaning of words in Homer and Solon (fr. 233). In another (fr. 205), the older man picks at unusual words in the young man's speech and connects them to problematic speakers in the public sphere in Athens.[8] Some terms he says belong to speakers in the Assembly and courts (ῥητόρων and ξυνηγόρων). Other terms he links to particular speakers. Alcibiades makes an early appearance here, a decade before his crucial role in the Sicilian expedition (cf. fr. 244), as does Thrasymachus, a shadowy figure for modern scholars (aside from the fiery character Plato makes of him in the *Republic*), but repeatedly cited in ancient accounts

---

7. *Clouds* was originally put on in 423 B.C.E., but this line comes from a section securely assigned to the revision of the play in ca. 417. See Kopff (1990), Storey (1993) and Henderson (1993).

8. See Chapter 2 and the Appendix for text, translation and discussion of this fragment.

of pioneers who developed rhetoric.⁹ Also cited is Lysistratus, but, whatever his reputation in 427, he is almost totally obscure now, even if he is to be identified with other scattered jokes about a Lysistratus in other plays.¹⁰

The obscurity of these references does not reduce the significance and seriousness of the matters Aristophanes addresses. It only reminds us that Aristophanes was writing and reacting to events and people before he could have the historical perspective of Thucydides and other sources years and centuries later. Gorgias had yet to visit Athens, and Aristophanes could not know that the strange turns of language he had already heard and dramatized would come to be reckoned the beginnings of an institutionalized program that would dominate education for more than a millennium. And yet the issues embedded in the brief fragments of Aristophanes' debut signal the same concerns as Thucydides' Cleon, as there is anxiety that showy, troublesome verbiage makes so marked an appearance in the language of public deliberation at Athens. Unfortunately, the remains of *Banqueters* do not permit productive speculation about how far Aristophanes dramatized and commented on the political and cultural stakes at risk in the deployment of this language, but his later career confirms these risks were consistently critical topics for him. After the military season of 427 and after Gorgias' visit, Aristophanes returned to the stage the next year with *Babylonians* (frr. 67–100), which, according to ancient testimony, in some form addressed the issue of Athens' governance of its empire and reportedly drew the ire of Cleon himself. How far and how directly Aristophanes staged and commented on the political institutions of Athens in these first two plays is not clear.¹¹ Based on the eleven surviving plays over the next four decades, it would not be surprising if Aristophanes had earlier dramatized and commented explicitly on the political bodies of the Athenian democracy and what role the new, unorthodox language played in them. Indeed, no extant play fails to address the bundle of issues raised by the historical accounts of 427.

In contrast to the historians, comic playwrights in Athens had to react, comment and develop their perspectives virtually in real time, very much as

---

9. AS.6–7, 10–11 and 13). Storey (1988) argues that the Thrasymachus of this fragment is not the same man cited in later sources. Cf. the Appendix and Aristotle, *Rhet.* 3.1.7.1404a12–16, where Aristotle says Thrasymachus commented on acting.

10. See Olson (2002, 285–86, on *Ach.* 855) for a survey of the problem; cf. the entry in the Appendix.

11. Σ *Ach.* 378 says Cleon brought Aristophanes before the Council. If, as some think, the scholiast had access only to other plays, this report might relate to events in *Babylonians* rather than to historical reality. *Banqueters* (fr. 216) and *Babylonians* (fr. 75) hint at trials in court. For a reconstruction of the feud between Aristophanes and Cleon, along with a helpful survey of relevant bibliography, see Storey (1995).

the speakers and the language were evolving to become, only after Aristophanes' lifetime, a specialized professional discipline and mainstay of political discourse. Such is the paradox and value of Aristophanes as witness and source for the early years of the development of rhetoric: he composed plays about the language without the benefit or restriction of a historical narrative to orient his observations; he embedded the phenomenon in the politics and culture of democratic Athens; he engaged in spectacle of the sort that Thucydides' Cleon finds contemptible; yet his comedies remain the most extensive explicit commentary contemporary with the crucial, but shadowy, invention of rhetoric across the first century of its development.

Thus the historical narratives are fundamentally unlike the testimony of Aristophanes' plays, but the account in Diodorus also typifies a perspective found in almost all surviving testimony about the oratory, speakers and theorizers of rhetoric from Aristophanes' lifetime, a narrative structured according to an Aristotelian template: initial creation followed by selective accretion and refinement as a discipline matures into a stable and sophisticated system. Thus Gorgias is a pioneer in some techniques, while other techniques are deprecated as rhetoric advances toward the system later authors could take for granted. By contrast, the attack Aristophanes mounts in 427 takes place well before our major sources composed their characterizations of Gorgias and his contemporary intellectuals, characterizations that became canonical. Plato, for example, was still an infant, decades away from launching his own historical narratives, which would relegate the thought and expression of Gorgias, Protagoras and others to the margins, and beyond, of productive intellectual pursuit. It is after Aristophanes' career is over that Plato, Isocrates, Alcidamas and others define and marginalize "Sophists" as those engaged in ephemeral verbal trickery.[12] Still later, when Aristotle composes the *Rhetoric* and includes an anthology of the development of rhetorical theory and practice, he inherits this formulation, new and old written sources are available to him, and he can take for granted that rhetoric is a discipline of fundamental civic and pedagogical importance. While Aristotle cites scripts of some plays for examples of rhetorical tropes, he scarcely looks to fifth-century Greek comedy for examples of rhetorical language, and never for historical context.[13]

---

12. On Plato's separation of "rhetoric" from philosophy, see McCoy (2007); and on Plato's engagement with drama and other genres in demarcating *philosophia,* see Nightingale (1995). On the way Plato construes drama as public rhetorical performance, see D. Carter (2011). For analogous studies of Isocrates and Aristotle, see McCabe (1994), Schiappa (1999, 162–201) and Haskins (2004). For Alcidamas in this context, see Muir (2001, vii–xv). On the issue more broadly, see Wardy (2009).

13. Aristotle cites *Babylonians* (fr. 92) for diminutives (*Rhet.* 3.2.15.1405b28–32) and a line

Except for imaginative extrapolations, scholarship during the Hellenistic, Roman and Byzantine periods hewed closely to Aristotle's narrative of rhetoric's birth and first century of development.[14] Until recently, modern scholarship maintained this allegiance to Aristotle, both in the way scholars narrated the development of techniques and in the way they evaluated and characterized early practitioners, as well as the exclusion of comedy, except for comparison of Aristophanes' *Clouds* to Plato's narrative of the antinomy between Socrates and the now so-called early Sophists.[15] In recent decades, however, scholars have engaged in a substantial revision of Aristotle's narrative and of his evaluation of intellectual activity in the fifth century.

The intellectuals now termed the Older Sophists have enjoyed a considerable rise in their stock.[16] Many hands have contributed to this resurgence, but G. B. Kerferd's work provides a sober review of the vicissitudes of the Sophists' reputation and has generated pragmatic approaches for subsequent study. As Kerferd illustrates, the Sophists long suffered at the hands of scholars and philosophers whose axiomatic precepts made them predisposed to fall in line with the criticisms leveled by Plato and Aristotle.[17] Conversely, in the last two decades, the ideas of the Sophists have benefited from recent schools of thought that allow greater interface with the intellectual challenges posed by Gorgias and others. In part, this has fostered a cottage industry in using the fragmentary, but provocative, remains of the Sophists' writings to articulate a sort of "sophistic rhetoric" for the modern, or post-modern, world.[18] The current study, however, seeks rather to

---

from an unspecified play of Aristophanes (fr. 649) for an antithesis (3.9.9.1410a28–29). Cf. Chapter 2 on Pericles for Aristotle's swipe at comic poets generally.

14. Cicero (*De inv.* 2.2.6) says that in his day, because of the success of Aristotle's summary history of early rhetoric, *nemo illorum praecepta ex ipsorum libris cognoscat, sed omnes, qui quod illi praecipiant velint intellegere, ad hunc quasi ad quendam multo commodiorem explicatorem revertantur,* "No one learns the precepts [of Aristotle's predecessors] from their own writings, but those who wish to know what principles they espoused come back to him [Aristotle] for a far more amenable explanation." Extant references to the early history of rhetoric are consistent with Cicero's characterization. Cf. Cole (1991b).

15. For typical examples of citing Aristophanes with respect to Plato's disparagement of Sophists, see McCoy (2007, 12, 39, 79 and 165, in contrast to Plato) and Romilly (1992, 83–89 and 134–43, supporting Plato). For an example of using Aristophanes to construct a modern critique of Socrates, see Nussbaum (1980).

16. The issue of who was a "Sophist" in antiquity is fraught with controversy, on which see Kerferd (1981, 42–58) and Schiappa (2003, 3–12). Because this study focuses on comedy's reaction to rhetoric, I am less concerned with whether any given individual should properly be reckoned a Sophist, although I will analyze comedy's use of the term σοφιστής in Chapter 2 and the Appendix. In any case, my aim is to cite and discuss any individual identified in comedy with speech making and language theory, regardless of whether the label "Sophist" applies.

17. Kerferd (1981, 4–12).

18. On the strengths and weaknesses of this approach, see Schiappa (1990b) and (1991). For an example of an updated version of this approach applied to democratic theory, see Crick (2010).

delineate the impact of intellectual investigation into language, including the techniques used in practical settings, against the political and cultural background of democratic Athens in the fifth century B.C.E. The contributions of this study to the reconstruction of a "sophistic rhetoric" should be construed as limited to two areas: making the evidence of Aristophanes and other fifth-century comic texts available and accessible for use in such reconstruction, and, in the process, clarifying the limits of historical reconstruction, since the study of the fragmentary remains of the Sophists' writing sometimes leads to claims that in the fifth century certain topics and techniques abided, when consulting other ancient sources strongly argues against such claims.[19]

When it comes to historical reconstruction, however, no component of the study of the Sophists has perhaps undergone so extensive a revision as that of the early history of rhetoric. The key points of the birth and development of rhetoric, from the mid-fifth century down to the mid-fourth century, that is, prior to Aristotle's *Rhetoric,* remained remarkably consistent from antiquity through most of the twentieth century.[20] The narrative begins on Sicily in the middle of the fifth century, where Corax and Tisias, in response to the pragmatic needs of the political environment, began laying out the precepts of speech composition and persuasive speaking. These precepts migrated to Athens via traveling teachers and intellectuals like Gorgias, along with a philosophical view that effective persuasion was an acceptable goal in itself, even at the expense of truth or justice. Plato reacted to this emerging tradition by separating rhetoric from philosophy proper and undermining the Sophists' claims to philosophical coherence. Later, Aristotle would acknowledge the risk of rhetoric, if someone "bent the ruler" (εἴ τις ᾧ μέλλει χρῆσθαι κανόνι, τοῦτον ποιήσειε στρεβλόν, *Rhet* 1.1.5.1354a) to deceive a jury (by making them angry, for example), but nevertheless offered a historical model for the development of rhetoric and an elaborate taxonomy of techniques, a summation of three generations of speakers refining various techniques and strategies.[21] For scholars following and detailing

---

19. An *argumentum ex silentio* is always difficult, but even so, reasonable caution and precision can be expected. For example, Consigny (2001, 43–44) makes a claim for the centrality of *kairos* to Gorgias' thought, but none of the texts he cites even use the term. It is one thing to acknowledge that ancient testimony indicates that Gorgias wrote about *kairos* (82 B13 DK), and even to attempt to reconstruct how such an idea fit into Gorgias' thought, but it is quite another to operate as if we have any text where Gorgias discusses the concept or even deploys the term. The presence, absence and limitations of meaning of key terms will be a recurring topic in this study.

20. Schiappa (1999, 3–10) catalogues seventeen points of agreement in the "standard" or "traditional" scholarly account of rhetoric prior to Aristotle.

21. On the unity of the *Rhetoric,* see Gross and Dascal (2001). On the problematic history of scholarship on the purpose and unity of the *Rhetoric,* see Poster (1997).

this scenario, the teaching of persuasive rhetoric was reckoned central to the Sophists' mission and fundamental for their popularity and success.

Since 1990, however, a new narrative has emerged. First, the centrality of rhetoric to the Sophists' teaching vanished with the recognition that there was effectively no evidence that the group of fifth-century intellectuals agreed on much of any central doctrine, that some of them were not known to have explored anything that could be construed as rhetoric, and that they did not promote doctrines consistent with what their later detractors held them responsible for. Indeed, the very word "rhetoric" (ῥητορική) was not available until well into the fourth century.[22]

A much less centralized and more diverse picture of the intellectual debate about language in the fifth century was now possible. Independently of each other, in 1991 Thomas Cole and Edward Schiappa offered fundamentally revised versions of the development of rhetoric prior to Aristotle.[23] Each in different ways saw Plato as a key figure in declaring rhetoric a focalized point of inquiry, not as reacting to an established discipline. For both scholars, Aristotle was thus capitalizing on a relatively recent development in having the techniques of speech composition and language manipulation formalized, but more importantly, in writing the *Rhetoric,* more than cataloguing established practices, Aristotle was actively shaping the history and methods of rhetoric into a system.[24] Thus, prior to Plato's inventive conceptual work (especially in *Phaedrus*), the study of "rhetoric" was fundamentally distinct from what followed and not simply a rudimentary core of what would become the taxonomy promulgated by Aristotle. For Cole, the explorations into language were "proto-rhetorical" at most and involved much more basic experiments with language against the backdrop of a transition from orality to literacy.[25] For Schiappa, the fifth century was an open marketplace of ideas in competition to determine the scope and methods for language exploration. Inspired by Kuhn's analysis of the way scientific research programs develop, collapse and reconstitute, Schiappa reckons Plato and Aristotle as key figures in establishing the "normal" research protocols for a new discipline, "rhetoric," but that the generation prior to Plato was engaged in much different work, reacting against their own predecessors

---

22. Schiappa (1990a), *pace* the objections of O'Sullivan (1993); cf. Schiappa (1994) and Pendrick (1998).

23. Cole (1991a) and Schiappa (2003, revised from 1991 edition).

24. See Wise (2008) for an analysis of Aristotle's *Poetics* that similarly finds him reacting to drama more as it was practiced in his own day than to fifth-century practice. Cf. the response to this thesis in Hanink (2011).

25. Cole (1991a, esp. 71–94). For convenience, I adopt his term "proto-rhetorical" for the cultural investigation into language that Old Comedy dramatizes and satirizes (cf. the Appendix).

(pre-Socratics like Parmenides, for example), and pursuing a wide range of intellectual exploration, much of it tied to the limits and capabilities of human speech.[26]

The reaction to Cole's and Schiappa's work has been debate and division, with scholars acknowledging, extending or rejecting the new narrative. Thus some engaged in the process of reconstituting the significance of what was rhetoric for the Sophists continue to push their characterizations beyond the traditional narrative, even if they do not necessarily follow Cole and Schiappa.[27] Some persist with the traditional model.[28] Others extend the new ideas into new areas, such as Ekaterina Haskins, who revisits the role of orality and literacy in Isocrates and Aristotle, and Michael de Brauw, who wrestles with the consequences of the new model for technical aspects of speeches, while David Timmerman, Schiappa and Christopher Tindale extend the theoretical discussion and probe the analytical consequences for our understanding additional fourth-century texts about rhetoric and the Sophists.[29]

Any stand in this debate involves characterizing what was transpiring with "rhetoric" (however defined) and language in the decades immediately prior to Plato's writings on the subject.[30] As productive as the discussion has been, it has remained limited in some respects. While an increasing number of texts have been brought to bear, these have been limited almost entirely to prose writings by and about the intellectuals in the debate. This choice already critically circumscribes the debate, since the choice to write technical prose in the fifth and fourth centuries was to declare allegiance to a certain range of cultural priorities.[31] So in some ways modern scholars work with a more limited type of sources than even Aristotle did, for drama, historiography and oratory play limited or no roles as resources for current attempts to understand the theory and practice at the time.[32] Needless to say, Aristotle's disregard for comedy persists. Once again, then, the testimony of Aristophanes is critical but underutilized, although his career, indeed the entire heyday of Old Comedy, spans exactly the period when rhetoric was

---

26. Schiappa (2003, esp. 77–81, 157–62) and (1999, esp. 10–13).

27. See Poulakos (1995) in general; Consigny (2001) and McComiskey (2002) on Gorgias; Mendelson (2002) on Protagoras.

28. Wardy (1996); Usher (1999); Pernot (2005).

29. Haskins (2004); Poulakos and Depew (2004); de Brauw (2007); Timmerman and Schiappa (2010); Tindale (2010).

30. For various recent perspectives on this debate and time frame, see Schiappa and Hamm, Gagarin, and Bons, all in Worthington (2007).

31. Cole (1991a, 115–38).

32. For some surveys, see Roisman (on Homer), Clay (on Hesiod), McDonald (on tragedy) and Fox and Livingstone (on historiography), in Worthington (2007). For Hubbard's contribution on comedy in the latter volume, see below.

said to have been birthed and developed. Unlike other authors of the period, however, he discusses the phenomenon explicitly and as it happens.

Scholarship on Aristophanes, in turn, has made limited exploration of the importance of rhetoric in his plays. Well before the sea change in the appreciation for the Sophists and the revision of the historical narrative of early rhetoric, Charles Murphy contributed some initial analysis of rhetoric in Aristophanes.[33] Consistent with the prevailing narrative of early rhetoric at the time, Murphy studies Aristophanes' plays for evidence of core techniques and structures from canonical rhetoric, quadripartite division and so on. He offers the provisional conclusion that Aristophanes was aware of basic core techniques and deployed them, and Murphy appends schematics of speeches from the plays to illustrate his point. No one continued Murphy's work for fifty years, until Maria de Fátima Sousa e Silva explored the topic again.[34] While she brings more text to bear, including fragments, her analysis and conclusions effectively repeat Murphy's tentative conclusions.

In the wake of the challenge of Cole and Schiappa, there has been an uptick in attention paid to rhetoric in Aristophanes, but of a limited or reactionary nature. D. M. MacDowell's survey of Aristophanes was the first to include a section about rhetoric in Aristophanes, however brief.[35] Neil O'Sullivan has been aggressive not only in rejecting challenges to the traditional narrative but also in contending that Greek comedy deployed formal critical terminology with regard to rhetoric and literary language, terminology that persisted in Hellenistic scholarship.[36] Subsequently Thomas Hubbard has come out upholding the idea that comedy reflects formal, organized rhetorical practice.[37]

O'Sullivan and Hubbard each approach the challenges of Cole and Schiappa by analyzing comedy of the fifth century to cull evidence for active rhetorical theory and practice reflected in the plays. In doing so, they share a methodology that skews their selection of comic material and their interpretation of the evidence in the plays. Both work backward from later models and theories of rhetoric and formal criticism, from periods when the terminology, infrastructure and evidence are much more detailed and extensive than they are for the fifth century, the period of the comic sources they mine. Focusing on somewhat different details, each cites terms and other supposed

---

33. Murphy (1938).
34. Sousa e Silva (1987–88).
35. MacDowell (1995, 131–32).
36. O'Sullivan (1992), (1993); cf. Rosen (2004), Hunter (2009, 10–52) and Pontani (2009). Bers (1997) provides some close technical readings on the reproduction of speech in drama.
37. Hubbard (2007).

parallels in Aristophanes, which they claim illustrate that components of rhetorical theory or analogous tools of rhetorical analysis are referred to in the plays. Such vestiges then become evidence for some disciplinary activity in the fifth century comparable to post-Aristotelian activity.

The issue of terminology encapsulates the debate, in that all sides agree that the presence and usage of formal terminology, sometimes called "metalanguage," is crucial for arguing the presence or absence of formal analytical activity. O'Sullivan argues at length that comedy, and Aristophanes' *Frogs* in particular, feature terminology that has a long tail of influence in later stylistic criticism, itself under the umbrella of rhetorical theory. Hubbard asserts that theoretical analysis could have been conducted that would not likely have survived in our written sources but that nonetheless "comedy clearly shows speakers engaged in self-conscious linguistic and discursive strategies."[38] The weakness of Hubbard's position becomes clear when he discusses specific terminology. He concedes there is nothing in Aristophanes comparable to the jargon found a century later in comedy.[39] Among words in comedy that "probably refer to current rhetorical terms," he finds only four, and only one holds up under scrutiny. Hubbard cites προοίμια from *Knights* 1343, but the context makes clear that it refers not to the first section of a speech (its meaning in canonical rhetorical theory later), but to a greeting, its standard meaning in the fifth century. The Sausage-Seller (now revealed as Agoracritus) is describing the earlier behavior of the Demos:

πρῶτον μέν, ὁπότ' εἴποι τις ἐν τ' ἠκκλησίᾳ,
"ὦ Δῆμ,' ἐραστής εἰμι σὸς φιλῶ τέ σε
καὶ κήδομαί σου καὶ προβουλεύω μόνος,"
τούτοις ὁπότε χρήσαιτό τις προοιμίοις,
ἀνωρτάλιζες κ'ἀκερουτίας.

First, whenever someone in the Assembly said,
"O Demos, I am your lover and I love you,
And I care about you and I'm the only one who cares for your welfare,"
Whenever anyone used *greetings* like this,
You would flap your wings and shake your horns. (*Kn.* 1340–44)

---

38. Hubbard (2007, 491) presents this argument as if it were one Cole and Schiappa would dispute; in fact, both agree that speakers engaged in techniques of persuasion, but each in his different way (despite Hubbard conflating them) finds this activity fundamentally distinct from the industry of rhetorical analysis a century later, a distinction Hubbard denies but does not discuss.

39. Hubbard (2007, 503); cf. Cratinus Jr. fr. 7.

Another term, τεκμήριον, is not technical at all. It is the word rhetoricians and orators use for "evidence," but it is the only noun available (as opposed to a number of verbs meaning "show," "demonstrate," etc.) and as such not formal or technical, but simply the standard word for referring to evidence. Nothing in its usage suggests it has a more restricted meaning in rhetorical contexts or that untrained speakers and audiences would have used any other, nontechnical word in its place. Hubbard speculates that Aristophanes in *Banqueters* (fr. 205) satirizes a term associated with Thrasymachus, ὑποτεκμήριον. The term is merely an inference from the verb in the fragment; the noun is unattested and the verb, ὑποτεκμαίρῃ, is scarcely attested except in this passage, which suggests that it is, like other words in the same passage, a coinage by Aristophanes mocking the unorthodox vocabulary of certain notorious speakers.[40] No one denies that intellectuals of the time deployed language in unorthodox ways and that comic poets took note of these eccentricities. Nonetheless, just because language use is unorthodox or speakers are talking about the differences does not mean their analysis of language corresponds to rhetorical theory of a century later. In all of surviving fifth-century comedy, only one word potentially corresponds to its usage in canonical rhetoric, ἀντίθετον.[41]

O'Sullivan makes a more complex argument, but with the same fundamental flaws. He seizes mostly on metaphors used in comedy to describe language, speaking and style. Terms describing loud and boisterous speakers also turn up in later authors describing style (e.g., ψόφος, "noisy," and variations on βρεντᾶν, "thundering"), from which O'Sullivan concludes the key terms in such metaphors were in fact nascent critical terminology that later rhetoricians and scholars inherited and used as formal analytical vocabulary. This conclusion goes well beyond the evidence. O'Sullivan does identify some parallels in terminology and metaphor between Aristophanes and rhetoricians of later times, but he never addresses the limitations of such parallels. It does not require formal critical analysis for a comic poet, or a Hellenistic scholar for that matter, to describe the language of a verbose speaker as some sort of storm or concise language as "thin" (λεπτός).[42] D. Müller, by contrast, makes the case that much metaphorical language in Aristophanes is parody, posing a fundamental challenge to O'Sullivan's

---

40. Pollux 9.151 uses the verb, but it does not illuminate this passage. Cf. Bonanno (1983, 62–63).

41. Aristophanes fr. 341 (not *antithesis*, as Hubbard quotes it). The fragment might be a later gloss and not fifth-century language at all. See the entries in the Appendix for this and the other terms discussed here.

42. O'Sullivan (1992, 107–23).

argument, in that Aristophanes' metaphors thus have a consistent, immediate referent in the dramas and orators being parodied, not in a system of formal vocabulary for criticism.[43] More recently, Andreas Willi probes the nature and limits of "technical language" in Old Comedy and finds that the technical vocabulary of literary criticism, even in *Frogs,* is all but lacking.[44] Ultimately, O'Sullivan has no more explicit or direct evidence than Hubbard that references to language or style in fifth-century comedy imply a formal analytical system. The persistence of some of the metaphors isolated by O'Sullivan can indicate that later critics used at least some of these metaphors to the point that they became ossified as technical terms,[45] but as far as fifth-century comedy is concerned, O'Sullivan's parallels at most suggest that later rhetoricians and scholars, because of their familiarity with classical texts, invoked, and expected their readers to recognize, metaphors culled from Aristophanes.

The arguments of O'Sullivan and Hubbard perhaps gain some traction among scholars because their conclusions are attractive. Proposing a direct parallel in comedy to canonical rhetoric offers greater hope of understanding and systematizing the interpretive work taking place in Aristophanes, in drama in general and in fifth-century Athens more broadly, and if that system has direct descendants in later writings, then the system and the diachronic progression of it offer more intelligibility for scholars. Moreover, with fragmentary material, such a model offers hope that we can organize scattered terminology in a systematic way and that fragments can be placed in some kind of relation to each other in the large puzzle of ancient comedy, drama and antiquity. This is much more appealing than the image of terminology that is simply not part of a larger system, which was deployed *ad hoc* and for a much more immediate and irrecoverable cultural context, and with no demonstrable *Nachleben.*

What hurts the efforts of O'Sullivan and Hubbard most is that they comb through comedy searching for and selecting material that fits the more familiar systems from later periods. Neither seeks to establish how fifth-century comedy treats the developments in language, the manners of speakers and the contexts in the plays, before they build a case around par-

---

43. Müller (1974). O'Sullivan (1992, 123 n. 112) finds Müller's conclusions "questionable" but offers no reason his own method is more reliable.

44. Willi (2003, 51–95, esp. 87–94). Willi responds to Denniston (1927) rather than to O'Sullivan, but the principle is the same. Willi concludes: "On the whole very little supports the claim that *Frogs* makes much use of an established technical language of literary criticism" (92). For a more sophisticated view of the genesis of literary criticism, see Ford (2002, esp. 188–208).

45. Hunter (2009) pursues this idea.

ticulars. Playwrights of all places and times, of course, dramatize events to reflect and comment on the world they experience. Aristophanes and his contemporaries dramatized trials, debates and other occasions where speakers employed persuasive language, but doing so does not require an established or nascent formalized system of critical terminology to describe speech making. Aeschylus dramatized persuasive speech making in the *Eumenides* in 458 B.C.E., and no scholar seriously contends that these speeches correspond to the canonical methods of a rhetorical speech, but, even though nothing in comedy corresponds any better, the idea that comedy must reflect formal rhetoric persists, primarily because the (inaccurate) historical progression promulgated by Aristotle contends it should.

Integrating Aristophanes' testimony into the narrative of early rhetoric requires analyzing his examples and comments in the context of his dramatization of the sociopolitical life of the Athenian democracy, for all his comments come in this context.[46] In this area, scholarly debate about Aristophanes' role, oriented with respect to the ideology of the Athenian democracy, has become lively. The same year Murphy's article on rhetoric in Aristophanes appeared, A. W. Gomme declared politics in Aristophanes a "threadbare topic," but the following decades have found scholars ever increasingly taking stands and elaborating reasons for and against claiming Aristophanes' allegiance to some political orientation.[47] While scholars in antiquity could associate Aristophanes' harsh treatment of public figures with the freedom of democracy, modern scholarship began by aligning Aristophanes with oligarchic and antidemocratic sympathies.[48] Jeffrey Henderson proposed a model wherein stage comedy serves as a safe venue to voice ideas fraught with ideological and political tension in the democracy.[49] In this sense, Aristophanes plays a role in the democratic process rather than criticizes it.[50] Into this fray Malcolm Heath issued a bracing and valuable

---

46. See Rhodes (1986, esp. 140–41) for the significance of speech making in Athenian politics in the later decades of the fifth century.

47. Gomme (1938).

48. For ancient examples of testimony that Aristophanes and Old Comedy represented democracy, see T62, 65–67, 80, 83b in PCG. Müller-Strübing (1873) is the starting point for modern discussion of Aristophanes' political orientation as oligarchic, but the most-often-cited modern expression of the idea is Ste Croix (1972); cf. the surveys in Henderson (1990), Walsh (2009) and Olson (2010a). For a refutation specifically of Ste Croix, see Pritchard (2012).

49. Henderson (1990).

50. Henderson (1998b) revisits and amplifies his model. Burian (2011) focuses on tragedy (cf. Chapter 6) but offers a generalized model comparable to Henderson's. Cf. Christ (1998, 104–17) on sycophancy in comedy, which, while playing on class tensions and aristocratic criticisms of democracy, nonetheless belongs to the broader civic ideology of Athens. Konstan (2010) analyzes Aristophanes' critique of Athens' war policy along the same lines. Rothfield (1999) argues, primarily out of passion,

critique of the criteria and argumentation employed by many in the debate, and pointed to several areas where the discussion merits more sustained and coherent analysis: comparison between public speakers on Aristophanes' stage and evidence from extant oratory, the presence or lack of discernible policies advocated or deprecated in Aristophanes' plays, and the imprecision of declaring the cultural and historical context for the reception of comedy by Aristophanes' audiences.[51] More recently, scholars have capitalized on work involving ideology, rhetoric and the ritual construction of citizenship.[52] Here again disparate conclusions continue. James McGlew finds comic protagonists, in pursuing their individual desire for pleasure,[53] oppose the aristocratically imposed ideal of physical and ethical self-restraint, while D. Rosenbloom finds comedy a component of criticism of democratic hegemony because it marginalizes the "new elite" as *ponēroi*.[54]

The focus on how citizens individually and collectively defined themselves through civic processes finds overlap with scholarship on rhetoric. Drawing on sociology and anthropology, scholars have constructed nuanced models for how citizens in democratic Athens, by participating as a group in ritualized collective decision making, both in political institutions (Assembly, Council, court) and theater, established, maintained and perpetuated the democracy. Josiah Ober and Barry Strauss provide a useful paradigm for comparing such rituals in the form of courtroom oratory and stage drama, even from different periods, leading to a productive cross-examination of each.[55]

The performance of ritual also requires a link to one more emerging strand in scholarship on ancient drama, that of performance criticism. Especially for tragedy, scholars have become increasingly imaginative with, and

---

for democratic partisanship. Sidwell (2009) proposes a democratic Aristophanes on the strength of an elaborate sequence of comic poets manipulating each other's identities in their plays, a scenario that strains credibility. Cf. Storey (2003, 281–88).

51. Heath (1998). Sommerstein (2005) responds to one of Heath's challenges by articulating practical enactments preferred in Aristophanes' vision of an "anti-democracy." Heath's critique is especially sharp toward Goldhill (1991, 167–22) and relevant to supporters of the idea of comedy in an insulated "carnival" environment. On the "carnival" model, see the survey in Reinders (2001, 10–14). Spielvogel (2003) attempts to make Aristophanes a moderate between the extremes of the Old Oligarch and radical democrats. B. Zimmermann (2005) tries to redefine the question with Freudian theory. Robson's (2009, 162–87) introductory essay on Aristophanes may suggest that currently the view of Aristophanes as antidemocratic still predominates. For orators' use of comedy, see Harding (1994) and Pontani (2009).

52. For example, Davidson (1997) and Zumbrunnen (2012).

53. McGlew (2002).

54. Rosenbloom (2002).

55. Ober and Strauss (1990), which builds on Ober (1989); cf. the overview of this sort of work in Wohl (2009).

sensitive to, the degree and manner in which ancient Greek playwrights constructed meaning on stage in addition to, and even in contradiction to, the direct verbal expression preserved in our scripts. Comedy has come rather later to the game, but full-length treatments of performance in comedy by Martin Revermann and Alan Hughes indicate much productive work is to come.[56] Such analysis will be critical for full description and analysis of Aristophanes' treatment of rhetoric and speakers in his plays. His comedies feature far more than verbal examples of political and rhetorical speech making. In four of the extant plays, Aristophanes stages parodies of the Assembly in action: *Acharnians*, *Knights*, *Thesmophoriazusae* and *Ecclesiazusae*. The deliberations of the Council constitute a reported scene in *Knights*, and the authority of the Council is crucial for the plots of *Peace*, *Lysistrata* and *Thesmophoriazusae*. The courts are the subject of routine jokes, in addition to generating virtually the entire plot of *Wasps*. Most famously and notoriously, Aristophanes builds most of an entire play, *Clouds*, around the perpetuation of such language. Indeed, every single extant play comments on speakers and language in relation to the function of the Athenian *polis* as a political and cultural system.[57] Aristophanes is not shy about blurring the distinction between the activity on stage and the functioning of these institutions outside the theater, such as when the personified Theoria in *Peace* is restored to the members of the Council seated in their prescribed area in the theater itself.

This study aims to weave together all these strands of scholarship to argue three overlapping points. (1) The references to orators and theorizing about rhetoric in Old Comedy confirm the newer paradigm of the early development of rhetoric, namely, that in the fifth century there was competition among intellectuals to determine the modes of formal analysis of language, not yet focalized under the rubric "rhetoric," but that rival models did not (as traditional histories do) concentrate on the arrangement of parts of speeches and the like. (2) Aristophanes and some other comic playwrights, initially at least, considered the use of proto-rhetorical language as inimical to the democratic process, but, following the challenges to the Athenian democracy in the wake of the disaster of the Sicilian expedition, Aristophanes reframes the problem as what formal rhetorical techniques the Demos should allow as a component of democratic debate. (3) Aristophanes' stance toward proto-rhetorical devices, and his depiction of Athenian democratic institutions more broadly, indicate he fundamentally operates within the mechanisms

---

56. Revermann (2006); Hughes (2012); and cf. Scharffenberger (2008).
57. See the Appendix for a catalog of these scenes.

of internal criticism of the Athenian democracy and not external, oligarchic opposition to it. These arguments unfold over six chapters, which proceed chronologically.

In the first chapter, "Sicilian Pioneers of Comedy and Rhetoric and Their Transmission to Athens," both stage comedy and rhetoric are reputed to have their earliest expression in the cities of Sicily in the mid-fifth century. Reliable information about the importance of developments on Sicily for the exponents of both rhetoric and comedy in Athens is scarce, but some links and parallels are worth exploring. The tradition of the Sicilians Corax and Tisias as "inventors" of rhetoric is now mostly discredited, but the intellectual milieu of Sicily certainly had an impact on Athens when Gorgias made his famous visit in 427 B.C.E. The relationship between Sicilian comedy and Athenian comedy is even less clear, but writings of the comic playwright Epicharmus would eventually reach Athens, at least in the form of philosophical forgeries. Among the genuine fragments of Epicharmus' comedies, there is at least one example of a play staging the deployment of subversive reasoning (of a type later linked with "rhetoric") used by a character in a sympotic and then forensic context. The forgeries under the name Epicharmus can explain why in fourth-century Athens there were also hesitant references to Tisias as a pioneer of rhetoric.

In Chapter 2, "Old Comedy and Proto-Rhetoric in Athens before 425 B.C.E.: The Age of Pericles," a survey of the fragments confirms the revised history, which expects that there is no established technical vocabulary referring to rhetoric and speech making. References to oratory in the fragments of Athenian comedy are dominated by Pericles. The references to him as a powerful, booming Olympian all turn on his speech making. Consistently in comedy, Pericles' effective use of public speaking marks a contravention of the democratic process rather than a component of it. By 426 B.C.E., Pericles is dead, new politicians are on the rise, Gorgias has made a successful and popular visit delivering speeches in his new, unorthodox prose style, and Aristophanes recognizes that quirky new language in public speaking is having a cultural impact on Athens.

The next chapter, "The Young Comic Playwrights Attack, 425–421 B.C.E.," capitalizes on the survival of a complete extant play of Aristophanes for each year in the period 425–421 B.C.E. (*Acharnians, Knights, Clouds, Wasps* and *Peace*) and a handful of suggestive fragments, which constitute the most thoroughly documented period for tracing how stage comedy reacted to the emerging changes in public speaking and how Aristophanes portrayed that language in operation in the democratic institutions of Athens, at a time of considerable internal debate and stress. In *Acharnians,* before his protagonist Dicaeopolis departs from the daily reality of Athens, Aristophanes stages the dysfunctional deliberations of the Assembly and has his chorus make sharp comments about the new aggressive and unfair language being used by young prosecutors in the courts. While scholars have previously focused on Diceaopolis' speech to the chorus as an example of a formally arranged specimen of rhetoric, it does not in fact conform to canonical principles. The real lesson in oratory is that when Dicaeopolis engages in the proper democratic deliberative process, he succeeds wildly, but he must conduct deliberations outside of their proper venue (the Assembly) to do so. The next year, in *Knights,* Aristophanes stages the action of the Assembly and analyzes the relationship between deceptive public speech and the proper decision-making process of the Demos. Crucial in the play is that, unfettered by deceptive and undemocratic speech, the judgment of the Demos will be sound, and the city will prosper. Next, *Clouds* turns to the underpinnings of the theorizing behind the new formal language. Aristophanes puts two Logoi on stage (in a way implicitly linked to Protagoras' famous opposing *logoi*) in order to reveal the moral damage caused by them (rather than allowing them to be morally neutral accounts of experience). Although the morally dubious qualities of the reasoning of the Sophists were established *topoi* later, *Clouds* in fact is our earliest example of transforming an idea of the Sophists from one morally neutral to one morally threatening to the community. Aristophanes returns to the language of political institutions in *Wasps,* where he again asserts that the judgment of the Demos, and hence the operation of the courts, will function properly once "rhetorical" and undemocratic speech making is removed from the equation. Finally, in *Peace,* Aristophanes celebrates the removal of the very sort of speakers whose deceptive and destructive speech making has hurt the city, and dramatizes a functioning Council and a prosperous city.

For the next chapter, "The Years of Confidence, 420–412 B.C.E.," only one complete play and a number of fragments are available, but they suggest a turn in the comic poets' perception of public speech. Eupolis in *Demes* reconstitutes Athenians of the past, notably including now a positive reference to Pericles as a powerful speaker (fr. 102). In the present, Alcibiades is now the speaker with an eerie ability to inspire Athenians with his speech, but references in comedy are too scanty to assess the early reaction on the comic stage. More important is the aggressive persuasion of Peisetaerus in *Birds,* where flattering speech considered undemocratic in the previous decade is now positive, because it is congruent with the imperial ambitions of the Athenian Demos.

In Chapter 5, "Crawling from the Wreckage, 411 B.C.E.," following the disaster in Sicily, the judgment of the Demos comes under new suspicion and threats. The Demos allows for the creation of the committee of Probouloi to rein in the Demos' own power. Oligarchic factions gain momentum, culminating in the violent coup of 411. The Probouloi and the various incarnations of the short-lived oligarchy all had a central ideological core: that the decision-making process for Athens should be restricted to fewer hands than that of the entire collective Demos. In this environment, Aristophanes stages *Lysistrata,* which supports expanding, rather than contracting, the number of those entrusted with contributing to the deliberative process. Women, legally barred from participating as citizens, appear as sober, devout and responsible administrators. Lysistrata's central speech calls for casting an even wider net to draw in as many people as possible to guide the city. The Proboulos, the official symbolizing the bottleneck in the deliberative process, is ridiculed and drummed off the stage. Lysistrata's speech making calls for the Demos' renewed authority. Then *Thesmophoriazusae* dramatizes a parody of the Athenian Assembly. Now formal speech in the Assembly functions in support of democratic decision making. In the atmosphere of the oligarchic government, Aristophanes dramatizes the functioning Assembly only among women at a closed festival, but it is a smoothly functioning democratic institution, not an oligarchic one.

In Chapter 6, "Tongues, *Frogs,* and the Last Stand," on the eve of the end of the Peloponnesian War, the ensuing reign of terror of the Thirty and the reconstituted democracy, Aristophanes staged another play that probed the foundations of public language in theory and practice, and specifically the moral hazard involved. Before *Frogs,* Euripides, while not a threatening figure, was long linked with sophistic reasoning and language in Aristophanes and other comic playwrights, but his recent departure from Athens, and the democracy's renewed interest in tragedy as its ritual core, made him a newly controversial and problematic figure. Once again, as in *Clouds,* Aristophanes exposes the problem, identifying it not as the language itself but as the underlying threat language poses to the spiritual health of the Demos. Whether it is Euripides or the leading politicians of the day, Aristophanes explicitly links the surface qualities of a speaker to his ability to contribute to the health of the Demos. With twenty years of support for the Demos behind him, Aristophanes can now even call for the support of the exiles from the coup of 411 and be rewarded with a crown from the Demos.

Despite his early antagonism to the formal prose techniques of public speaking in the 420s and the reservations that resurface in *Frogs,* Aristophanes lives to see just such language become not the antithesis of democratic decision making, but the very language of democratic institutions after the democracy is renewed in 403 B.C.E. Aristophanes was right that elite speakers could, and at times did, use their access to this specialized language to achieve ends contrary to the best interests of the Demos, but he comes to reconcile that the elites can deploy such techniques in democratic institutions and the Demos can still sit in collective judgment and lead Athens to prosperity.

The Appendix itemizes the following: (1) formal terminology and techniques pertaining to rhetorical theory and oratorical practice (a crucial catalog, since much of the revision of the history of fifth-century "rhetoric" hinges on the presence and absence of specific terms); (2) portrayals of and references to historical figures, both intellectuals associated with new trends in language (i.e., the "Older Sophists") and public figures in Athens deploying such language; (3) representations in comedy of democratic institutions (Assembly, Council, courts), which are particularly important to an analysis of comedy's portrayal of rhetoric, in theory or practice, as the context of its commentary, and often the dynamic of a scene, convey as much meaning as any explicit statements within comedy.

The conclusions reached in this study will not, of course, settle the wide-ranging debates in any of the major areas of scholarship it addresses, but it is my hope that the analysis provided here will prove greater than the sum of its parts. The evidence of Aristophanes and Greek Old Comedy has a role to play in the ongoing revision of the early history of rhetoric. The political allegiances of Aristophanes will assuredly remain a contentious topic, but it is, in my opinion, healthy and productive that this is so. I hope everyone can agree that Aristophanes did not intend his plays merely to reinforce the status quo, in his own day or for anyone coming to his work in other times and places. His treatment of language and his staging of the political institutions in his own community merit consideration, as does his staging of the city of Athens, both as a physical space and as an ideological construct. Whether for the purpose of reconstructing Aristophanes' original spectacle or of preparing a performance for modern audiences, an improved grasp of the stage dynamics of Aristophanes' most topical material helps achieve the immediacy and impact for which he strove. Finally, however valuable the current study may be, I hope that research into Greek comedy, itself such a madcap blend of traditions, will continue to combine knowledge, insights and contributions from diverse explorations to create a fruitful and entertaining revue.

1

Sicilian Pioneers of Comedy and Rhetoric and Their Transmission to Athens

εἰσὶ δὲ καὶ ψευδεῖς ἀντιθέσεις, οἷον καὶ Ἐπίχαρμος ἐποίει·
τόκα μὲν ἐν τήνων ἐγὼν ἦν, τόκα δὲ παρὰ τήνοις ἐγώ.

There are also false antitheses, such as when Epicharmus wrote,
"Sometimes I was among them, and other times I was with them."

—Aristotle, *Rhet.* 3.9.10.1410b3–5, quoting Epicharmus fr. 145

Both comedy and rhetoric have Sicilian pioneers who preceded the better-preserved and better-known later Athenian practitioners. Also common to the early history of both comedy and rhetoric is that recovering the accomplishments of these pioneers is hobbled by limited fragmentary remains and by later pseudographic sources that distort what little information has been preserved. These difficulties raise substantive issues for reconstructing and understanding the transmission of Sicilian traditions to Athens, with consequences for the revised history of early rhetoric and how Athenian comedy responded to it.

THE SICILIAN FOUNDERS OF RHETORIC IN THE FIFTH CENTURY

The reputed founders of the discipline of rhetoric were Sicilians from the middle of the fifth century named Corax and Tisias. Ancient sources recite that, after the Sicilians had thrown out their tyrants and began establishing democracies, especially in Syracuse, there grew a need for effective speech making in public debate, and one source links this need to the disputes over the distribution of property.[1] This scenario would put their activity in the 460s and 450s. From this start, then, would develop an environment in which persuasive speech was paramount, methods to that end increasingly valuable, and in turn from this environment would arise a speaker and thinker like Gorgias, who then makes his famous embassy to Athens in 427 B.C.E. Other links can be inferred for the transmission from Sicily to Athens. Cephalus, father of the orator Lysias, for example, was a wealthy immigrant in Athens but was originally from Syracuse.

Much of this early Sicilian narrative is insecure and controversial. First, the historicity of Corax has fallen into doubt. He is not attested in the earliest sources, and patterns in later sources indicate that he may be a doublet or nickname ("crow") for Tisias.[2] In any case, most of the post-Aristotelian accretions to the story of these founders can be dispensed with for purposes of historical reconstruction. The limited references just to Tisias even in the classical period are problematic in themselves. He is first named in Plato's *Phaedrus* (266e–67e), of the fourth century, linked to arguments from probability. One difficulty is a comment Plato adds at one point about Tisias: ὁ Τεισίας ἢ ἄλλος ὅστις δή ποτ' ὢν τυγχάνει καὶ ὁπόθεν χαίρει ὀνομαζόμενος, "Tisias, or whoever else he might be and wherever he might take his name from" (273c). If Tisias already had the nickname Corax, perhaps this is an oblique reference to it, but it also suggests Plato is aware of a slipperiness with regard to Tisias' name and ideas. Later, Aristotle makes him the first name among pioneers of rhetoric, but not the first overall, being Τεισίας μὲν μετὰ τοὺς πρώτους, "Tisias after the first ones" (*Soph. el.* 33.183b31), the others not being named, again a hint that, even for Aristotle, Tisias was not simply "the founder" of rhetoric. Because Aristotle has just been talking about the growth, through accretion, of the skills of rhetoric, scholars used to take Aristotle to mean that Tisias established the basic division of speeches (a claim later scholars of antiquity were happy to

---

1. AS (AV.6–11).
2. Cole (1991b).

infer as well), but in the wake of the work of Cole and Schiappa, this claim does not hold.³ Taking a fresh look at what Plato says of Tisias in *Phaedrus,* Michael Gagarin makes a strong argument that the significant development associated with Tisias was not speech division or just probability arguments, but specifically the reverse-probability argument (e.g., a smaller man argues that it was improbable that he would attack a larger man, but the larger man counters that, because he would likely receive blame, it is improbable that he would have started a fight).⁴ This would be a significant step toward applying arguments to either or both sides of a dispute and thus represents substantial progress toward more sophisticated, and sophistic, argumentation. Even if Gagarin is right, though, it does not explain why Plato and Aristotle are vague about Tisias as an individual or why his contribution would become a topic of interest and debate roughly a century after he supposedly laid the foundation for rhetorical speech making, points that will be taken up again later in this chapter.

SICILIAN COMEDY IN THE FIFTH CENTURY

Sicily was a creative center for drama in the early and middle fifth century, attracting Aeschylus early on to the court of Hieron of Syracuse, where he staged new plays. Sicily developed its own brand of stage comedy, but, as with rhetoric, its relationship to later Athenian productions is unclear and still debated.⁵ Of the handful of names known of these early Sicilian comic playwrights, only the fragments of Epicharmus provide more than the slightest material for study. The limited testimony points to a career including, but not necessarily limited to, the 480s and 470s and also including a probable meeting with Aeschylus. It is possible that his life and career extended into the 460s and beyond, but no surviving fragment or testimony requires a date beyond the 470s.⁶ Consequently, while it would be illuminating if Epicharmus' comedy reflected the activities of Tisias, the burgeoning democracies, or rhetorical practice and theory as they were developing in Sicily, there are no sure indications of this activity. The paucity of fragments means it is imprudent to draw any conclusions from this absence of evidence, but there

---

3. See Roberts (1904) for an example of how this framework can affect historical reconstruction. Roberts argues that the fragmentary rhetorical treatise on *POxy.* 410 was authored by Tisias himself in the 420s.
4. Gagarin (1994) and (2007).
5. Kerkhof (2001, 133–77).
6. See Olson (2007, 6–12) and Rusten (2011, 59–60) for an overview.

is one provocative fragment that raises issues for the legacy of both Sicilian rhetoric and comedy for later Athenian practice.

In the interest of thoroughness, what follows presents everything from Sicilian comedy that pertains to speakers and language. In terms of speakers, no fragment or testimony names or describes someone using rhetorical language or refers to someone otherwise linked with the history of rhetoric. Aristotle cites Epicharmus himself, but only to quote a single line as an example of a false antithesis (*Rhet.* 3.9.1410b3 = Epicharmus fr. 145, quoted above).

Because a crucial part of the revision of the history of early rhetoric focuses on the development of specifically technical vocabulary for rhetoric, it would be helpful to know if early Sicilian comedy reflected knowledge of any technical vocabulary with regard to rhetoric. No such vocabulary appears, and this is consistent with the arguments of Cole and Schiappa that such terminology develops a century later, but remains are too scanty for this argument from silence to constitute certainty.[7] Epicharmus did title one of his plays Λόγος καὶ Λογίνα (The Word and the Female Word).[8] The three brief fragments of the play, however, give no help with the title or much of the content of the play. The longest fragment, at three lines, refers to Zeus ordering a meal for Pelops, which suggests that, like the majority of Epicharmus' fragments, this one has a mythological setting (fr. 76). One fragment, a single line, lists seafood (fr. 78). The last fragment, a couplet, mentions another Sicilian comic poet, Aristoxenus, introducing iambic verse (fr. 77). The single line of Aristoxenus' writing to survive mentions the word ἀλαζονία, which is later applied to orators and rhetoricians, among others, but here modifies prophets (μάντεις).[9]

Epicharmus did use dialogue and thus opened the door to scenes of debate, although there is almost never enough of a fragment to indicate scene or context. Athenian drama makes extensive use of formal debate, and Athenian comedy in particular will explicitly link debate to philosophical and political institutions, but there are only potential hints at such material in Epicharmus. Five brief fragments, none linked to named plays, are consistent with the staging of discussion or debate within a play, but none requires that such a scene occurred:

---

7. Cf. Schiappa (1999, 3–84) on the importance of stable terminology for focalizing a discipline.

8. Readers may be alert to the gender bias in this translation, which, however, reflects the gender bias in the Greek; λόγος is grammatically masculine and would culturally be read, unmarked, as masculine, while the neologism λογίνα would be read as marked, for indicating female gender; how Epicharmus handled the gender dynamics is completely unknown.

9. See MacDowell (1990) on the history and use of ἀλαζών and related words.

Fr. 144 (unmetrical)

ἀρτίως τε γὰρ λέλεκται, καὶ εὐθέως φαίνεται οὐ καλῶς ἔχον.
As soon as it has been said, it immediately seems to be wrong.

Fr. 161

τὰ πρὸ τοῦ δύ' ἄνδρες ἔλεγον, εἷς ἐγὼν ἀποχρέω.
For what two men said before, I myself am sufficient.

Fr. 163

ἀλλὰ καὶ σιγῆν ἀγαθόν, ὅκκα παρέωντι κάρρονες.
But it's good to be silent, when your betters are present.

Fr. 175

ἅμα τε καὶ λόγων ἀκούσας ἀδύμων
at the same time listening to sweet words

Fr. 184

οὐ λέγειν τύ γ' ἐσσὶ δεινός, ἀλλὰ σιγῆν ἀδύνατος[10]
You are not inspiring at speaking, but incapable of staying quiet.

Nothing in these statements allows inferences about context, so there is no way to determine if such comments occurred in the topical political atmosphere found in Aristophanes and other Athenian comic poets. While in general most of the fragmentary quotations from Epicharmus have mythological contexts, there is some evidence that he explored more topical issues and set them in less remote settings. Among direct quotations, one fragment could require a more immediate setting and address civic life: the speaker charges the addressee with making the city uncultured (ἀγρὸν τὰν πόλιν ποιεῖς, fr. 219).

Beyond these isolated lines, the extant fragments are too brief to convey how Epicharmus staged scenes or constructed plots. The papyrus remains

---

10. This line, preserved in Gellius, might be the earliest appearance of the phrase δεινὸς λέγειν "awesome at speaking", which was used pejoratively of court speakers in Athens in the fourth century (e.g., Plato, *Apol.* 17b; Lys. 12.86; Isoc. 21.5; Dem. 22.66). The notoriety of the phrase, however, also makes the line a reasonable candidate for forgery (a problem to be addressed later in this chapter).

of *Pyrrha and Prometheus* (fr. 113) offer strands of hundreds of lines and, while not complete enough to provide coherent flow, do confirm the use of dialogue between characters and, so far, no participation by a chorus. The most extensive evidence, however, for what sort of scenes Epicharmus staged arrives yoked with a perennial philosophical problem and the most important extant link between him and the Athenian intellectual milieu.

As with the pioneer in rhetoric, Tisias, the earliest references to Epicharmus come in mid-fourth-century Athenian authors (e.g., the gnomic frr. 236 and 271 from Xenophon *Mem.* 2.1.20). By far the most important comes from Plato's *Theaetetus* (152e), where Socrates and Theaetetus are discussing the philosophical problems of perception and change, and whether change over time makes an individual a being distinct from who he was at an earlier time. Socrates groups Epicharmus with thinkers who agree that identity changes over time. A fragmentary commentary on papyrus explains Epicharmus' position on this issue in large part by summarizing how he dramatized the problem (fr. 136):

Ἐπίχαρμος, ὁμιλήσας τοῖς Πυθαγορείοις, ἄλλα τέ τινα εὖ ... κεν δράματ ... οὖ αὐξομένου, ὃ λόγῳ ἐφοδικῷ καὶ πιστῷ ἐπέραινε. οὐ μὴν ἀλλ' ὡς ἄφοδοι γίνονται πρόσοδοί τε ἐναργές, εἰ οὐχ ἑστώς τις γίνεται μείζων ἢ ἐλάττων· εἰ δὲ τοῦτο, οὐσίαι ἄλλοτε ἄλλαι γίνονται διὰ τὴν συνεχῆ ῥύσιν. καὶ ἐκωμῴδησεν αὐτὸ ἐπὶ τοῦ ἀπαιτουμένου συμβολὰς καὶ ἀρνουμένου τοῦ αὐτοῦ εἶναι διὰ τὸ μὲν προσγεγενῆσθαι, τὰ δὲ ἀπεληλυθέναι, ἐπεὶ δὲ ὁ ἀπαιτῶν ἐτύπτησεν αὐτὸν καὶ ἐνεκαλεῖτο, πάλιν κἀκείνου φάσκοντος ἄλλο μὲν εἶναι τὸν τετυπτηκότα, ἕτερον δὲ τὸν ἐγκαλούμενον.

Epicharmus, through his association with the Pythagoreans, in plays well explored (?) issues, including the problem of growth, which he accomplished with a methodical argument and proof. It is not obvious how approach becomes departure, if someone fixed does not become bigger or smaller. But if this happens, essences sometimes become different through constant flux. And he made comedy of this by having the same man requested to pay his share at a symposium and then refuse on the basis of becoming and departing, and, when the one who invited him struck him and was indicted, he in turn claimed to be someone other than the one who did the beating and who was indicted.

The commentary suggests six actions: (1) one man invites another to a symposium, and (2) when the guest refuses to pay his share, (3) he argues that he is no longer the same man who accepted the invitation; (4) the host in turn beats the guest, and (5) when indicted for battery, (6) he argues that he is no longer the man who did the beating. Plutarch alludes to these events in Epicharmus briefly, but perhaps with additional information (*De Sera num. vind.* 15.559a–b, also cited in fr. 136):

ταῦτά γε τοῖς Ἐπιχαρμείοις ἔοικεν, ἐξ ὧν ὁ αὐξόμενος ἀνέφυ τοῖς σοφισταῖς λόγος, ὁ γὰρ λαβὼν πάλαι τὸ χρέος νῦν οὐκ ὀφείλει, γεγονὼς ἕτερος, ὅ τε κληθεὶς ἐπὶ δεῖπνον ἐχθὲς ἄκλητος ἥκει τήμερον· ἄλλος γάρ ἐστι.

It's like this with the Epicharmians, among whom the argument arose about growth: for the one who owed a debt now does not owe it back, because he is someone else, and the one who was called to dinner yesterday is uninvited today, for he is someone else.

Plutarch's reference is brief but adds the additional element of someone refusing to pay back a debt by the same reasoning (he is no longer the same individual who incurred the debt). Aristotle also cites Epicharmus briefly in the context of repaying debts (*NE* 9.7.1167b17 = fr. 142). It is possible that Plutarch and Aristotle allude to an element from the plot of Epicharmus' play. The two pieces of testimony together strongly suggest that Epicharmus treated the issue at some length. At a minimum, the plot developments require some extended narration. If the storyline was not staged in the play, but only reported or narrated within a monologue, the entire sequence of events would still require a long-enough speech to explain who the two men are, and relate the invitation, the subsequent refusal, the violence, and the dialogue after the violence. A fully staged version of the events would contain the meal, potentially the invitation earlier in the play, certainly the slapstick, and potentially also a separate, subsequent scene in court playing out the indictment. Taken together, these scenes could make up a substantial portion of a play or an entire short one.

Supporting the idea of a staged version of events is fragment 146 (= Olson A15), which indicates that Epicharmus did stage sympotic scenes with dialogue in them. A short dialogue features two characters talking about behavior at symposia, with one character articulating how drunkenness leads to violent behavior and thence to legal trouble and finally to punishment.

† ἐκ μὲν θυσίας θοίνα
ἐκ δὲ θοίνας πόσις ἐγένετο.
(Β.)   χαρίεν, ὥς γ' ἐμοὶ <δοκεῖ>.
(Α.) ἐκ δὲ πόσιος κῶμος, ἐκ κώμου δ' ἐγένεθ' ὑανία,
ἐκ δ' ὑανίας δίκα, <'κ δίκας ἐγένετο καταδίκα>,
ἐκ δὲ καταδίκας πέδαι τε καὶ σφαλὸς καὶ ζαμία

   †A sacrifice leads to a feast,
and feast leads to drinking.
(B.)   Sounds good to me, at least!
(A.) But drinking leads to wandering the streets drunk;
   wandering the streets drunk leads to acting like a pig;
   acting like a pig leads to a lawsuit;
   <a lawsuit leads to being found guilty;>
and being found guilty leads to shackles, stocks and a fine.
(following the supplements of Dindorf in line 2 and Meineke in line 4, as printed and translated by Olson)

This fragment has a certain sociopolitical content, insofar as it expresses, in a compressed form, causality between unrestrained symposiastic behavior and punishment for that behavior meted out by established legal institutions. It is tempting to say that the scenario fits a democratic environment, since punishment is meted out through lawsuits and courts, with no reference to a local ruler, but such a suggestion is speculative. Nonetheless, combined with the summary testimony, this fragment makes a case that Epicharmus devoted a substantial portion of at least one comedy to dramatizing philosophical, civic and political tensions. It is thus the closest to evidence that Sicilian comedy, or at least Epicharmus, incorporated the issue of sophistic reasoning in a sociopolitical context, including political institutions like courts. Only the reasoning is highlighted in the testimony, however. No reference points to the particular manner or techniques either party used when constructing a speech in support of their position. Thus while the evidence is valuable in several ways, and the silence about speech-making techniques is not at all proof that Epicharmus did not raise the issue, there is no reference to any activity that would match any definition of "rhetoric."

Scholarship for the most part has studied this evidence with an eye toward parallels in later Athenian dramatic technique. Epicharmus was not the last comic poet to stage satire of communal and even political institutions through a sympotic situation. R. Kerkhof looks to Strepsiades in

Clouds and Philocleon in *Wasps* as potential *Nachleben*.[11] Likewise scholars have been drawn to other fragments for the speech of a parasite and various aspects of mythological parody in Epicharmus as direct predecessors of such material in later Athenian comedy.[12] With regard to the symposiastic setting, Kenneth Rothwell provides much evidence that many core techniques of Athenian comedy had their origins in performances at symposia.[13] If there is any direct link between Epicharmus and Athenian comedy, the institution of the symposium might provide it.[14] This is not to claim additional influence for Epicharmus on Athenian comedy except to suggest that it could be valuable to see this scene in Epicharmus as fundamental for Greek stage comedy's method of engaging its audiences with topical and cultural issues.

The philosophical issue debated here also has a legacy that raises further issues for the links between Sicily and Athens, with suggestive parallels to the transmission of early rhetoric. A series of forged writings in Epicharmus' name circulated and became popular. The date and origin of the various forgeries can be determined only within general limits, but Aristotle's pupil Aristoxenus is the earliest person we know of who specifically identified one of these works as a forgery (by identifying its true author, Athenaeus 14.648d = Aristoxenus fr. 45 Wehrli and cited in PCG as Epicharmus Ψευδεπιχάρμεια Ti). Circulation of these forgeries in the late fourth and early third centuries would also be consistent with a reference in Alexis to writings of Epicharmus (fr. 140 = Olson G3).

Among the forgeries was a work by an otherwise unknown Alcimus entitled *To Amyntas*. Alcimus evidently claimed that Plato had plagiarized a significant amount of doctrine from Epicharmus, and cited forged Epicharmic writings to make his case. One of these doctrines was Plato's position on the problem of growth and change.[15] Diogenes Laertius (3.11) preserves

---

11. Kerkhof (2001, 171–73) explores this topic with particular reference to the influence of Epicharmus for the rustic characterization of Strepsiades in *Clouds*.

12. See Olson (2007, 55) for bibliography.

13. Rothwell (2007, 6–35).

14. The possibility of a genetic link from sympotic scenes in Epicharmus to those in Athenian comedy also suggests that symposiastic contexts were core to comic performance, and it is worth exploring if it remained so more than has been appreciated to date. We are relatively well equipped to explore this possibility, since, because of Athenaeus, our remains of Greek comedy derive overwhelmingly from sympotic scenes. This is not to say that every symposium was the topic of philosophical or topical debate, or that every list of fish hints at intellectual discourse, but there might be more there than we realize if we are not just looking for civic, public contexts such as we are accustomed to in Aristophanes, or domestic scenes such we are accustomed to in New Comedy. Translocation of civic debate will be crucial in Aristophanes' plays (see Chapters 3–6). Cf. Wilkins (2000, 320–31) and Carrière (2003).

15. See *Prot.* 356e for the simile of odd/even and lesser/greater numbers, likely the reference for the forgery.

the forgery from Alcimus, which provides a glimpse of how Epicharmus' dramatic writings could be later reconstituted (Pseudepicharmia fr. 276):

(A.) αἰ πότ' ἀριθμόν τις περισσόν, αἰ δὲ λῇς πότ' ἄρτιον,
ποτθέμειν λῇ ψᾶφον ἢ τᾶν ὑπαρχουσᾶν λαβεῖν,
ἦ δοκεῖ κα τοί γ' <ἔσθ'> ωὑτὸς εἶμεν;
(B.)   οὐκ ἐμίν, γα κα.
(A.) οὐδὲ μὰν οὐδ' αἰ ποτὶ μέτρον παχυαῖον ποτθέμειν
λῇ τις ἕτερον μᾶκος ἢ τοῦ πρόσθ' ἐόντος ἀποταμεῖν,
ἔτι χ' ὑπάρχοι κῆνο τὸ μέτρον;
(B.)   οὐ γὰρ.
(A.)   ὧδε νῦν ὅρη
καὶ τὸς ἀνθρώπους· ὁ μὲν γὰρ αὔξεθ,' ὁ δέ γα μὰν φθίνει,
ἐν μεταλλαγᾷ δὲ πάντες ἐντὶ πάντα τὸν χρόνον.
ὃ δὲ μεταλλάσσει κατὰ φύσιν κοὔποκ' ἐν τωὐτῷ μένει,
ἕτερον εἴη κα τόδ' ἤδη τοῦ παρεξεστακότος.
καὶ τὺ δὴ κἀγὼ χθὲς ἄλλοι καὶ νῦν ἄλλοι τελέθομες,
καὖθις ἄλλοι κοὔποχ' ωὑτοὶ καττὸν αὐτὸν αὖ λόγον.

(A.) Then if someone to an odd number, or to an even one if you want,
wants to add a pebble or to take one away that is lying there,
does it seem to stay the same to you?
(B.)   Certainly not to me.
(A.) Nor, if to a thick measure someone wants to add
an additional amount, or to cut away from what is present,
would that measure remain?
(B.) No.
(A.)   So now look at
people: one grows and another shrinks,
and they are all in the process of change all the time.
But what changes naturally never remains in the same state:
it would be something other than that from which it transformed.
Even you and I were one thing yesterday but now become different,
and will never be the same again by the same reasoning.

The testimonia in fr. 136, the example of fr. 146 (cf. fr. 147 = Olson A14 for another snatch of dialogue in a sympotic setting) and the text of this forgery encapsulate the difference between fifth-century stage comedy and later writings under the influence of the Platonic style of promulgating philosophical doctrine. The speakers in the forgery bluntly lay out the philosophical topic with no hint of the stage action implied in frr. 136 and 146. This forgery served the purpose of trying to discredit an Athenian philosopher, but Epicharmus did dramatize the topic, and Plato seems to have been aware of the original dramatization. This gives some idea of how complex and problematic the reception of Sicilian influence in Athens could be, more so now through the fragmentary state of all these sources.

THE RECEPTION OF SICILIAN COMEDY AND RHETORIC IN ATHENS

Comparison of the evidence for the Sicilian pioneers of comedy and rhetoric does not yield certainty about the interrelation of the two genres, but it is suggestive and allows for some provisional conclusions. A chronology combining the two will be helpful. Aristotle would have Epicharmus established as early as the sixth century, nearly back to the time of Pythagoras, but other evidence points to a *floruit* in the 480s and 470s (not entirely incompatible with Aristotle, but it suggests his chronology should not be pushed to expect too much precision). Tradition, presumably Aristotelian, held that, following the overthrow of tyrants in the 460s, Tisias was a critical pioneer in developing techniques for speech making in the new democracies. Aristotle claims that Epicharmus and Sicilian comedy were the first to incorporate μῦθοι, "stories," into their comedies, and then cites Crates, active in the 450s and 440s, as the first Athenian comic playwright to do so (*Poetics* 1449b5–9). As noted above, Aristotle is circumspect in citing Tisias, and scholars have been rightly cautious with regard to how accurate Aristotle could have been about Epicharmus. Even the idea that Sicilian comedy was a crucial influence on Athenian comedy by the time of Crates is only an inference from Aristotle's brief statement.

The relevance of Tisias or the comic playwrights for Athenian practice, in either comedy or rhetoric, in the fifth century is not clear. Despite efforts to discern Sicilian influence on Athenian drama, "no positive evidence exists to suggest that Sicilian comedy (or other texts assigned to Sicilian comic playwrights) directly influenced any Attic author before the time of Plato and Xenophon."[16] Much the same is true for Tisias. Even if Gagarin is right about Tisias' importance for the development of the reverse-probability

---

16. Olson (2007, 11).

argument, its impact in Athens was limited at best until the time of Plato.[17] The early attempts at defining the proper components of a speech and their order, which the traditional narrative of the early development of rhetoric ascribed to Sicilian pioneers, is not yet in evidence in Athenian oratory from the fifth century.[18]

In Plato's *Phaedrus,* Tisias emerges as a topic of contemporary debate. Both Plato and Aristotle are cautious in referring to him. Around this same time, Plato cites Epicharmus in *Theaetetus*.[19] Aristotle cites and discusses Epicharmus in a limited way, but by this point Epicharmus was a poet of the distant past. If there was some chain of influence on Athens, direct or indirect, at the latest by the generation after Aristotle, Epicharmus' comedies were not circulating sufficiently to prevent the drastic rewrites of them. Rather than present an archaic Doric Sicilian comic scene, Alcimus presents a rewrite to make it contemporary and modern by fourth-century standards. Alcimus and others took the authentic fifth-century Sicilian Epicharmus and reinvented him as an authoritative ancestor in the development of fourth-century Athenian philosophy. Likewise, for both Plato and Aristotle, whatever circulated under Tisias' name in the fourth century was problematic enough for each of them to be circumspect in the way they referred to him, but they, too, faced the prospect of an authoritative mid-fifth-century Sicilian predecessor to Athenian achievement. There is no way to determine if the stories or writings attributed to Tisias were bald forgeries, rewrites of real material, or in fact authentic, but the coexistence of authentic and forged writings for Epicharmus, some used explicitly to discredit Plato, indicates there were parties ready, willing and able to insert Sicilian predecessors, of dubious veracity, into the narrative of the history of ideas, and specifically to try to claim credit for fundamental ideas prior to Athenian contributions.

Whatever the historical Tisias said, did or wrote to be invoked as a Sicilian founder of rhetoric is now beyond productive speculation, but the scenario reinforces Cole's and Schiappa's contention that formalized disciplinary study of rhetoric originated in fourth-century Athens, not fifth-

---

17. The First Tetralogy (Antiphon 2.2.3 and 2.2.6) makes use of the reverse-probability argument, but whether this results from a connection to the historical Tisias cannot be determined. See Gagarin (1997) 14.

18. Timmerman and Schiappa (2010, 153–70).

19. The date of composition of *Phaedrus* is still a matter of some dispute, but most evidence favors a late composition, close in time to *Theaetetus.* See Rowe (1986, 120–21). In the context of the idea that Sicilian influence is suddenly the rage near the mid-fourth century, while it is too much to say it is additional evidence, it is interesting that *Phaedrus* makes much of the oratory and rhetoric of Lysias, the son of a Syracusan.

century Sicily. Such a conclusion should not be taken as a disparagement of Sicilian accomplishments in speech making in the fifth century, but merely a lament that we can no longer recover what those accomplishments were. Had we access to even the slimmest of references to Tisias prior to his resurrection in the fourth century, we might find, as with Epicharmus, a vital and creative force, though perhaps in a rather different form than extant testimony leads us to expect. The diversity of the surviving fragmentary evidence is, however, perhaps a reminder of the wild and woolly ways that drama and oratory can intertwine in the milieu of the Greeks in the classical period.

In Athenian comedy, scenes that can seem like elaborations on the one found in Epicharmus do exist, such as the elaborate trial and Philocleon's subsequent disruptive behavior at a symposium in *Wasps*. Still, nothing allows us to confidently infer that Aristophanes or other Athenian comic playwrights reacted to or incorporated either comic or rhetorical traditions as Sicilian. For the purposes of the rest of this study, then, in analysis of Athenian comedy of the fifth century and for the duration of Aristophanes' career, Sicilian predecessors for both comedy and rhetoric will be considered beyond the playwrights' line of sight, except for individuals and ideas for which there is other evidence of links to Athens. Thus Gorgias' visit and reputation in the city provide a demonstrable link to Sicilian tradition, but the point is that Gorgias developed a distinct presence and reputation in Athens, as did other non-Athenians, and similarities to Sicilian rhetoric or comedy do not have resonance simply because of the pioneering creativity that flourished there. The next chapter, then, turns to Athenian stage comedy prior to the availability of the first complete extant comedy in 425 B.C.E., focusing on the fragmentary evidence for its engagement with intellectuals and their pursuit of language, along with testimony about the effects of these pursuits on the language used in public discourse.

2

Old Comedy and Proto-Rhetoric in Athens before 425 B.C.E.

The Age of Pericles

TOPICAL AND HISTORICAL SCOPE

The historical range for this study in general is the fifth century down to 404 B.C.E., the year of Athens' surrender to Sparta at the end of the Peloponnesian War and the year of the encore performance of Aristophanes' *Frogs*. The following year saw the reconstitution of the Athenian democracy, and subsequent comedy sees changes in form and topic; thus the fourth century merits a separate study utilizing criteria appropriate to the times and generic differences.[1] The aim of the current chapter is to survey and analyze evidence for comedy's reaction to proto-rhetorical and linguistic phenomena in Athens prior to 425 B.C.E. It is impossible to marshal all the relevant evidence and be absolutely strict about chronological borders. All evidence from comedy during this period is fragmentary, and while a number of fragments can be roughly assigned to the fifth century, it is frequently impossible to determine whether they originated before or after 425. By default this floating material will be cited in this chapter. In addition, several authors have careers that span both sides of the 425 divide, and again it is not always, or often, possible to place fragments within their career. Generally speaking,

---

1. See Ober (1989, 35–38) for the period 403–322 B.C.E. as suitable for synchronic study. On fourth-century comedy in general, see Arnott (2010).

however, Crates and Cratinus will be the focus of this chapter, even though Cratinus' career extends a few years beyond 425. On the other hand, Eupolis will appear in subsequent chapters for the most part, although his career begins a few years before 425.[2] Fragments of still lesser-attested playwrights of the time (most notably Hermippus, Pherecrates and Phrynichus), even if their careers spanned 425, are included in this chapter.[3] In some cases, the main text discusses fragments on a topic, and a note will discuss parallels that must belong to later years, although there is no noticeable change because of the chronological difference. For the most part, references to historical individuals in the comic fragments tend to be linked to later periods, so there is little discussion of them here, aside from Pericles. Fragments utilizing specific terminology, which are especially likely to be difficult to date, find a home in this chapter by default. This placement should not meaningfully distort the analysis and conclusions here. The chapter does not argue that comedy's treatment of proto-rhetoric fundamentally changed in or around 425; the arrangement merely reflects the state of the evidence. Subsequent chapters will be able to capitalize and focus on Aristophanes' extant plays, although they will incorporate evidence from contemporaneous fragments where available and relevant.

Following these principles, this chapter proceeds through the evidence for comedy's reaction to burgeoning rhetoric roughly as follows: (1) the terminology in comedy referring to language and speakers, primarily in public political discourse, but also with reference to developments in intellectual pursuits; (2) references to groups and individual speakers characterized in some way by their language or their link to developments in language study; (3) references to the public institutions in Athens where oratory and public displays of language took place, namely, the Assembly, Council, and courts; (4) comedy's depiction of language and speakers in the "Age of Pericles," since some distinctive issues arise with regard to Pericles himself.[4]

TERMINOLOGY

Consistent with recent research into the development of early rhetorical theory, and as with Sicilian comedy, the fragments of Old Comedy do not

---

2. The career of the comic playwright Plato falls wholly later, however, so he will be discussed in Chapters 4–6, on the last two decades of the fifth century.

3. On Pherecrates' dates, see now Olson (2010b).

4. The Appendix has entries for most of these items but groups all the fifth-century evidence topically rather than chronologically.

include the word ῥητορική or any of the formal terms canonized in the curriculum of rhetoric from the late fourth century onward, such as names for parts of speech.[5] The comic Phrynichus mentions τῇ διαθέσει τῶν ἐπῶν ("the arrangement of words," fr. 58), but there is no context. Some words appear that in the next century and later have different connotations for rhetoric and so merit glossing for their usage in the fifth century. Chief among these is the term σοφιστής, which at this point refers broadly to performers and to those who have some prestige for their wisdom.[6] In Old Comedy it never refers to the intellectuals now known as the Sophists.[7] Cratinus calls a group of poets a swarm of sophists (σοφιστῶν, fr. 2). Eupolis applies the term to a rhapsode (fr. 483). A σοφιστής is addressed in Eupolis fr. 388, but given parallel usage, this is most likely someone who in modern terms would be identified as a poet or performer.[8]

Another key term associated with the sophistic movement in the fifth century is εἰκός, which carries the overlapping meanings of both "proper" and "probable." Arguments based on the principle of probability were a hallmark of fifth-century thinkers and speakers engaging in the new, rational means for constructing arguments, examples being best preserved in the speeches of Antiphon.[9] Consistent with Old Comedy's antagonistic stance toward the new intellectuals and their distinct language, comic idiom never uses εἰκός in an argument built on probability. The term always carries the value-laden, more traditional sense of "proper." Thus Pherecrates deploys the term in a fragment probably spoken by a young man to an elder, perhaps his father: "it is proper (εἰκός) for me to be in love but past your season" (fr. 77). Cratinus says the tragedian Acestor will get a beating unless he tidies

---

5. On the chronology of ῥητορική in particular, see Schiappa (1990a). Cf. the entries in the Appendix for προοίμιον and ἀντίθετον, and the Introduction, 13–14.

6. Kerferd (1950).

7. Plato anachronistically retrofits the term to fifth-century intellectuals, most notably at *Prot.* 311e–12e, dramatically set in the 430s but composed ca. 380 B.C.E. In this passage he takes care to debate and define the term, since it is a contentious term in the mid-fourth century. This distinction can still be underappreciated, as shown by Tell (2009), who seems not to understand fifth-century usage. Tell (2011, 21–38) does subsequently recognize and explore the problem. Athenaeus records that the term was also commonly used to refer to comic performers (14.621d–e), but the source and dating for the reference is unclear.

8. Plato the comic playwright wrote a Σοφισταί, in which he identifies Bacchylides (a fluteplayer, not the choral poet) as a σοφιστής (fr. 149).

9. Whether or not the attribution to Antiphon is correct, the *Tetralogies* make considerable use of probability arguments and come closest to this time period; see Zuntz (1949). Antiphon 5 and 6, belonging to the 410s, also incorporate this manner of argumentation. The defense speech of Palamedes attributed to Gorgias also makes much use of this type of argumentation. See Schiappa (1999, 36) on this term in early rhetoric and some scholars' speculative use of it. Cf. Tindale (2010, 69–82).

up his business, where εἰκός could yield either sense, but certainly there is some hint of propriety ("he deserves it," fr. 92).¹⁰

In general, Old Comedy does not describe speeches with technical vocabulary, nor does it ever respect or praise a formal or ornate speech that would later be deemed "rhetorical." Positive references to speech making do not involve formal or sophisticated rhetoric. Other qualities or purposes are required for a positive evaluation. Serving the public good is a laudable goal for a speech, so Cratinus fr. 52 wishes victory to whoever speaks best (λέγων τὸ λῷστον) for the city.¹¹

Any speech is likely to provoke a response. Debate and competition were long ingrained in Greek culture, and speakers paired in debate were enshrined in the legal and political system of democratic Athens. Whatever the reputation of sophistic debate, refusal to engage in dialogue is unhealthy in comedy. The standard term for responding in a debate is ἀντιλέγειν, and that for engaging in conversation is διαλέγεσθαι.¹² A participant should also "listen back" (ἀντακούειν), as the speaker in Crates fr. 45 commands someone to do.¹³ A fragment on a strip of papyrus seems to trace the contrast between the good old days and current decadence (adesp. 1095; note the arrival of cosmetics, symposia and dancing in lines 15–16). Near the end of the fragment, the speaker says someone does not (if the supplement to the damaged text is correct) reply, possibly in debate at a symposium. Two lines later a character emphasizes, and laments, a respondent's complete silence (σιγᾷ κοὐδὲν γρύζει;).¹⁴ In Phrynichus fr. 19 (= Olson B21), the recluse is characterized in part by not engaging in conversation (ἀδιάλεκτον).¹⁵

10. Cf. the entry for εἰκός in the Appendix.

11. Similarly, Aristophanes describes a manner of speaking that avoids the extremes of urban decadence and slavish crudeness (fr. 706):

διάλεκτον ἔχοντα μέσην πόλεως,
οὔτ' ἀστείαν ὑποθηλυτέραν
οὔτ' ἀναλεύθεραν ὑπαγροικοτέραν

He keeps his dialogue with the city moderate,
neither urbanly submasculine
nor too crude like those not freeborn.

Along analogous lines, the speaker of Eupolis fr. 108 promises to stop using circular talk (τοῦ κύκλῳ ... λόγου). For an overview of the problematic phrase διὰ τῶν χωρίων in the next line, see Telò (2007, 606–8). "Talking around" is attested in Hermippus (fr. 89 περιλέγειν) and is potentially negative.

12. Cf. adesp. 572, where λεσχαίνειν is equated with διαλέγεσθαι.

13. Cf. similar commands in Euripides at *Supp.* 569 and *Hec.* 321.

14. Cf. *Wasps* 741, *Peace* 96–97, and Crates fr. 4 for similar phrases; however, they do not illuminate the current passage.

15. On the broader history of citizens not engaging in Athenian democracy, see L. B. Carter

When speakers do engage each other, in lieu of technical vocabulary, comedy opts to describe and characterize rhetorical speech with colorful metaphors. In Pherecrates fr. 56, an unidentified speaker is silent, until the verbal torrent has poured out (χαράδρα κατελήλυθεν). Another voice breaks out sharply and loudly (ὥστ' ἀνέρρωγεν τὸ φώνομ' εὐθὺς ὀξὺ καὶ μέγα, Pherecrates fr. 153). In Phrynichus fr. 3 (= Olson J14), an old man fears younger men who scratch up their elders with words, although they speak sweetly (τούτοις οἷς ἡδυλογοῦσι μεγάλας ἀμυχὰς καταμύξαντες). Other passages find something "hard to reckon" (adesp. fr. 587, δυσλογεῖν, or perhaps "to speak harshly of"). Cratinus fr. 476 has speakers "talk to the details" (μικρολογεῖσθαι).[16] More common than getting lost in the details is sheer vapidity. Hermippus fr. 21 has λεπτολογία, "refined talk," glossed as the equivalent of ἀδολεσχεῖν; and Cratinus fr. 342 has ὑπολεπτολόγος (here applied to Aristophanes for resembling Euripides), which covers similar territory.[17]

The tongue (γλῶττα), as the organ of speech and synecdoche for language, generates its own group of metaphors. In these metaphors, the tongue consistently implies negative or less than candid speech (which will be significant for its use with reference to Pericles; see below), in contrast to the mouth (στόμα).[18]

Comedy indulges in creating neologisms, even as it criticizes other speakers for using unorthodox language. The longest fragment from Aristophanes' first play, *Banqueters*, hinges on the issue of orthodox language. A delinquent son is using unusual terminology, and at each phrase the father angrily identifies contemporary individuals associated with the phrasing. The passage (fr. 205) begins with the son calling his father old-fashioned by using a unique diminutive of σόρος (any sort of container for the dead; this along with the other items means his father is material for a funeral):[19]

—ἀλλ' εἶ σορέλλη καὶ μύρον καὶ ταινίαι.
—ἰδοὺ σορέλλη· τοῦτο παρὰ Λυσιστράτου.
—ἦ μὴν ἴσως σὺ καταπλιγήσῃ τῷ χρόνῳ.

(1985), Christ (2006) and, for Old Comedy in particular, Ceccarelli (2000). Storey (2011, 3: 399) wonders if this fragment belongs to Eupolis' *Kolakes*.

16. So also Eupolis fr. 469.

17. Eupolis uses κενολογήσω, "I will talk empty" (fr. 456). Cf. Aristotle, *Rhet.* 1393a17, where he is bringing subjects to a close and saying it would be pointless to say more.

18. See entry for γλῶττα in the Appendix for examples.

19. Cf. Bonanno (1983) for a detailed analysis of the rare words in this fragment. Adesp. fr. 932 records other compounds of σόρος used as insults to the elderly, both σορόπληκτος and σοροπλήξ meaning "coffin-striker." Cf. Pollux 10.150.

—τὸ καταπλιγήσῃ τοῦτο παρὰ τῶν ῥητόρων.
—ἀποβήσεταί σοι ταῦτά ποι τὰ ῥήματα.
—παρ' Ἀλκιβιάδου τοῦτο τἀποβήσεται.
—τί ὑποτεκμαίρῃ καὶ κακῶς ἄνδρας λέγεις
καλοκἀγαθίαν ἀσκοῦντας; —οἴμ' ὦ Θρασύμαξε,
—τίς τοῦτο τῶν ξυνηγόρων τερατεύεται;

SON: You're just a coffinette, sweet oil and wreaths.
FATHER: Look at that "coffinette"! That's from Lysistratus!
SON: I bet you'll be tripped down in time.
FATHER: "Tripped down"! That's from those *rhetores* [see below for more on this term].
SON: These very speeches will get away on you.
FATHER: That "will get away on" is from Alcibiades!
SON: Why do you evidence against and disrespect men
Cultivating gentlemanliness?
FATHER: Ahh! Thrasymachus,
Which of those legal types talks such hocus-pocus?

Another fragment (fr. 233) features part of the same debate, but about words in older authors such as Homer and Solon, still a type of discussion associated with the new intellectualism, since it hinges on the idea of analyzing language. Nonetheless Aristophanes and other comic playwrights themselves coin words and phrases to condemn the unusual language of speakers associated with the new intellectualism. Cratinus fr. 381 coins λυπησιλόγος for someone who causes pain with their words, and describes running down someone with words like running over them with a horse (fr. 389, ἐφιππάσασθαι λόγοις).[20] Such mouthings at a symposium might come from στωμυλῆθραι δαιταλεῖς, "mouthy banqueters" (adesp. fr. 115 dub.). Suetonius (adesp. frr. 930–31) collects several heavy compound creations used to characterize busybodies in the agora, some attested from Aristophanes' extant plays but also others not known from other comic remains, including πολυκαλινδήτους, "lots of rolling." It is important to keep in mind that these more isolated items could apply equally well to speakers or situations quite apart from those using formal rhetoric (e.g., to a lyric poet). It is also telling that such vocabulary tells us little about comedy's characterization and evaluation of a speaker. Aeschylus, Cratinus and Cleon, accord-

---

20. Such might be the goal of a politician engaged in knock-down politics (πολιτικοκοπίαν in Sannyrio fr. 7 and πολιτικοκοπεῖν f glossed at Plato fr. 113 as λοιδορεῖν and κωμδορεῖν).

ing to comedy, all use torrential language, but this does not imply any more broadly what a comic poet says about the individual speakers.[21]

PRACTITIONERS

As it happens, of all the fragments securely dated before 425 B.C.E., aside from those connected to Pericles, only Aristophanes fr. 205 names speakers linked to unorthodox language.[22] First is Lysistratus. There may be multiple men named Lysistratus referred to by Aristophanes in various plays and by Antiphon and Andocides in speeches, but there is no definitive way to separate them or establish them under a single identity.[23] None of the other references play on Lysistratus' manner of oratory or speaking. Fr. 205 also provides the earliest reference to Thrasymachus of Chalcedon, unless Ian Storey is correct that this Thrasymachus is not the famous Sophist.[24]

The generic term for a speaker, ῥήτωρ, had a broader range than English "orator" (as a professional speaker or someone especially skilled in delivering speeches), often corresponding more to "politician" in the sense of someone publicly engaged in policy debate. The early sense of ῥῆσις as communal judgment or decree, going back to Homer but also in early comedy (Crates fr. 59), perhaps also contributes to the sense of ῥήτωρ as politician.[25] The early references to ῥήτορες in Old Comedy do not mention them in the act but refer to them more as a species. Crates wrote a play entitled Ῥήτορες, but the sole surviving line mentions only a simile about Cephisian turnips (fr. 30). The passage from Aristophanes' *Banqueters* quoted above (fr. 205) links them directly with strange, new phrasing.[26] Another fragment uses the

---

21. Note O'Sullivan (1992, 106–29) on this metaphor, but these passages do not imply, as O'Sullivan argues, a coherent, formal system of vocabulary for such metaphors. Cf. Scharffenberger (2007, 232–36) on the metaphors used of Aeschylus in *Frogs,* and see the Introduction, 14–16.
22. Alcibiades will be discussed in Chapter 4, in the context of his prominent role in the events of the 410s.
23. MacDowell (1971, 238).
24. Storey (1988). Cf. the entries for practitioners in the Appendix.
25. Connor (1971, 116 esp. n. 51).
26. Later, the comic playwright Plato uses the heads of the mythological Hydra to comment on their ever-growing numbers:

ἢν γὰρ ἀποθάνῃ
εἷς τις πονηρός, δύ' ἀνέφυσαν ῥήτορες·
οὐδεὶς γὰρ ἡμῖν Ἰόλεως ἐν τῇ πόλει,
ὅστις ἐπικαύσει τὰς κεφαλὰς τῶν ῥητόρων.
κεκολλόπευκας· τοιγαροῦν ῥήτωρ ἔσῃ.

metaphor of "knocking them out" (ἐκκροτεῖν, adesp. fr. 596) in the sense of crafting *rhetores* with tools, but no surviving reference describes them as the product of a school or particular training.[27]

In addition, there is the strictly pejorative term ἀλαζών ("faker"), which in the fifth century is applied to a range of characters employing pretentious quackery, but all of whom use decidedly verbal trickery, whereas in later periods it is used of a wider range of braggarts and fools. Cratinus might, appropriately enough, pair it with κομπός, "noise" (fr. 375), while adesp. fr. 438 mentions a λόγων ἀλαζόνα ("faker in his words").[28]

INSTITUTIONS

While Aristophanes' extant plays amply demonstrate that fifth-century comedy dramatized political and social institutions, the fragments of earlier times are too brief or too obscure to allow analysis of their broader depiction of intellectual and political life and the role of formal oratory within it. Nonetheless, the shards from such depictions at least confirm some of the general trends in Aristophanes' complete plays. Aristophanes dramatizes directly or reports explicitly on the three main institutions of the Athenian democracy (the Assembly, the Council and the courts), and he projects an anxiety about the role of the new intellectual style of speech in each of them. The fragments of Old Comedy are too slight to assert definitively that other comedies dramatized these institutions and incorporated the role of rhetorical speech in their presentation. It seems likely, however, that when Thugenides composed a play called Δικασταί (*Jurors*) and someone asks, τί, ὦγάθ' ἀντιδικοῦμεν ἀλλήλοις ἔτι; "Sir, why do we keep suing each other?" (fr. 1; cf. Phrynichus fr. 89, which uses the same verb), it is quite reasonable to believe that the play staged issues in the court and addressed issues of how citizens spoke there, but no details are available. A more colorful version of the comment comes in Telecleides (ἀλλ' ὦ πάντων ἀστῶν λῷστοι

If just a single rascal dies, two *rhetores* grew in their place,
because we don't have an Iolaus in the city
to cauterize the *rhetores*' heads.
You've been butt-fucked, so you'll end up a *rhetor*. (fr. 202 = Olson E9)

Plato, *Euthydemus* 297c uses the image of the Hydra as a mistress of sophistry (σοφιστρία), whose κέφελαι τοῦ λόγου ("heads of speech") grow back.

27. This is true even in *Clouds*, where training in the new philosophy and way of speaking is a major concern; *pace*, for example, Piltz (1934). Cf. Chapter 3.

28. MacDowell (1990), and cf. the entry in the Appendix.

σεῖσαι καὶ προσκαλέσασθαι,/παύσασθε δικῶν ἀλληλοφάγων, "You who are the best of all cities at shakedowns and indictments, stop the cannibalistic lawsuits," fr. 2), which probably represents the chorus addressing the spectators, but whether the issue was part of the fabric of the play or belonged only to an isolated passage is unrecoverable now. Cratinus punningly expresses concern for justice in the courts when someone worries ὥστε δίκας τ' ἀδίκους νικᾶν ἐπὶ κέρδεσιν αἰσχροῖς, "that the result be unjust cases winning for shameful profits" (fr. 353).

Consequently this survey ends by noting a few isolated words that are suggestive of the broader issues comic playwrights adduced when addressing issues germane to the democracy, including what form the functional language of that democracy should be. The adespota include δικομήτρα glossed as "the mother and generator of cases and sycophants" (fr. 590), δικολύμης "pain-of-a-lawsuit" (fr. 591) and πυθμὴν δικῶν "root of lawsuits, i.e., a sycophant" (fr. 649).[29] We end at the beginning, where a character wonders how a speech will begin: ἄγε δή, τίς ἀρχὴ τῶν λόγων γενήσεται; "Come on, what will be the beginning of the speech?" (Cephisodorus fr. 13).

PLUTARCH, COMIC PLAYWRIGHTS AND PERICLES

καὶ οἷς ἡ διατριβὴ ἐπὶ ταῖς τῶν πέλας ἁμαρτίαις, οἷον χλευσταῖς καὶ κωμῳδοποιοῖς· κακολόγοι γάρ πως οὗτοι καὶ ἐξαγγελτικοί.

And [there are] those who spend their time on the faults of those around them, such as comedians and comic playwrights, since they are sort of gossips and muckrakers. Aristotle, *Rhet.* 2.6.20.1384b9–11

So runs Aristotle's only discussion of comic playwrights in his *Rhetoric*, as he is explaining the benefits of circumscribing the use of rhetoric, especially in a political environment.[30] This contempt for comic playwrights has a long history and is crucial for understanding the evidence for comedy's treatment of Pericles. Ancient sources waver between the idea of Pericles as inspiring leader and imperious bully.[31] Comedy, however, overwhelmingly fronts the

---

29. Cf. τριπτὴρ δικῶν, "mortar for pounding lawsuits" (*Ach.* 937) of the sycophant Nicarchus; Christ (1998, 54).

30. On the political tensions in the *Rhetoric*, see Berlin (1992), Most (1994), Sprute (1994) and Jacob (1996).

31. Connor (1971, 119–28) and Stadter (1989, xxxviii–xliv).

latter image but is also nearly the only contemporary source referring to him.[32] The bias in, and the necessity of, referring to these sources were evident to Plutarch, and thus sources of frustration for him. When discussing the scandals surrounding Phidias, he comments (13.15–16.160e):

[10] δεξάμενοι δὲ τὸν λόγον οἱ κωμικοὶ πολλὴν ἀσέλγειαν αὐτοῦ κατεσκέδασαν, . . . καὶ τί ἄν τις ἀνθρώπους σατυρικοὺς τοῖς βίοις καὶ τὰς κατὰ τῶν κρειττόνων βλασφημίας ὥσπερ δαίμονι κακῷ τῷ φθόνῳ τῶν πολλῶν ἀποθύοντας ἑκάστοτε θαυμάσειεν . . . ; οὕτως ἔοικε πάντη χαλεπὸν εἶναι καὶ δυσθήρατον ἱστορίᾳ τἀληθές, ὅταν οἱ μὲν ὕστερον γεγονότες τὸν χρόνον ἔχωσιν ἐπιπροσθοῦντα τῇ γνώσει τῶν πραγμάτων, ἡ δὲ τῶν πράξεων καὶ τῶν βίων ἡλικιῶτις ἱστορία τὰ μὲν φθόνοις καὶ δυσμενείαις, τὰ δὲ χαριζομένη καὶ κολακεύουσα λυμαίνηται καὶ διαστρέφῃ τὴν ἀλήθειαν.

The comic playwrights picked up the story and splattered Pericles with charges of great corruption, . . . and why should anyone be astonished that men who live like satyrs offer up sacrifices of slander of their betters, as if to the evil deity of jealousy . . . ? In this way, it seems the truth is entirely difficult and hard to capture by research, since later writers find that time covers over and blocks their knowledge of events; while contemporary research into the deeds and lives, both because of jealousy and hostility and through favoritism and flattery, damages and distorts the truth.

Rhetoric poses a fresh set of problems for Plutarch, though ones intertwined with comedy.[33] Pericles had a reputation for powerful oratory, among both supporters and detractors, but Plutarch wrestles with this component of Pericles' leadership, sensitive to the morally gray area involved in overwhelming a citizen audience with the power, rather than the substance, of a speech. The tension surfaces, for example, when Plutarch discusses Pericles being termed an Olympian god. Plutarch asserts that the reputation reflects a range of Pericles' accomplishments, but concedes that in comedy the epithet referred specifically to his oratory (8.2–3, partly cited as adesp. 701):

---

32. Podlecki (1998, 169–78) surveys the references in comedy to Pericles. Sidwell (2009, 147–53) and Bakola (2010, 181–208, 213–20) provide more extensive readings of Pericles in the fragments.

33. See Stadter (1989, xxxviii–xliv, lxiii–lxx) for Plutarch's rhetorical dilemma and his use of comic sources. Cf. Yunis (1991) for an analysis of how Thucydides puts a positive spin on Pericles' rhetoric.

διὸ καὶ τὴν ἐπίκλησιν αὐτῷ γενέσθαι λέγουσι· καίτοι τινὲς ἀπὸ τῶν οἷς ἐκόσμησε τὴν πόλιν, οἱ δ' ἀπὸ τῆς ἐν τῇ πολιτείᾳ καὶ ταῖς στρατηγίαις δυνάμεως Ὀλύμπιον αὐτὸν οἴονται προσαγορευθῆναι· καὶ συνδραμεῖν οὐδὲν ἀπέοικεν ἀπὸ πολλῶν προσόντων τῷ ἀνδρὶ τὴν δόξαν. αἱ μέντοι κωμῳδίαι τῶν τότε διδασκάλων σπουδῇ τε πολλὰς καὶ μετὰ γέλωτος ἀφεικότων φωνὰς εἰς αὐτόν, ἐπὶ τῷ λόγῳ μάλιστα τὴν προσωνυμίαν γενέσθαι δηλοῦσι, "βροντᾶν" μὲν αὐτὸν καὶ "ἀστράπτειν," ὅτε δημηγοροίη, "δεινὸν δὲ κεραυνὸν ἐν γλώσσῃ φέρειν λεγόντων."

So they say he had his surname: although some think it was from the means by which he beautified the city, and others from his ability as a statesman and a general, that he was called Olympian, it is not unlikely that his reputation resulted from many things associated with the man. But the comedies of the playwrights at the time who let loose lots of sounds, both seriously and to get a laugh, show that he got this surname primarily because of his speech: they spoke of him as "thundering" and "lightning" [*Ach.* 531] when he spoke to the people publicly, and as "carrying an awesome thunderbolt on his tongue."

A little later Plutarch again addresses Pericles' success as an orator, this time in laudatory terms. To offset the association of his rhetoric with tyranny, and criticism from the comic playwrights, he cites new authorities and reframes Pericles' accomplishments (15.2–3):

ἔδειξε τὴν ῥητορικὴν κατὰ Πλάτωνα ψυχαγωγίαν οὖσαν καὶ μέγιστον ἔργον αὐτῆς τὴν περὶ τὰ ἤθη καὶ πάθη μέθοδον, ὥσπερ τινὰς τόνους καὶ φθόγγους ψυχῆς μάλ' ἐμμελοῦς ἁφῆς καὶ κρούσεως δεομένους. αἰτία δ' οὐχ ἡ τοῦ λόγου ψιλῶς δύναμις, ἀλλ', ὡς Θουκυδίδης φησίν, ἡ περὶ τὸν βίον δόξα καὶ πίστις τοῦ ἀνδρός, ἀδωροτάτου περιφανῶς γενομένου καὶ χρημάτων κρείττονος.

He demonstrated that rhetoric is, to use Plato's words, "a leader of the soul" [*Phaedrus* 261a, 271c] and that its paramount task is pursuit of the character and emotions, as if they were the strings and sounds of the soul, in need of harmonious touch and fingering. The cause was not simply the power of his speech, but, as Thucydides says [2.65], the reputation of his life and the trust placed in the man as one who was utterly free of corruption and beyond bribes.

The strategy Plutarch employs here typifies much reception of the interplay between comedy and rhetoric. Where comic playwrights of the time linked Pericles' speech to power and imperiousness, Plutarch reconstructs the effectiveness quite differently. By citing Plato (albeit from a passage, and using a term, that was not necessarily laudatory), Plutarch enlists an important ally, because Plato was such a critic of rhetoric. If Plutarch can find a way to harmonize Pericles' rhetoric with something Plato approves, then clearly Pericles' oratory is to the good and not of a sophistic variety. Plutarch follows this by invoking Thucydides and concluding that Pericles led in fact by his individual moral authority, not by the techniques of his speech making. In the process, Plutarch nullifies the criticism of comedy. The comic authors were jealous entertainers who did not appreciate the noble superiority of Pericles and thus did not recognize the true cause of the success of his oratory. Plutarch accomplishes this reinterpretation by invoking Plato and Thucydides as canonical authorities, and also the tradition from the fourth century onward of subjecting rhetoric to higher pursuits such as philosophy. In this way, Plutarch belongs to the long tradition of dismissing fifth-century accomplishments in language and oratory, along with comedy's voice in the debate, by invoking fourth-century critiques.

Nearly all of comedy's extant reaction to Pericles derives from Plutarch's biography, but it is still possible to make discerning observations despite this filtering. Modern scholars have especially seized on the statement in the hypothesis for Cratinus' *Dionysalexandros* that κωμῳδεῖται δ' ἐν τῷ δράματι Περικλῆς μάλα πιθανῶς δι' ἐμφάσεως ὡς ἐπαγηοχὼς τοῖς Ἀθηναίοις τὸν πόλεμον, "In the play, Pericles is satirized very felicitously by innuendo as having brought the war upon the Athenians" (44–48, trans. Bakola).[34] E. Bakola soberly reviews the history of allegorical readings of Pericles that have flowed from this statement, although, after solid criticism of such efforts, he offers an overly confident reading of the play's remains.[35] Stimulating as many interpretations of the *Dionysalexandros* have been, Bakola's careful study of how limited an application such statements in ancient hypotheses generally have to comic plots and content in general indicates that many of these readings are primarily speculative.

---

34. McGlew (2002, 25–56) uses this statement to, in a sense, invert Plutarch's criticism of comedy's criticism. McGlew sets Cratinus' satire of Pericles against the ideals for the citizen in Thucydides' version of Pericles in the Funeral Oration. Where Thucydides' Pericles has citizens subordinate their individual desires to Athens and to the state's goals, comedy celebrates and promotes the individual citizen's desire in a way that becomes paradigmatic for the comic protagonist. Cf. Davidson (1997) and Farenga (2006, 424–70).

35. Bakola (2010, 180–208).

When it comes to Cratinus' and other comedians' characterization of Pericles' rhetoric, a limited but substantive conclusion emerges. The evidence consists of only a handful of lines, but they are consistent, as Plutarch admitted was broadly true, in reckoning Pericles' oratory as the embodiment of him as an imperious, superhuman tyrant. Two fragments containing images similar to that of oratory as thunder and lightning (Telecleides fr. 48 and adesp. 288) might refer to Pericles' oratory, but their context has not been preserved. Fragments of Cratinus confirm that he employed the characterization of Pericles as Zeus (frr. 73, 118 and 258 = Olson E12). For speech, Cratinus draws on the metaphor of the tongue as an instrument of troublesome speech when he calls Pericles "the greatest tongue of the Greeks" (μεγίστη ... γλῶττα τῶν Ἑλληνίδων, fr. 324).[36] Another fragment of Cratinus might elaborate on what Pericles can do with his tongue (from *Dionysalexandros,* possibly Athena's offer in the parody of the judgment of Paris):

γλῶττάν τε σοι
δίδωσιν ἐν δήμῳ φορεῖν
καλῶν λόγων ἀείνων,
ᾗ πάντα κινήσεις λέγων.

... gives you a tongue of beautiful eternally flowing words to bring to the Demos with which you will move them all when you speak. (fr. 327 = Olson B16)

Cratinus likewise has Pericles lead with words (λόγοισι προάγει, about building the Long Walls) but move nothing in fact (fr. 326). Another fragment criticizes him as "king of the satyrs," for Pericles does not raise a spear himself but nonetheless provides bold speeches about the war (ἀλλὰ λόγους μὲν/περὶ τοῦ πολέμου δεινοὺς περέχῃ, Hermippus fr. 47 = Olson E14).[37]

For Plutarch and modern historians, it is a source of frustration that events from the comic stage infiltrated the historical record, but it can be illuminating for understanding comic practice. Anecdotes about Pericles' companion Aspasia, of dubious historical value, might have their origins in depictions of the couple on the comic stage. Plutarch reports that the comic poet Hermippus prosecuted Aspasia for impiety and operating a brothel, but

---

36. Cf. entry for γλῶττα in the Appendix and above.
37. "King of the satyrs" can refer to the perennially cowardly Silenus who regularly graces the stage in satyr plays. On satyrs in Cratinus' *Dionysalexandros,* see Bakola (2010, 81–117, esp. 84 n. 8).

that Pericles' weepy appeal in court saved her (*Pericles* 32, partly quoted as Hermippus T2 in PCG). Depending on how garbled this report is, it could mean at least that in a play of Hermippus, he had the chorus or a character relate a satirical trial and acquittal of Aspasia. If Hermippus actually included a scene or more of such a trial, including actors portraying Pericles and Aspasia, it would be the earliest known example of the staging of an Athenian political institution at work, the earliest staging of public figures in this way, and possibly of staging speeches and oratory. Another report has Aspasia assist Pericles in composing his orations (Callias fr. 21; cf. Cratinus fr. 259 [= Olson E13]), which again reads like stage satire, though there is no indication whether it was more than a passing comment.[38] When discussing Aspasia's trial, Plutarch adds that a certain Diopeithes brought a bill in support of public prosecution of atheists (32.1). Whether this brief reference recalls history, comedy, or a blend of the two, Diopeithes was a known name on the comic stage.[39]

Plutarch was well aware that appraisal of Pericles changed over time and that he had a reputation in retrospect that turned many of his negatives, such as his penchant for imperiousness, into virtues, such as integrity in leadership (39.4–5).[40] Plutarch does not apply this perspective to the comic sources he cites, but his observation holds true for them. All the comic fragments from Pericles' lifetime are negative. Only a decade or more after his death comes the famous laudatory description of the power of his speaking, from Eupolis' *Demes,* where Pericles was one of four figures from Athens' past to reappear.[41] If the passages in *Acharnians* (524–33) and *Peace* (603–28), where Pericles even after death is an imperious Olympian bully responsible for the war, are any indication, however, it did take some years for Pericles' stock to rise.

CONCLUSION: COMEDY AND RHETORIC BEFORE 425 B.C.E.

The above surveys lead to two generalizations. First, as is consistent with the revised history of early rhetoric, comedy does not reflect the use of the technical vocabulary or techniques documented from the fourth century

---

38. On the depiction of Aspasia in Greek comedy, see Henry (1995, 19–28).
39. See the entry in the Appendix.
40. Cf. *Gorgias* 518e1–19d5 for Plato's more cynical take on the idealizing of leaders of the past, including Pericles.
41. See Chapter 4 for discussion.

onward. The terminology found in early Athenian comedy for "rhetorical" language, speaking and its practitioners is not technical vocabulary, the core of which was canonized a century later and subsequently expanded and elaborated, nor is it even a direct forerunner of such terminology. Rather the fragments of Old Comedy, like Aristophanes' complete extant plays, employ comic and satirical terms, highly evaluative, almost exclusively pejorative, and often also drawing on comedy's own tradition of colorful, creative metaphors and neologisms to attack sophistic language.[42] Instead, comic criticism addresses unusual language and oratory deployed for negative purposes, but does so by creating comic neologisms to identify critical issues. As such, it is a comic playwright's means for asserting the superiority of the comic stage's own language, backed by comedy's distinct cultural authority, as superior to the emerging prose rhythms that will, nonetheless, come to dominate the discourse of the democracy in the coming generations.[43] Once again, the source of comic vocabulary resides not in a formal system of criticism, but in a tradition opposed to such systems.[44]

Second, comedy's aggressive stance toward speakers and their speeches appears in a political context. The sharp attacks on Pericles, including a substantial portion aimed at his oratory, establish that comedy was in the business of policing politics and the beat included oratory, comprising its manner, technique and purpose, for improper use of oratory was embedded in tyranny and was *a fortiori* antidemocratic. Unfortunately, the fragments prior to 425 B.C.E. provide almost no coherent sense of how scenes and actions in the lost comedies dramatized the workings of this activity in the mechanisms of the democracy to supplement what we have in Aristophanes' extant plays. Only the garbled testimony about Hermippus' prosecution of Aspasia might provide a glimpse of a more extended report or scene devoted to a dysfunctional political institution. In this sense, the fragments of Aristophanes' *Banqueters* that deal with language use (frr. 205 and 233) are not so novel, except that the debate transpires between a father and son, with no indication that their dialogue takes place in a public, political space. Translocation out of appropriate public space will be a crucial device in the complete plays for cornering and exploring issues involved with public oratory and language exploration in general, however, beginning in 425 B.C.E., in *Acharnians,* in the next chapter.

---

42. Müller (1974).
43. Ober (1989).
44. See the Introduction, 12–16 on how this contradicts the positions of O'Sullivan (1992) and Hubbard (2007); cf. Bakola (2010, 24–29).

The Young Comic Playwrights Attack, 425–421 B.C.E.

> ὑποδύεται ὑπὸ τὸ σχῆμα τὸ τῆς πολιτικῆς ἡ ῥητορική.
> Rhetoric puts on the appearance of politics.
> —Aristotle, *Rhet.* 1.2.7.1356a27–28

Aristotle laments the role of rhetoric in political deliberation and even idealizes political decision making that is devoid of rhetoric, but when Aristophanes composed comedies for performance in the 420s B.C.E., he had no reason to reckon the novel turns in language of the time as fundamentally distinct from political discourse. Indeed, the presence of unorthodox language in public debate and Gorgias' speech making, successful both as performance and for its political achievement, could only have testified that the language that came to be called "rhetoric" was enmeshed in the deliberations of the Athenian democracy. Since for Aristophanes it was also established that comedy engaged the political environment of the democracy, including the language of its prominent citizens (Chapter 2), it is no surprise that *Acharnians* of 425 B.C.E. dramatizes the language of democratic debate not in terms of adherence to the formalized system of "rhetoric" of the next century, but in terms of the current debate about spectators, deliberation and democracy.[1]

---

1. Athenian theater's relationship to democratic deliberation is much debated. For study of

It is telling, by contrast, that when scholars have searched Aristophanes' *Acharnians* for examples of speech making under the influence of rhetoric, they have turned to Dicaeopolis' speech to the chorus (496–556), several episodes into the play, and bypassed completely the opening scene, set in the Assembly of Athens, where speeches about public policy would normally take place.[2] It is logical to turn to Dicaeopolis' speech, of course, since the scene in the Assembly does not feature, and indeed cuts off, any debate or opportunities for speech making. Instead, the type of debate that belongs in the Assembly, about public policy, takes place near Dicaeopolis' home. Racing ahead to the full speech overlooks this translocation, overlooks that Aristophanes makes an issue of the fact that speech making and deliberation do not take place in the Assembly, where they should. This emphatic absence means spectators of the play have reason to be watching for a speech, and that the speech finally arrives in an unexpected locale is significant. It is a repeated and core argument of this study that Aristophanes is purposeful in transferring the setting of speeches and oratory and that restoring the deliberative process to its normal location is equally meaningful. The plays of 425 to 421 B.C.E. not only involve translocation of the deliberative process, and of the act of speech making within it; such transfers are central to the action and the basic cause-and-effect of each play. *Acharnians, Knights, Clouds* and *Wasps* all feature processes central to the democracy (public debate, trial by jury, education) stalled in their normal and proper locations and translocated to other environments. In each play, the underlying assumption, usually explicit, sometimes implicit, is that a normal and healthy process takes place in its proper public democratic institution. In this sense, Aristophanes' comedies are grounded in an ideology consistent with a functional and empowered democracy, and criticisms of its failures or errors should be construed in this context. Moreover, the translocation process works both ways. When Aristophanes celebrates the happy restoration of Athens in *Peace,* he translocates authority and the deliberative process away from its nontraditional location back to its proper democratic home, in this case the Council. In *Acharnians,* however, Aristophanes carefully and consistently dramatizes and emphasizes translocation away from the traditional and proper location for deliberation, the Pnyx, and the traditional and proper occasion, the Assembly.

---

modern theories about democratic deliberation and Aristophanes, see Zumbrunnen (2012), and for tragedy's engagement with this issue, see Goldhill (2009), Hall (2009) and Hesk (2011), with the important response by Heath (2011). Cf. the Introduction.

2. Murphy (1938, 101–4); Harriott (1986, 27–36); Sousa e Silva (1987–88, 99–102).

THE ASSEMBLY IN *ACHARNIANS*

At the original performance of *Acharnians* in 425 B.C.E., the set in the Theater of Dionysus, before any performers appeared, might or might not have signaled to the spectators that the setting is the Pnyx, but the script is unambiguous that this is the setting. In the same scene that indicates this setting, however, the play repeatedly sounds notes of dislocation and frustration. Throughout the monologue that opens the play, Dicaeopolis harps on the theme that the deliberative process is occurring in the wrong places (1–39). His first example, Cleon coughing up money to the Knights (5–8), is predicated on an attempt by Cleon to short-circuit deliberation, but an attempt that rebounds on its instigator. Unfortunately, Dicaeopolis does not specify the location of this example, presumably because the audience would have known it without prompting. If, as many scholars have argued,[3] the passage refers to a scene in *Babylonians* of the previous year, then this first event, a public political action, "a worthwhile thing for Greece" (ἄξιον γὰρ Ἑλλάδι, 8), takes place not where it should (a court, or perhaps the Council and Assembly), but in the theater. The next events, good and bad (a tragedy by Theognis, the music of Moschus, Dexitheus and Chaeris, 11–16), all take place in the theater.[4] If political justice has taken place in the theater, and otherwise the theater is the site of pleasure and pain, what is happening in the political arena? Dicaeopolis soon explains: nothing, because the Pnyx is deserted when it should be in session (19–20). Instead, the spectators are in the Agora, not deliberating or giving speeches but engaging in talk without substance (λαλοῦσι, 21; cf. the Appendix). They specifically stay out of the physical space of the Assembly (22).[5]

Even the Prytaneis are not present in the Assembly (23). When they do arrive, late, they are coming not to engage in the business of the Assembly but instead to scramble for the seats that will provide the best view (23–26).[6]

---

3. Olson (2002, 66–68) provides a survey of the issues. On the thorny issues the passage raises about the censorship of Old Comedy, see the debate in Sluiter and Rosen (2004).

4. Brockmann (2003, 27–41) argues that Theognis was directing a revival of Aeschylus' *Persians* here. Sidwell (2009, 293–95) incorporates this notion into a chain of antidemocratic targets from Pericles to Eupolis. If by chance the lines do refer to a revival of *Persians*, there could be a political alignment at issue, but the evidence is slight at best. Cf. Chapter 6.

5. How the σχοινίον . . . μεμιλτωμένον functioned is not certain, for which cf. Olson (2002, 73); but the metaphor is clear: people are actively avoiding the border that would have them in the physical space of the Assembly and engaged in its processes. Shear (2011, 131–34, 269–85) analyzes the conversion of the Agora into markedly democratic space in the fourth century, but *Acharnians* long predates this transformation.

6. See Olson (2002, 75) for a survey of the textual and interpretive problems in these lines, but

The absence of substantive deliberation in contrast to eager viewing recalls the criticism found in Thucydides, where Cleon rebukes the audience at the Assembly along analogous lines: σοφιστῶν θεαταῖς ἐοικότες καθημένοις μᾶλλον ἢ περὶ πόλεως βουλευομένοις ("You resemble seated spectators before performers more than those deliberating about their city," 3.38.7).[7] The Prytaneis race to be seated spectators rather than civic deliberators. Thus Aristophanes, in his satire of the deliberative processes, maintains the same contrast as Thucydides.

Next Dicaeopolis makes explicit that the proper business of the Assembly, deliberating about peace, has no value (27), and he invokes the entire political community (ὦ πόλις πόλις), but in vain, for at this point there is no place where the desired process is taking place. Now Dicaeopolis begins reconstituting the Assembly and attempting to create a space for the process he desires.[8] In contrast to the Prytaneis, he himself always attends the Assembly ahead of everyone and then sits alone (28–29). With no deliberative process transpiring, Dicaeopolis feels the pull of other locations, his *deme* in particular, which is notably free of the invitations and sales pitches of the Agora (32–36). Lest this wistful thinking suggest that Dicaeopolis is merely at the Pnyx to get the best seat as a spectator of the oratorical displays, he explains his purpose exactly (37–39):[9]

νῦν οὖν ἀτεχνῶς ἥκω παρεσκευασμένος
βοᾶν ὑποκρούειν λοιδορεῖν τοὺς ῥήτορας,
ἐάν τις ἄλλο πλὴν περὶ εἰρήνης λέγῃ.

So consequently, I've come totally prepared
to shout, interrupt and abuse the speakers,
if anyone speaks about anything except peace.

As for formal rhetorical technique, in modern terms, Diceaopolis' monologue to this point can be labeled a priamel, but this structure does not correspond to any outline or component in ancient Greek rhetoric and is not geared to resemble or recall a piece of oratory.[10] It does, however, set

---

the purpose of the Prytaneis' actions seems clear.

7. Cf. the Introduction, 3–5.

8. Cf. McGlew (2002, 57–78), for whom it is crucial that Dicaeopolis here pursues personal desire rather than state-sanctioned sacrifice.

9. Cf. the entries on shouting and screaming in the Appendix.

10. Edmunds (1980, 26–33) analyzes *Ach.* 1–39 as a priamel, setting up the opposition between poetry and politics. Race (1982, x; cf. 36 n. 11) notes that no ancient rhetorician describes a figure

up the expectation that there should be a functional Assembly and that the spectators should be fully engaged in the deliberative process. Aristophanes, having built up this expectation, establishes suspense and tension until the anticipated speech making takes place. That he delays the speech and the deliberative process until well after the Assembly is adjourned says as much about the absence of functional process at the Assembly as it does about the functional deliberations once they occur.

After Dicaeopolis' initial monologue, the Assembly does begin (with the Prytaneis entering just as Dicaeopolis describes, 40–42, confirming Dicaeopolis' reliability as an interpreter of events), and Aristophanes continues to set the expectation of deliberation against the frustration of this expectation. The herald confirms that parties are now within the physical space of the meeting (43–44).[11] One citizen, Amphitheos, is present and immediately ready to initiate the deliberation about peace (45), as Diceaopolis earlier called for, but he is just as quickly removed from the space (54). When Dicaeopolis objects to the failed attempt at deliberation, the herald responds by telling him to sit down and be quiet (κάθησο, σίγα, 59), an inversion of the behavior Dicaeopolis came ready to engage in and which he has established as proper engagement in the deliberative process. For the rest of the proceedings of the Assembly, Dicaeopolis comments but cannot participate (60–166).[12] Forced ironically to be a spectator of what is said, he now offers perspective for the benefit of the spectators of the play, but his comments only reinforce the distance between the activities around the Pnyx and the proper business of the Assembly (note especially 101–7, where Dicaeopolis literally interprets the speech of Pseudartabas).[13] Eventually, the language of the Assembly proves functional only to terminate dialogue entirely. Addressing the Prytaneis, Dicaeopolis shuts down the Assembly (169–72; Dicaeopolis' call, ἀπαγορεύω μὴ ποιεῖν ἐκκλησίαν, in 169 mirrors the herald's question at the beginning of the meeting, τίς ἀγορεύειν βούλεται, 45).

---

comparable to the priamel. Compton-Engle (2001) compares this speech with Silenus' opening catalog of πόνοι in Eur. *Cyc.* 1–40 against the backdrop of tragic priamels. Motifs like ὦ πόλις πόλις (27) have their parallels in drama rather than extant oratory (cf. the same phrase in Eupolis fr. 219 and Sophocles, *OT* 629). For two quite different analyses of the entire prologue, see Gordziejew (1938) and Platter (2007, 42–62).

11. The script does not specify whom the herald moves inside the area, but the key point is that participants are now explicitly within the borders of the functional territory of the Assembly, and the deliberative process should follow.

12. See Buis (2008, 250–62) for a close reading of the tensions in the diplomacy with foreign nations in this scene.

13. See Slater (2002, 42–49) on Dicaeopolis as actor, spectator and liaison with the audience.

With the dysfunctional Assembly ended, paradoxically, the deliberative process Dicaeopolis has sought now begins almost immediately. Amphitheos returns and Dicaeopolis quickly negotiates his thirty-year peace (175–203). While about the Pnyx deliberation and dialogue result in no consequence, now cause and effect take place. The peace treaty brings on both the chorus of Acharnians (204–36) and Dicaeopolis' celebration of the rural Dionysia (237–79). The confrontation between them begins with the chorus refusing to listen at all (280–327, esp. 295, 298, 303, 323–24). Dicaeopolis will manage to compel a deliberative process, but he still cannot use what should be the appropriate institution and venue, so he turns to the resource he has invoked several times already: tragedy.

As Helene Foley has argued in detail, Aristophanes has Dicaeopolis invoke tragedy through much of *Acharnians* to bolster the play's broader political themes.[14] The protagonist finally engages in the deliberative process that was a nonstarter in the Assembly and opposed by the chorus of Acharnians. Armed by Euripides and clothed in tragedy, Dicaeopolis finally compels permission from the chorus to address them, ἄνδρες οἱ θεώμενοι, "gentlemen spectators" (496), and begins his speech (497). This form of address can appear metatheatrical or in some way discordant with the illusion of the environment of the play, but it is not, really. It simply resumes and maintains a metaphor that was already implicit in Dicaeopolis' monologue at the beginning of the play, when he criticizes the Prytaneis for their lackadaisical commitment to deliberation, combined with their enthusiasm for a good show of speeches (again cf. the rebuke of Thucydides' Cleon of those at the Assembly as mere spectators of speeches: θεαταὶ . . . τῶν λόγων, 3.38.4). Dicaeopolis was reduced to such a spectator during the Assembly in the play, and so the spectators of *Acharnians* have at least some reason to expect, and some of them even to look forward to, an occasion finally to watch someone in the play deliver a speech.

DICAEOPOLIS' SPEECH (496–556)

The speech Dicaeopolis gives here serves as a good example of how previous attempts to align speech-making practice in Aristophanes' plays with the dictates of later rhetorical theory can look logical in their bare outline but not hold up under closer examination. Charles Murphy's 1938 article is the

---

14. Foley (1988) closely analyzes this dynamic. Biles (2011, 56–96) concentrates on the poetic allegiances Aristophanes builds through Dicaeopolis to achieve victory. Cf. P. Wilson (2007) on the issues related to victory in competition in this model.

most often cited study of rhetoric in Aristophanes, and he devotes his most detailed analysis to this speech.¹⁵ His scheme is the following:

1. Προοίμιον, 496–512
2. Πρόθεσις, 513–14
3. Πίστεις, 513–54
   a. 515–22. The Athenian sycophants were unjust to Megara in the matter of confiscation.
   b. 523–29. The rape of the harlots, begun by the Athenians, led directly to the war.
   c. 530–34. Pericles introduced the Megarian decree for personal reasons.
   d. 535–39. We refused to reconsider the decree.
   e. 540–54. (*Refutatio*) "What should you have done under similar circumstances?"
4. Ἐπίλογος, 555–56

Murphy's scheme relies on the axiom that the canonical divisions of speech (prologue, narrative, proof, epilogue) are already fixed and widely accepted.¹⁶ Even without this underlying assumption, however, the scheme does not match Dicaeopolis' speech. Murphy describes the proem as "unusually elaborate," as he must, since it includes many statements not required, and not typical, of a προοίμιον. It certainly does not resemble a προοίμιον as given as an example in *Knights* 1344 (see below), which is an initial statement of praise and flattery. When Dicaeopolis says (496–98):

μή μοι φθονήσητ', ἄνδρες οἱ θεώμενοι,
εἰ πτωχὸς ὢν ἔπειτ' ἐν Ἀθηναίοις λέγειν
μέλλω περὶ τῆς πόλεως.

Don't bear me ill will, gentlemen spectators,
if I am a beggar and yet among the Athenians I
intend to speak about the city.

Murphy finds here the device of diminution (ἐλάττωσις), but these lines are also a direct parody of lines from Euripides' *Telephus* (fr. 703), so we

---

15. Murphy (1938, 101–4).
16. Usher (1999, 22), who persists in propping up the older model, offers a taxonomy like that found in Murphy, except in even stronger terms, saying that the divisions here "one may assume to have been available to a speechwriter plying his trade from about 420 B.C."

would have to accept that Aristophanes is borrowing the device from Euripides' original speech.[17] Even if we accept this identification, it seems that the lines do more to establish Dicaeopolis in his parodic character than repeat any rhetorical device from Euripides. If there is any establishment of rhetorical formality here, it disappears entirely in the next few lines as Dicaeopolis (and in some fashion Aristophanes) declares the authority of comedy to speak on justice (499–501). This statement and the following lines on the environment at the Lenaea (502–8), far from continuing in the manner of a properly formal rhetorical speech, instead emphasize that we are anywhere but in a location typical for a forensic speech.

αὐτοὶ γάρ ἐσμεν οὑπὶ Ληναίῳ τ' ἀγών,
κοὔπω ξένοι πάρεισιν· οὔτε γὰρ φόροι
ἥκουσιν οὔτ' ἐκ τῶν πόλεων οἱ ξύμμαχοι
ἀλλ' ἐσμὲν αὐτοὶ νῦν γε περιεπτισμένοι·
τοὺς γὰρ μετοίκους ἄχυρα τῶν ἀστῶν λέγω.

For it's just us, and it's the contest at the Lenaea,
And there're no foreigners yet. Neither the tribute
Nor the allies from the other cities have arrived.
But at this point we are the processed grain,
Because the immigrants are the bran. (504–8)

Murphy labels the last line here a προκατάληψις,[18] as it preempts a potential objection from the audience, but there is no reference to such an objection, as opposed to later in the speech when Aristophanes is perfectly willing to refer to such objections (540). Rather the line is the last detail in his description of the gathering.

The next section in the scheme (513–14) is the following:

---

17. For formal rhetorical technique in Euripides' *agons*, see Lloyd (1992, 19–36). Scholarship on rhetoric in tragedy has yet to recognize the developments in the recent research on the development of fifth-century rhetoric. Gallagher (2003) attempts a detailed linkage of the *agon* in *Electra* with the Sophists' rhetorical doctrines. For an analysis of "rhetoric" in Euripides, very broadly defined, see Mastronarde (2010, 207–45). For Euripides' appropriation of late fifth-century philosophy generally, see the extensive catalogs in Egli (2003) and the survey in Dillon (2004). More superficially, see Conacher (1998). Cf. Chapter 6. Sansone (2012) explores drama (primarily tragedy) and the invention of rhetoric. I regret that it arrived too late for me to engage with its novel thesis.

18. This line is deleted by N. G. Wilson, because of the difficulty of the metaphor. See Whitehead (1977, 39–41) and N. G. Wilson (2007a, 26). This is not germane to my discussion of Murphy's analysis, but I agree with Wilson that the line and its characterization of metics is entirely inconsistent with other statements in Aristophanes. On the issue of inclusion in deliberation with regard to foreigners and others, see below on *Knights* (72–73), and Chapter 5 on Lysistrata's central speech.

ἀτὰρ, φίλοι γὰρ οἱ παρόντες ἐν λόγῳ,
τί ταῦτα τοὺς Λάκωνας αἰτιώμεθα;

Since everyone here at the speech is friends,
Why do we blame the Spartans for this?

Murphy calls this is a πρόθεσις, a declaration of the subject of the speech, but the couplet is barely even that. The first line has nothing to do with such a declaration, and the second line simply picks up the thought in the few previous lines, still part of Murphy's προοίμιον, where Dicaeopolis cites the damage the Spartans inflicted on his own farm. Murphy elides the problem by saying the section "continues the attempt to win favor" (102) and invoking the authority of the *Rhetoric to Alexander* that a πρόθεσις should come at the end of a προοίμιον when the speaker faces prejudice (29.1437b34–38a2).

Murphy does not point out, however, his unorthodox privileging of the πρόθεσις, for he elevates it to the status of the second section in the speech, when it is not normally a division at all. Why he does so becomes evident with the next section of his scheme. Because there is nothing that corresponds to the narrative (διήγεσις) and proofs (πίστεις) to yield a quadripartite division of the speech, Murphy elevates the πρόθεσις, declares the third section the πίστεις, and, to cover the διήγεσις, says: "The proofs consist mainly of a narration of certain facts." This makes the section seem more like a narrative than a set of proofs. Whether the section is a narrative, a set of proofs or both at the same time, it violates the canonical quadripartite division of a speech by not having separate sections devoted to narrative and proof, to say nothing of being in canonical order. Murphy's scheme downplays this problem and reckons the πρόθεσις a full division to mask the deficiency.[19]

The scheme ends with a two-line so-called ἐπίλογος (555–56):

ταῦτ' οἶδ' ὅτι ἂν ἐδρᾶτε· τὸν δὲ Τήλεφον
οὐκ οἰόμεσθα; νοῦς ἄρ' ἡμῖν οὐκ ἔνι.

I know that's what you would have done. And we don't think
so of Telephus? Then we're really out of our minds.

---

19. The underdifferentiation of narrative and proof is a notorious problem for those insisting that the canonical principles of classical rhetoric were in force in the fifth century. Even Usher (1999, 23–24) has to acknowledge the nebulous evidence for narrative sections in early speeches. See Timmerman and Schiappa (2010, 137–70) for attempts to analyze early oratory using established fifth-century narrative patterns instead of fourth-century ones.

Like the first lines of the speech, these are direct parodies of Telephus' speech in Euripides (fr. 710) and signal the conclusion to Dicaeopolis' parody more than constituting any formal peroration. If Dicaeopolis' speech resembles any formal oratorical structure, it is that more common of fifth-century speeches, loosely inspired by ring composition from oral poetry and with a body containing a sequence of arguments.[20]

More important than the structure of Dicaeopolis' speech is its effect: the members of the chorus react to what he has said. Some members stand their ground and remain opposed to Dicaeopolis' position, but others defend both his position and his right to speak (557–65). In this way, even those opposed to Dicaeopolis are at least involved in the process on the terms Dicaeopolis described them (ready to insult and stop any speaker not addressing the topic he wishes; cf. lines 37–39). Far from mere spectators, the full chorus is now active deliberators.

Cause and effect are important here. Once Dicaeopolis engages in the deliberative process after disbanding the Assembly, from the moment he begins negotiating with Amphitheos, his speech has real effect. Once he completes his speech, half of the chorus joins him; when the other half invokes Lamachus, Dicaeopolis repels him, too, and the full chorus explicitly acknowledges that his speech has proven successful deliberation for the people of Athens (627–28):

ἀνὴρ νικᾷ τοῖσι λόγοισιν, καὶ τὸν δῆμον μεταπείθει
περὶ τῶν σπονδῶν.

The man has won with his speeches and convinced the Demos about his treaty.

Dicaeopolis remains dominant throughout the rest of the play, easily repelling challengers and unwanted visitors. The process that brought him to this point, however, is exactly the one he came to the Assembly to enact: engagement with speakers and deliberation about policy. When it cannot take place at the Pnyx, Aristophanes shows that the appropriate location does not support the process, but that the democratic process itself does function, and exceptionally well. Dicaeopolis enacts it, and all benefits flow to him as a result.[21]

With this fundamental point established, that the democratic process

---

20. Timmerman and Schiappa (2010, 157–67).

21. P. Wilson (2007) elegantly explores the tension between Dicaeopolis' success, Aristophanes' victory in festival competition and the prosperity of the community at large.

does work but it is currently not operational in the appropriate and established political institution, Aristophanes has his chorus deliver the *parabasis*, wherein he can discourse more on the deliberative process. Addressing the spectators seated in the theater (πρὸς τὸ θέατρον, 629), an area where the deliberative process remains functional, the chorus says (630–32):

> διαβαλλόμενος δ' ὑπὸ τῶν ἐχθρῶν ἐν Ἀθηναίοις ταχυβούλοις,
> ὡς κωμῳδεῖ τὴν πόλιν ἡμῶν καὶ τὸν δῆμον καθυβρίζει,
> ἀποκρίνασθαι δεῖται νυνὶ πρὸς Ἀθηναίους μεταβούλους.
>
> Slandered by the Athenians who are quick in their deliberations,
> on the charge that he mocks the city and degrades the Demos,
> he must answer now, before the Athenians change their judgments.

He raises the issue of the Athenians' rush to judge and the instability of their judgment with two *hapax* epithets, ταχυβούλοις and μεταβούλους.[22] Nonetheless, Aristophanes and his chorus are engaging in the deliberative process by presenting policy recommendations in a public speech. The speech raises two issues with regard to the deliberative process: attention paid to outside influence, and simple flattery (633–35):

> φησὶν δ' εἶναι πολλῶν ἀγαθῶν ἄξιος ὑμῖν ὁ ποιητής,
> παύσας ὑμᾶς ξενικοῖσι λόγοις μὴ λίαν ἐξαπατᾶσθαι,
> μήδ' ἥδεσθαι θωπευομένους, μήδ' εἶναι χαυνοπολίτας.
>
> The poet says he deserves rich compensation,
> because he stopped you from being too much deceived by foreign speeches,
> and from enjoying being flattered and from being gape-open citizens.

Aristophanes has dramatized this deceptive influence earlier in the play, the scene of the Assembly, where such deliberation as there was consisted of flattery and deception by ambassadors and foreigners. Now he gives examples, and these are examples of προοίμια as Aristophanes knows the term, flattering prefaces to a speech (635–40):

> πρότερον δ' ὑμᾶς ἀπὸ τῶν πόλεων οἱ πρέσβεις ἐξαπατῶντες
> πρῶτον μὲν ἰοστεφάνους ἐκάλουν· κἀπειδὴ τοῦτό τις εἴποι,

---

22. Reinders (2001, 156–59) studies these terms in the context of Aristophanes' vocabulary for the Demos and class distinctions in general.

εὐθὺς διὰ τοὺς στεφάνους ἐπ' ἄκρων τῶν πυγιδίων ἐκάθησθε.
εἰ δέ τις ὑμᾶς ὑποθωπεύσας λιπαρὰς καλέσειεν Ἀθήνας,
ηὕρετο πᾶν ἂν διὰ τὰς λιπαράς, ἀφύων τιμὴν περιάψας.

Previously ambassadors from the allied cities tricked you,
first by calling you "violet-crowned": at the moment anyone said that,
just "violet-crowned," you'd sit at the tips of your asses.
And if anyone really buttered you up by saying "Glistening Athens,"
he'd get anything for that "glistening," wrapping you in honor worthy of sardines.

Aristophanes returns to the value of what he does and explains what is and what should be happening: he is demonstrating how democracy functions, so the allied states will learn about democracy, too, not flatter the Athenians in a dysfunctional deliberative environment (641–42):

ταῦτα ποιήσας πολλῶν ἀγαθῶν αἴτιος ὑμῖν γεγένηται,
καὶ τοῖς δήμοις ἐν ταῖς πόλεσιν, δείξας ὡς δημοκρατοῦνται.

For doing this, he deserves rich compensation,
and for showing the Demoi in the allied cities how democracy works.

After an extended example of the value that foreigners like the King of Persia recognize in the comic poet, he again declares how the deliberative process works (656–58):

φησὶν δ' ὑμᾶς πολλὰ διδάξειν ἀγάθ', ὥστ' εὐδαίμονας εἶναι,
οὐ θωπεύων οὐδ' ὑποτείνων μισθοὺς οὐδ' ἐξαπατύλλων,
οὐδὲ πανουργῶν οὐδὲ κατάρδων, ἀλλὰ τὰ βέλτιστα διδάσκων.

He says he'll teach you plenty of valuable things, so you'll prosper,
Without flattering or dangling rewards or diddling you
Or resorting to any means or sprinkling you, but just teaching you the best.

For the *pnigos*, the chorus taunts Cleon and dares him to do what he can (659–64). Naming Cleon now identifies him as a bottleneck in the deliberative process, one who engages in the sort of flattery and deception Aristophanes has been criticizing.

It is ironic in retrospect that Thucydides puts in Cleon's mouth some of these same metaphors to describe and berate the dysfunctional deliberative process, but the parallel imagery toward different ends suggests the possibility that the terminology of spectators and dysfunctional deliberation was not original with either Thucydides or Aristophanes and, more significantly, that the authors had quite different perspectives on the nature of, and solution to, the problem of the deliberative process not yielding positive results. Although Thucydides does not explicitly state a solution to the problem, he offers a positive portrait of Pericles and his domination of the political processes, praising the fact that he led the Demos rather than the other way around (2.65.8–9). As we have already seen, comedy did not react to Pericles this way, indeed quite the opposite. Moreover, Aristophanes in *Acharnians* continues depicting Pericles as a damaging arrogant tyrant (524–34), consistent with comedy's criticisms during Pericles' lifetime, so there is additional reason to believe that Thucydides and Aristophanes diverged in their representation and evaluation of politics and individuals. That both of them despised Cleon does not mean they did so from a similar political orientation. Thucydides describes Periclean democracy as such in name only, with the man himself prudently guiding Athens, but characterizes Cleon as an ignorant, violent fool, with the two leaders having in common only their ability to criticize the Demos and yet to compel it to act.[23] Aristophanes finds the deliberative process in the Assembly (and the Council, as other plays show) to be the key to the democracy and trusts the Demos' judgment. Dicaeopolis narrates Pericles' role in the war as resulting from petty personal vengeance (524–30). Personal aggrandizement will be core to Aristophanes' charges against Cleon in *Knights*, too. Both Pericles and Cleon eviscerate the deliberative process by driving the Demos along with flattery and contempt rather than discussing policy. And while Aristophanes (at least satirically) promotes himself as a teacher of integrity and respect, and although Thucydides nowhere explicitly refers to comic playwrights, it seems a safe conclusion that the historian did not consider comedy a source of valuable advice for Athens in times of crisis.

In the remaining sections of the *parabasis,* Aristophanes turns to the processes in another anchor of democratic institutions, the courts. The elderly chorus members first complain about the rough and unjust treatment they suffer from young prosecutors. As is typical of comedy of the fifth century, *rhetores* are a sort of species of creature unleashed by the spectators (ὑπὸ νεανίσκων ἐᾶτε καταγελᾶσθαι ῥητόρων, 680), but in turn the prosecu-

---

23. Pope (1988) argues that Thucydides criticized factionalism in Athens rather than democracy as an ideology or government. Yunis (1991) argues that Thucydides equates Periclean rhetoric with instruction of the Demos, in contrast to demagoguery, which is negative for the Demos and therefore criticized by Thucydides.

tors hunt the weak old men with verbal round rocks and traps tripped with words (στρογγύλοις τοῖς ῥήμασιν ... σκανδάληθρ' ... ἐπῶν, 686–88). After the generic criticism, Thucydides son of Milesias becomes the example, again a reminder that Aristophanes and comedy stand in opposition to Pericles and his brand of politics, here to the point of sympathizing with Pericles' most prominent opponent. As regards terminology, as in *Banqueters* (fr. 205), there seems no particular distinction between ῥήτορες (680) and συνήγοροι (685, 705), and Thucydides' prosecutor uses substanceless talk (λάλῳ, 705), as does Alcibiades (καὶ λάλος χὠ Κλεινίου, 716).[24] Aristophanes will flesh out the issues in the courts fully three years later in *Wasps*.

But for his play of the next year, Aristophanes keeps his focus on the Pnyx, the functioning of the Assembly and the man who wielded his power there.

RULING DEMOS: *KNIGHTS*

Knights concentrates on the tensions and failures in the deliberative process every bit as much as, indeed more than, *Acharnians,* and Aristophanes is more emphatic about the key to successful deliberation, and the benefits that result from it. The focus is different, though, in that *Knights* bores in on components and participants who received only passing attention in *Acharnians*. Whereas in *Acharnians* the Prytaneis are tagged as the failures of the Assembly for being mere dithering spectators, now the collective will of the Demos becomes central to restoring the process. Cleon's flattery and deception of the Demos is a topic the chorus mentions obliquely in the *parabasis* of *Acharnians,* but now Cleon becomes the critical barrier to a functional democracy. Success in the deliberative process for Dicaeopolis meant prosperity for him. Now the functional judgment of the Demos, not only at the Assembly but also in the Council, means Athens restored to the imperial greatness of its pre-Periclean days.

The location of the deliberative process also remains crucial in *Knights,* and activity on the Pnyx in particular. Demos is introduced as belonging to the Pnyx as his deme (Δῆμος Πυκνίτης, 42).[25] Cleon is projected as a giant monster with one leg in the Assembly (76). The dynamic of deliberation is

---

24. Cf. the entries for all these terms and individuals, plus that for Euathlos, in the Appendix. Like most editors, I follow Hamaker's emendation of Κεφισοδήμῳ to Κεφισοδήμου in line 705.

25. See Reinders (2001, 61–70, 123–30) for a breakdown of Aristophanes' characterization of the Demos.

problematic in ways similar to that described in *Acharnians*. Where there the Athenians are quick to judgment, quick to change their minds and easily deceived by flattery, in *Knights*, Demos is (41–43)

ἀκράχολος,
Δῆμος Πυκνίτης, δύσκολον γερόντιον
ὑπόκωφον.

quick to anger,
Demos of Pnyx, cranky, a little old man
and deaf.

The barrier to the deliberative process is the same deceptive flattery dramatized and criticized in *Acharnians*, but here it is Cleon in the form of the Paphlagonian slave who embodies this problem (ἤκαλλ' ἐθώπευ' ἐκολάκευ', ἐξηπάτα, "He fawns, sucks up, flatters, deceives" 48). There is no deliberation or debate, not even from the race of *rhetores*, for Cleon stands ready and flicks them away (ἑστὼς ἀποσοβεῖ τοὺς ῥήτορας, 60). The slaves Demosthenes and Nicias are reduced to deliberating about the best way to commit suicide (80–100). Demosthenes' solution is to get drunk, because then the rewards of good deliberation follow (90–94):

οἶνον σὺ τολμᾷς εἰς ἐπίνοιαν λοιδορεῖν;
οἴνου γὰρ εὕροις ἄν τι πρακτικώτερον;
ὁρᾷς, ὅταν πίνωσιν ἄνθρωποι, τότε
πλουτοῦσι διαπράττουσι, νικῶσιν δίκας,
εὐδαιμονοῦσιν, ὠφελοῦσι τοὺς φίλους.

You dare to dispute that wine leads to thinking?
Could you find anything more effective than wine?
You see, when people drink:
They get wealthy. They prosper. They win their cases.
They're blessedly happy. They help their friends!

Lubricating the deliberative process yields victory and success. To make success appear simultaneously traditional and democratic, Aristophanes makes it come in the form of the traditional formula of helping one's friends and harming one's enemies. He explicitly includes the ability to help friends, while harming enemies comes in the form of winning court cases against them, using an established process via a democratic institution. Even drunkenness is a virtue if it leads to deliberation, and just starting to drink starts the mind on the process (99–100):

ἢν γὰρ μεθυσθῶ, πάντα ταυτὶ καταπάσω
βουλευματίων καὶ γνωμιδίων καὶ νοιδίων.

If I get drunk, I'll sprinkle everything here
with little resolutions, thoughts and ideas.

Once again, deliberation is stalled in the Assembly but the process itself emerges elsewhere: for the moment, in the drunken talk among slaves in the house of Demos. Again as in *Acharnians,* once the deliberative process begins, translocated and wine-addled as it is here, progress begins immediately. Fortified with drink, Demosthenes has Nicias steal the Paphlagonian's oracles. The oracles describe the succession of "sellers" who control the affairs of the city (ἕξει τῆς πόλεως τὰ πράγματα, 130). Cleon is characterized substantially by his speaking (137):[26]

ἅρπαξ, κεκράκτης Κυκλοβόρου φωνὴν ἔχων

A thief, a shrieker, with the voice of roaring Cycloborus.

When Cleon's successor, the Sausage-Seller, arrives, Demosthenes describes his future as a decidedly antidemocratic leader (164–67):

τούτων ἁπάντων αὐτὸς ἀρχέλας ἔσει,
καὶ τῆς ἀγορᾶς καὶ τῶν λιμένων καὶ τῆς Πυκνός·
βουλὴν πατήσεις καὶ στρατηγοὺς κλαστάσεις,
δήσεις φυλάξεις, ἐν πρυτανείῳ λαικάσει.

You will be the "Commander of the People" for all of them,
over the Agora, the harbors and the Pnyx.
You'll smash the Council! You'll cut down the generals!
You'll lock 'em up! You'll jail 'em! You'll suck cock in the Prytaneum!

---

26. There may be vestiges of allusions to Cleon's oratory earlier in the play. In 103, he is licking, λείξας, a common metaphor for embezzlement but also an easy pun on forms of λέγω (λείξας/λέξας). In 115 he farts and snores, πέρδεται καὶ ῥέγκεται, sometimes a metaphor for oratory; cf. Major (2002). On the terms here, cf. the entry for the tongue in the Appendix.

Succeeding Cleon means continuing the status quo, only more so. This status quo, with Cleon flattering and deceiving the Demos, while he keeps any other deliberative input at bay, points the way to monarchy and tyranny. Aristophanes reinforces the undemocratic direction in tone and content. The unique form ἀρχέλας means "commander of the host," but Aristophanes has just used τὰς στίχας . . . τὰς τῶνδε τῶν λαῶν, "the rows of this host" (163), to refer to the spectators of the play in the theater, so the title here more likely is just picking up on λαῶν to say that he will be ruler of the assembly present.²⁷ The reference to abusing the Council and imprisoning people emphasizes the antidemocratic nature of the power described, since the oath for the Council specifically forbade imprisoning Athenians (Dem. 24.14). Adding the Prytaneum to this sequence, when Cleon had just recently been granted seating and meals there, associates his privileges with aristocratic monarchy rather than with democratic reward.

The conversation soon turns to the credentials of the rising star. Here a crucial new term makes its earliest appearance (191–93):

ἡ δημαγωγία γὰρ οὐ πρὸς μουσικοῦ
ἔτ' ἐστὶν ἀνδρὸς οὐδὲ χρηστοῦ τοὺς τρόπους,
ἀλλ' εἰς ἀμαθῆ βδελυρόν.

Leadership of the Demos doesn't belong to the educated
man anymore or one beneficial in his manner,
but instead to the ignorant and disgusting.²⁸

After working through the details of an oracle, Demosthenes echoes the sentiment (217–19):

τὰ δ' ἄλλα σοι πρόσεστι δημαγωγικά,
φωνὴ μιαρά, γέγονας κακῶς, ἀγοραῖος εἶ·
ἔχεις ἅπαντα πρὸς πολιτείαν ἃ δεῖ.

You have the rest of what it takes to lead the Demos:

---

27. Raaflaub (2003, 80) observes that the political associations of ἀρχή at this time are positive compared to those of tyranny, but the non-Attic contraction to -α throws the word into a different register; see, for example, Aeschylus, *Persians* 297, where it is used by the Persian Queen of Persian leaders.

28. N. G. Wilson 2007a, 42 rightly obelizes line 193, and I have no better solution to offer, but, if his suspicion is right that a line has dropped out here, nothing suggests that an addition would alter the connotation of the key term under discussion here, δημαγωγία.

> a polluted voice, bad family, a background in the Agora.
> You have everything necessary for civic life.

It seems that δημαγωγία and related terms are new at this time, in fact being attested for the first time in these two passages.[29] The term does not surface in Aristophanes again until *Frogs*, nearly twenty years later, where it is linked to the unpleasant Archedemus (419). The only other instances in Greek comedy provide little help. First is someone who is "worthy to be a demagogue" at Eupolis fr. 99.23 from *Demes*. The identity of this demagogue here and in the following lines remain the subject of much debate and uncertainty.[30] The other instance is far from certain. Adesp. fr. 1094 consists of two strips of papyri containing the middle of some thirty-five lines, not enough to allow for continuous sense. The words that survive point to political content (repeated use of πολίτης, δῆμος, etc.). Line 4 begins]αγωγός, and δημ]αγωγός seems a reasonable restoration. This would be the only attested use of this exact noun in Old Comedy, but, in fact, it is not certain that this fragment comes from comedy at all.[31]

The two instances in *Knights* do not come loaded with the negative connotation that the word later acquires of "demagoguery." Rather, the appearances seem to expect that the terms are neutral or even slightly positive and that Aristophanes is redefining them in a sharply negative way. The development from and contrast with ἀρχέλας earlier is also significant. The two terms are parallel in one sense (ἀρχ- and -αγω indicating leadership; λάος and δῆμος indicating the communal body they lead). Aristophanes sets up ἀρχέλας as distinctly lofty and antidemocratic, which can then suggest an aristocratic leadership. The cynical definition of δημαγωγία is still operating in the context of antidemocratic leadership, but it additionally removes any possibility of aristocracy.

Thus Aristophanes further denigrates Cleon's influence. Pericles' aristocratic arrogance was bad enough for democracy, but Cleon has all the bad traits and represents nothing more than an ever-spiraling kakocracy. Such is the outcome in the absence of democratic deliberative process. Until Demos finally makes a meaningful judgment, *Knights* steams ahead in pursuit of the painfully logical ramifications of Cleon's influence. The Knights, good and noble citizens who hate Cleon, along with the spectators, and even the gods will support the Sausage-Seller out of opposition to Cleon (225–29). Such

---

29. See Connor (1971, 109–10) for the history of δημαγωγός in the politics of Athens in the last third of the fifth century.

30. Storey (2003, 149–60).

31. Gigante (1957), but Austin notes in PCG that the extant text suits trochaic tetrameters, leaving the possibility open for the text to belong to comedy.

support seems paradoxical until one realizes Aristophanes' underlying thesis: the only remedy for kakocracy is to restore the process. Without restoring the judgment and integrity of the deliberative process, overthrowing Cleon or any other poor leader will just result in even worse leadership, because that is all the current dysfunctional system permits. More than permitting the downward spiral, the current situation promotes and accelerates the ruin of Athens.

The outsized *agon* that consumes much of the play from this point onward is devoted to dramatizing this point. Currently the system leads to ever-worsening leadership; only an alert Demos will stop the cycle. When the moment comes, it more than stops the cycle; it completely reverts Demos and Athens to the mighty city that repelled the Persians and amassed an empire without suffering the tyranny of Pericles.

Once Cleon (nominally as the Paphlagonian) and the chorus of Knights arrive on stage (235–72), sparring in violence, flattery and deception dominates the debate between the Sausage-Seller and Cleon. Distorted public language forms an intrinsic part of the problem.[32] A number of comments address speaking, oratory and their role in the democratic process. One exchange confirms Cleon using shrieks and shouts to lead the city (the Sausage-Seller asks: καὶ κέκραγας, ὥσπερ ἀεὶ τὴν πόλιν καταστρέφεις; "So you shriek, as you always do when you tear the city down?" and Cleon responds: ἀλλ' ἐγώ σε τῇ βοῇ . . . , "I'll use my shouting . . . ," 274–75; cf. the same threat at καταβοήσομαι βοῶν σε, 286, and the entry in the Appendix). Demosthenes adds a comment that Cleon represents a decline even from Pericles (οὗ Περικλέης οὐκ ἠξιώθη πώποτε, "Even Pericles never deserved this," 283).[33] Another exchange indicates that deliberation will not be allowed to rise even to a verbal level (294–95):

ΠΑ.
διαφορήσω σ' εἴ τι γρύξει.
ΑΛ.
κοπροφορήσω σ' εἰ λαλήσεις.[34]

---

32. See Simmons (2012) for more on the terminology Aristophanes uses to characterize Cleon here.

33. On the points of contact between references to Cleon's honor in *Knights* and inscriptional evidence, see Rhodes (2010, 160).

34. Wilson (2007a, 45) follows Blaydes' emendation to λακήσει here in place of λαλήσεις, saying: "I prefer to see in the text a more vigorous term that can be traded as an insult." As a principle, this is fine, but it does not suit the context here, where the verb should be parallel to γρύξει in the previous line. Moreover, λακάω is not attested with reference to aggressive or insulting behavior in Aristophanes. In line 167 above, it is part of the Sausage-Seller's imagined luxurious life in the Prytaneum, and at *Th.* 57, it is something Agathon enjoys doing. The point here should be that, if

PAPHLAGONIAN
I'll plunder you, if you just gurgle.
SAUSAGE-SELLER
I'll shit you under, if you babble.

Cleon's nonverbal shrieking replaces even any vocalizing aimed toward deliberation. The chorus provides a vivid image, amplifying Cleon to a supersized monster over the Greek world (303–12):

ὦ μιαρὲ καὶ βδελυρὲ κρᾶκτα,[35] τοῦ σοῦ θράσους
πᾶσα μὲν γῆ πλέα, πᾶσα δ' ἐκκλησία,
καὶ τέλη καὶ γραφαὶ καὶ δικαστήρι,' ὦ
βορβοροτάραξι καὶ τὴν πόλιν ἅπασαν ἡμῶν ἀνατετυρβακώς,
ὅστις ἡμῶν τὰς Ἀθήνας ἐκκεκώφωκας βοῶν.

You polluted, disgusting shrieker, with your boldness
the whole earth is full, the entire Assembly,
the taxes, the lawsuits, the courts.
Mudthrasher, you've churned our whole city into chaos.
You've made Athens deaf from your shouting!

They continue shortly, inverting a crucial bit of political terminology (324–25):

ἆρα δῆτ' οὐκ ἀπ' ἀρχῆς ἐδήλους ἀναίδειαν, ἥπερ μόνη
προστατεῖ ῥητόρων;

From the start, didn't you show shamelessness,
The only "Protector of the Politicians"?

Given that Cleon earlier was swatting *rhetores* away from Demos, it seems odd that here it is a problem for them to be protected or that Cleon might be party to shielding them. The key to the chorus's charge, however, is the perversion of the title, which should be προστάτης τοῦ δήμου, "protector of the Demos." W. R. Connor argues that the term was fresh in the 420s and

---

Cleon even tries to engage in his normal blabber, the Sausage-Seller will stop him. Accordingly, I have retained the MSS reading here.

35. See Parker (1997, 160–63) for the metrical problems here with the MSS's καὶ (κε)κράκτα, for which Meineke's κρᾶκτα is an imperfect emendation. Depending on the depth of the corruption here, it is possible that the -κρα- root is itself corrupt, which would affect my reading slightly, but no satisfactory solution is available.

one a leader like Cleon could use to suggest he was more devoted to the city than to his circle of friends, as an aristocrat was prone to be, but the term nonetheless nervously has associations that such a "protector" could leap for monarchy or tyranny.[36] If Cleon used the term positively of himself, as seems likely, Aristophanes has reason not to use it, or rather to use it only in a negative form. Having the Knights make this charge and making them criticize the lack of a προστάτης τοῦ δήμου also draws support for the Demos from an aristocratic class. This is shrewd, for it gives the Knights more than a personal motivation for objecting to Cleon, and thus Aristophanes depicts an allegiance between the Knights and the mass Demos but does so without denigrating their nobility or elite status. Once again, then, Aristophanes embeds the idea that restoring the authority of the Demos is the goal, while Cleon is an impediment to such restoration.

In lieu of προστάτης τοῦ δήμου, tainted by its association with Cleon, Aristophanes seems to prefer a more venerable variation on it, the ἐπίτροπος τοῦ δήμου, "trustee of the people," implying that a leader should be a trusted administrator of the will of the Demos.[37] The Sausage-Seller is amazed at the idea that he might undertake such a responsibility (212), and the phrase anchors the mock solemnity of the prophecy that the Sausage-Seller will one day guide the city (427). Later in the play, Demos for the first time threatens to discharge Cleon, saying he will no longer be the Demos' steward (ταμίας, 948), and Cleon, now in the presence of Demos and hoping to conceal his true ambitions, tries to hold onto the position by using the same subservient language (εἰ μή μ' ἐάσεις ἐπιτροπεύειν, 949).[38]

But earlier in the play, as the *agon* mounts, the Knights raise the stakes still more with their next charge against Cleon (326–27):

ᾗ σὺ πιστεύων ἀμέργεις τῶν ξένων τοὺς καρπίμους,
πρῶτος ὤν· ὁ δ' Ἱπποδάμου λείβεται θεώμενος.

Trusting in that shamelessness, you milk the fruitful of the foreigners,
You, "Number One," while the son of Hippodamus[39] is left watching.

---

36. Connor (1971, 110–15).
37. Connor (1971, 127 n. 68). Thrasymachus (85 B1 DK) uses the term favorably when referring to the good government of Athens by its elders in the past. Cf. the praise of the past rule of Athens by the chorus at *Knights* 565–80. Aristotle, *Rhet.* 3.8.1408b25 has children cry out that a freedman will choose Cleon as his ἐπίτροπος. In the Council, there was the presiding but limited office of ἐπιστάτης τῶν πρυτάνεων (Arist. *Ath. Pol.* 44.1); cf. Rhodes (1972, 23–24).
38. Cf. *Peace* 648, where the city misses its ἐπίτροπος.
39. N. G. Wilson finds the metrical response here and the identification of Hippodamus problematic (2007a, 45–46), but Sommerstein (1980, 47–48) makes a convincing case for the identification.

Several strands are woven together here, each belonging to broader ideological preferences Aristophanes trumpets more explicitly in other passages. First, the son of Hippodamus, Archeptolemus, is elsewhere in the play cited for proposing peace with the Spartans (794). In addition, although Archeptolemus was of non-Athenian extraction (for this and probably for lobbying efforts on behalf of other foreigners, he is linked to them here), he was a rare case of a foreigner holding citizenship in Athens. As Aristophanes does regularly, he expects that advice and deliberation from an inclusive body, including the voices of non-Athenians, are beneficial to Athens.[40] Finally, Archeptolemus is marginalized as a spectator, the recurring metaphor of an individual who is present but plays no meaningful role in policy deliberations, although here prevented against his will. Having tacitly lamented the absence of the authority of the Demos and implied the need for more inclusive deliberation, the chorus can cheer the only option left, the Sausage-Seller as the new leader. "Show us how worthless a decent upbringing is" (νῦν δεῖξον ὡς οὐδὲν λέγει τὸ σωφρόνως τραφῆναι, 332), they comment sardonically.[41] The Sausage-Seller and Cleon in turn spar for the right to speak and over the ability to do so (335–43). Cleon offers a dismissive image of someone trying to participate in the deliberative process (344–50):

ἰδοὺ λέγειν. καλῶς γ' ἂν οὖν σὺ πρᾶγμα προσπεσόν σοι
ὠμοσπάρακτον παραλαβὼν μεταχειρίσαιο χρηστῶς.
ἀλλ' οἶσθ' ὅπερ πεπονθέναι δοκεῖς; ὅπερ τὸ πλῆθος.
εἴ που δικίδιον εἶπας εὖ κατὰ ξένου μετοίκου,
τὴν νύκτα θρυλῶν καὶ λαλῶν ἐν ταῖς ὁδοῖς σεαυτῷ,
ὕδωρ τε πίνων κἀπιδεικνὺς τοὺς φίλους τ' ἀνιῶν
ᾤου δυνατὸς εἶναι λέγειν. ὦ μῶρε, τῆς ἀνοίας.

Look at that "speaking"! It'd be just great if some issue fell to you.
You'd get it all torn up and raw and treat it just fine!
You know what I think happened to you? What happens to the masses.
If you do a good job speaking for some little case sometime against a
    resident foreigner,
chattering all night and blathering to yourself in the streets,

---

40. Cf. Chapter 5 on *Lysistrata* for a more extended example of this principle. Sommerstein (1980, 48) also notes that Archeptolemus is a rare politician whose actions elicit sympathy from Aristophanes, the others being Demosthenes (whom even Sommerstein acknowledges seems to have been a democrat, if anything) and possibly Thrasybulus.

41. On the aristocratic associations of σωφρών, see Neil (1901, 204), Dover (1974, 56–60, 66–69, 119–21) and Papageorgiou (2004a).

drinking water, rehearsing, annoying your friends,
you think you're capable of giving a speech! You moron! What an idea!

The passage provides a rare vivid image of a speaker preparing, and also a rare acknowledgment of the craft and preparation involved. Aristophanes also laces it with antidemocratic expressions. Rather than δῆμος, Cleon uses πλῆθος, consistent with an oligarch's view of the Demos.[42] He describes a minor case against a *metic*, when the chorus has just recently established and defended the role of foreigners in advising Athens.[43] In general, Cleon dismisses the ability of anyone to speak meaningfully on public policy, a right central to the democracy and one defended by Aristophanes (e.g., *Ach.* 557–65) and enshrined in the twin democratic principles of *parrhesia* and *isegoria*.[44] The Sausage-Seller responds to this image by denigrating the substance of Cleon's own oratory and reiterating the antidemocratic result (351–52):

τί δαὶ σὺ πίνων τὴν πόλιν πεποίηκας, ὥστε νυνὶ
ὑπὸ σοῦ μονωτάτου κατεγλωττισμένην σιωπᾶν;

So what do you drink to handle the city and make it so that now
It's silent from being tongued down by your singularity?

A silent city means the democratic deliberative process is not taking place, the only noise coming from Cleon, and his weapon of choice, the tongue, regularly indicates poor or troublesome language.[45] To outdo Cleon, the Sausage-Seller boasts he will use his throat instead to dominate the *rhetores* (λαρυγγιῶ τοὺς ῥήτορας, 358).

So far the contested space for deliberation is the Pnyx and the occasion the Assembly. In *Acharnians,* the Prytaneis from the Council received criticism for their apathy toward the business of the Assembly, but the Council itself was never mentioned. In *Knights,* the rivalry between Cleon and the Sausage-Seller now expands beyond the Assembly. "I'll jump on the Council and stir it by force" (ἐγὼ δ' ἐπεισπηδῶν γε τὴν βουλὴν βίᾳ κυκήσω, 363), promises Cleon as part of his assurance he will dominate the city more than the Sausage-Seller can (cf. the promise at 166 that the Sausage-

---

42. Connor (1971, 203); Reinders (2001, 39–55).
43. Whitehead (1977, 39–41) surveys Old Comedy's references to metics, limited as they are, and finds them, on balance, benevolent.
44. On these terms, see Raaflaub (1980, 11–23).
45. See Chapter 2 and the Appendix.

Seller will dominate the Council). In the midst of ever-mounting threats of physical domination from the Sausage-Seller, Cleon claims protection in his control of the Council (395–96):

οὐ δέδοιχ' ὑμᾶς, ἕως ἂν ζῇ τὸ βουλευτήριον
καὶ τὸ τοῦ Δήμου πρόσωπον μακκοᾷ καθήμενον.

I'm not afraid of you as long as the Council House lives
And the face of the Demos sits booby-faced.

Cleon has now laid claim to two of the three democratic institutions where the Demos is supposed to promulgate its will, the Council and Assembly. After more sparring, Cleon again invokes the Council as the *agon* is about to move there (475–79):

ἐγὼ μὲν οὖν αὐτίκα μάλ' ἐς βουλὴν ἰὼν
ὑμῶν ἁπάντων τὰς ξυνωμοσίας ἐρῶ,
καὶ τὰς ξυνόδους τὰς νυκτερινὰς τὰς ἐπὶ τῇ πόλει,
καὶ πάνθ' ἃ Μήδοις καὶ βασιλεῖ ξυνόμνυτε,
καὶ τἀκ Βοιωτῶν ταῦτα συντυρούμενα.

Right now I'll go to the Council!
I'll tell them about all y'all's conspiracies,
the nighttime meetings against the city,
and everything you swore to the Persians and their King,
and being thick in cheese[46] with the Boeotians!

As the Sausage-Seller and Cleon leave the stage to resume their conflict at the Council itself, the chorus of Knights devotes part of its *parabasis* to praise of their ancestors for their military glory on behalf of Athens (565–80). They add specifically that the generals of old would never have stooped to asking Cleon's father for state maintenance in the Prytaneum. In addition to attacking Cleon's privilege yet again, they set up the image of the glorious ancestors who will be invoked at the end of the play when Demos is restored and rejuvenated.[47]

---

46. Pollux 6.130; among many phrases Pollux lists to provoke the Demos (πρὸς τὸν θορυβοῦντα τὸ δημόσιον), he objects to this metaphor when Demosthenes uses it (19.295), as here, to indicate sedition.

47. See Edmunds (1987a 253–56 = 1987b, 39–41) and Hubbard (1991, 78–83) for more detailed analyses of the ideological dynamics in this section.

Meanwhile, the contest before the Council might inspire hope that some substantial deliberation will ensue. The Demos is absent from the proceedings, however, and the Prytaneis behave very much as they did at the Assembly in *Acharnians:* responsive only to deception and flattery, taken in more by show than by discussion and deliberation. Within the Sausage-Seller's report of the meeting are some important characterizations of speaking and oratory. When Cleon arrives, he is letting loose with thundering words, reminiscent of the negative portrayal of Pericles as an arrogant, domineering Olympian (ὁ δ' ἄρ' ἔνδον ἐλασίβροντ' ἀναρρηγνὺς ἔπη, 626). It is no surprise that, in order to outdo Cleon, the Sausage-Seller prays for boldness (θράσος, 637; cf. the chorus's image of Cleon's θράσος filling the world at 304) and a tongue (637; cf. 352 of Cleon using his tongue to subdue Athens, Chapter 2 and the Appendix). For his first utterance, the Sausage-Seller shrieks (ἀνέκραγον, 642; cf. 137, 274 and 303 of Cleon). He wins the Council's attention, not with policy or discussion, but by deception in the form of good news about cheap sardines. The Council responds by gaping (ἐκεχήνεσαν, 651), just as the *parabasis* of *Acharnians* described the Athenians doing in response to flattery (635). Like the Prytaneis at the Assembly in *Acharnians,* the members of the Council are more interested in trivialities and corruption, so when Cleon desperately tries to regain the attention of the Council by saying a Spartan ambassador comes to seek a peace treaty, the members remain fixated on the sardines and make their own shriek this time, for the Prytaneis to adjourn the meeting (ἐκεκράγεσαν, 674). By these means, supplemented by tossing in a bribe of coriander to season to sardines, the Sausage-Seller declares victory. It is a victory over the Council as much as it is over Cleon.

Cleon returns unfazed, and more sparring ensues as the competition staggers toward the next phase of the *agon.* Cleon swears he will ruin the Sausage-Seller, invoking the honorary seating he enjoys because of his victory at Pylos (702). The Sausage-Seller retorts (703–4):

ἰδοὺ προεδρίαν· οἷον ὄψομαί σ' ἐγὼ
ἐκ τῆς προεδρίας ἔσχατον θεώμενον.

Privileged seating! I look forward to seeing you
out of the front row and watching from the back!

In response to Cleon enjoying the sort of seats even the Prytaneis scramble for and being a leading participant in activities, the Sausage-Seller inverts both privileges by sending him to the back and making him a spectator, a nonparticipant. The citation of Cleon's privileges, again mentioning the Prytaneum in a few lines (709), heightens the distance between Cleon and the humble service and victory of the Knights' ancestors celebrated in the *parabasis*. Immediately, the rivalry turns to the Demos (710–23). After the keenly felt absence of the Demos and the consequences of the absence of his judgment, this section of the battle promises to be the climax. Whoever holds sway over the Demos undeniably holds the power.

When Demos emerges, both rivals immediately engage in the flattery that has so far proven effective in place of deliberation. Familiar characterizations of the broken deliberative process recur here, from the shouting (728) typical of Cleon to Cleon's claim he is being bullied by the younger generation (731). Cleon calls for a meeting of the Assembly so Demos can judge his most devoted lover: Cleon or the Sausage-Seller. Translocation is again an issue. In *Acharnians* the deliberations of the Assembly at the Pnyx were dysfunctional, but deliberations could occur outside of it, such as at Dicaeopolis' home. The Sausage-Seller indicates the same dynamic holds now. The collective judgment of the Demos is operative at home but not on the Pnyx (752–55):

οἴμοι κακοδαίμων, ὡς ἀπόλωλ'. ὁ γὰρ γέρων
οἴκοι μὲν ἀνδρῶν ἐστι δεξιώτατος,
ὅταν δ' ἐπὶ ταυτησὶ καθῆται τῆς πέτρας,
κέχηνεν ὥσπερ ἐμποδίζων ἰσχάδας.

Oh poor me! I'm dead. The old man
At home is the smartest man around,
But when he's sitting on that rock there,
He gapes[48] like he's mashing dried figs.

The discursive debate that follows on the Pnyx fails as substantive deliberation and reiterates the established cancers on the political process.[49] Cleon brags of the violent and distorted public service by which he dominates the Council (774–76). In response, the Sausage-Seller reminds Demos how he won victory at Marathon, which should have provided better material

---

48. "Gaping" is a repeated metaphor for lack of meaningful participation in the deliberative process. See *Ach.* 635, 651 above; and *Kn.* 1119 and *Wasps* 695 and 1007 below.

49. Rhodes (2010) details the points of contact between this scene and documentary evidence for the procedures of the Assembly, establishing both that Aristophanes was familiar with the actual proceedings of the Assembly and that the scene reflects events there. Cf. Chapter 5 and Haldane (1965) for an even more detailed example from *Thesmophoriazusae*.

for tongues now (782). Cleon keeps any overtures for peace away from the Demos (794–96). Out of jealousy, Cleon investigates the activities of assholes to prevent active ones from generating *rhetores* (878–80). Conversation with a pressed olive leads to clearer thinking than do the corrupt proceedings on the Pnyx (805–8).

On the other hand, a few lines begin to reveal the true principles of success, as Aristophanes depicts them, which consistently refer to the glory days of Athens' ascendancy as the democracy that repelled the Persians and built an empire, featuring the heroes of the pre-Periclean age. When the Sausage-Seller invokes the martial prowess of Marathon and Salamis, the Demos asks if he belongs to the family of the tyrant killer Harmodius (781–86). While tyranny and monarchy are the enemies of democracy, for the Demos to rule all of Greece is a positive and laudable goal (797–801). Both Cleon and the Sausage-Seller agree on Themistocles as a figure who benefited Athens greatly (812–19).[50]

After the contest in oracles comes to a draw (997–1108), Demos declares that he will hand the reins of the Pnyx over to whichever of them can do more for him (ὁπότερος ἂν σφῷν εὖ με μᾶλλον ἂν ποιῇ, / τούτῳ παραδώσω τῆς Πυκνὸς τὰς ἡνίας, 1108–9). As a setup for this last round in the contest, Aristophanes reinforces some basic vocabulary for the popular political order. The chorus of Knights addresses the Demos, making explicit that the absolute power of the Demos is a good thing (1111–14):

ὦ Δῆμε, καλήν γ' ἔχεις ἀρχήν, ὅτε πάντες ἄνθρωποι δεδίασί σ'
ὥσπερ ἄνδρα τύραννον.

Demos, your rule is glorious when all people fear you like a tyrant.

The problem is not the rule of the Demos, only the obstructions to the Demos' good judgment (1115–20):

ἀλλ' εὐπαράγωγος εἶ,
θωπευόμενός τε χαίρεις κἀξαπατώμενος,
πρὸς τόν τε λέγοντ' ἀεὶ
κέχηνας· ὁ νοῦς δέ σου
παρὼν ἀποδημεῖ.

But you tend to lose your way,

---

50. Cf. the discussion of Braun (2000) in Chapter 4.

when you enjoy being flattered
and deceived.
You always gape when someone is speaking,
away from home when you are right there.

The deception, flattery and gaping are familiar motifs by this point, and the closing words pick up the metaphor of translocation. The pun on the word Demos (ἀπο-δημ-εῖ) reinforces the idea that the judgment of the Demos is missing from the location where productive deliberation is supposed to take place. For the first time, however, Aristophanes turns the tide by dramatizing the will of the Demos as superior to the "protector of the Demos" who seems to be in power (1121–30):

νοῦς οὐκ ἔνι ταῖς κόμαις
ὑμῶν, ὅτε μ' οὐ φρονεῖν
νομίζετ'· ἐγὼ δ' ἑκὼν
ταῦτ' ἠλιθιάζω.
αὐτός τε γὰρ ἥδομαι
βρύλλων τὸ καθ' ἡμέραν,
κλέπτοντά τε βούλομαι
τρέφειν ἕνα προστάτην
τοῦτον δ,' ὅταν ᾖ πλέως,
ἄρας ἐπάταξα.

You've lost the brains under your hair
if you don't recognize I'm sane. I willingly
act stupidly like this.
Because I like
crying for my daily sustenance
and I want to fatten up the thief,
that singular "Protector."
And when he's full,
I'll sacrifice him on the altar.

Commentators have rightly found this sudden assertion surprising, because Demos has not hinted at this awareness previously, and because Demos will again have to shake off his doldrums later in the play, but they have missed how the statement is crucial and logical in the resolution to the problem Aristophanes has presented.[51] Repeatedly, in different ways, Aristophanes has

---

51. Reinders (2001, 170–92) reviews the problem and concludes, like many scholars, that Aris-

stated and dramatized that the only means to Athens' prosperity is rule by the judgment of the Demos via the deliberative processes of the democracy. He has been paving the way for the play's conclusion where the rejuvenated Demos will restore Athens' pre-Periclean, pre-demagogic, pre-"Protector" glory. At some point, the Demos needs to participate and lead by rendering his judgment, so Aristophanes simply has Demos assert his awareness and leadership. It may not be fine dramatic construction, but it is ideologically consistent and logical. Next, the second half of the exchange reinforces the idea and the vocabulary. The chorus of Knights praises the shrewdness of Demos with a pun (πυκνότης, 1132, punning on πυκνίτης, the mock demotic from line 42) and alludes to the title of προστάτης τοῦ δήμου, which Demos had invoked, but here they praise his fattening up of supposed public servants (as if they were literally slaves of the Demos) on the Pnyx (δημοσίους τρέφεις/ἐν τῇ πυκνί, 1136–37). Demos then again asserts his awareness of the politicians' larceny and that he will use audits to force return of their ill-gotten gains (1145–50).

For the next stage of the *agon*, even when Demos does not make explicit his awareness of the flattery of the competitors, every line is consistent with being delivered ironically, sardonically and knowingly. As the *agon* resumes, Cleon and the Sausage-Seller engage in a contest of flattery (1151–1208).[52] After a series of spiraling offers, Demos resets the decision for the final time (1209–10):

τῷ δῆτ' ἂν ὑμᾶς χρησάμενος τεκμηρίῳ
δόξαιμι κρίνειν τοῖς θεαταῖσιν σοφῶς;

So now, what evidence seems best to the spectators for me to use to judge you wisely?

For the first time in either *Acharnians* or *Knights,* all the elements are together for proper and successful deliberation. There are spectators to the speeches, but now the Demos will render wise judgment on the Pnyx. In rapid succession, Demos investigates what each suitor holds back in his basket for himself (1211–25), ignores Cleon's defense that he stole for the good of the city (1226–29), and the oracle about Cleon's downfall is confirmed (1230–52). The Sausage-Seller takes the crown from Cleon, but the real

---

tophanes voices serious criticism of the Demos but mutes and calibrates it.

52. Note that at 1196–98 the Sausage-Seller distracts Cleon by imagining some foreign ambassadors are nearby, ready for robbing, again playing on Cleon's propensity for abusing, rather than capitalizing on, the contributions of foreigners in the deliberative process.

climax is the assertion of, and subservience to, Demos and his judgment. The Sausage-Seller explains his role this way (1261–63):

καὶ μὴν ἐγώ σ', ὦ Δῆμε, θεραπεύσω καλῶς,
ὥσθ' ὁμολογεῖν σε μηδέν' ἀνθρώπων ἐμοῦ
ἰδεῖν ἀμείνω τῇ Κεχηναίων πόλει.

But now I will serve you well, Demos,
so you can agree that you have never seen anyone
better for the city of Gawkers.

Aristophanes shifts the vocabulary now. Rather than flatter (θωπεύω, e.g., *Ach.* 635–39; *Kn.* 48, 1116), the Sausage-Seller will serve the Demos (θεραπεύσω, which Cleon laid sole claim to doing at 59 and 799), but with the crucial difference that the Demos' judgment is the ultimate arbiter, even if the Athenians are still, satirically, the same passive gawkers at the Assembly.

The final scene in the play displays the thoroughly positive results from the restoration of Demos' judgment to the deliberative process. The Demos is now the peer of Aristides and Miltiades of the old days of Marathon (1325, 1334).[53] Athens can now be violet-crowned without flattery (ἰοστέφανοι, 1329). Monarchy or tyranny in an individual is to be fought and resisted, but tyrant, monarch and king are welcome attributes of Demos ruling Greece (τύραννον, 1114; τὸν τῆς Ἑλλάδος ὑμῖν καὶ τῆς γῆς τῆσδε μόναρχον, 1330; ὦ βασιλεῦ τῶν Ἑλλήνων, 1333).[54]

Because the language of public discourse was the primary sign of the dysfunctional deliberative system, it is the first item to distinguish the newly rejuvenated and restored Demos from his former failures. In response to Demos' initial inquiry about how he used to behave, Agoracritus explains with a by-now familiar image of flattery (1340–44):

πρῶτον μέν, ὁπότ' εἴποι τις ἐν τ' ἠκκλησίᾳ,
"ὦ Δῆμ', ἐραστής εἰμι σὸς φιλῶ τέ σε
καὶ κήδομαί σου καὶ προβουλεύω μόνος,"
τούτοις ὁπότε χρήσαιτό τις προοιμίοις,
ἀνωρτάλιζες κἀκερουτίας.

First, whenever anyone in the Assembly said,

---

53. On such invocations generally, see Rhodes (2011a).
54. The view presented here generally agrees with those of Henderson (2003, esp. 168) and Kallet (2003). For a contrary view (that Demos as Tyrannos is pejorative), see Raaflaub (2003).

"Demos! I'm your lover and I love you,
and I'm the only one who worries and makes your proposals!"
Whenever someone used these types of greetings [*prooimia*],
you'd flap your wings and shake your horns.

Agoracritus goes on to reprise the issues of deception (1345, 1357) and deafness to reason (1347–48), familiar from earlier passages in the play and in *Acharnians*. Now, under the rejuvenated Demos, *rhetores* and *synegoroi* will no longer ply their deceitful ways, not because they will be blocked from speaking, but because Demos will render sensible judgment on them (1350–63). A series of policy reforms follows (1364–95). One specifically addresses the shifty talk of young provocateurs (1375–80):

τὰ μειράκια ταυτὶ λέγω τἀν τῷ μύρῳ,
ἃ τοιαδὶ στωμύλλεται καθήμενα
"σοφός γ' ὁ Φαίαξ δεξιῶς τ' οὐκ ἀπέθανεν.
συνερτικὸς γάρ ἐστι καὶ περαντικός,
καὶ γνωμοτυπικὸς καὶ σαφὴς καὶ κρουστικός,
καταληπτικός τ' ἄριστα τοῦ θορυβητικοῦ."

I mean those punks there in the myrrh,
who sit and mouth off like this:
"That really wise Phaeax avoids death so cleverly.
Because he's cooperative, conclusive,
idea-impressitive, clear, strikitive,
and most repressative of the provocative."

Little is known of Phaeax,[55] but the repeated application of the termination -ικός is typical of comedy's method for dealing with unorthodox language. While the termination is an established and productive one in Greek, most authors apply it to inanimate or abstract nouns, while comedy applies such words derogatorily of people.[56] The next few lines further illustrate how the language of the Demos differs from that of uppity, elite young speakers (1381–83):

Ἀλ.
οὔκουν καταδακτυλικὸς σὺ τοῦ λαλητικοῦ;

---

55. On Phaeax, see Eupolis frr. 2 and 116; cf. Storey (2003, 73) and the entry in the Appendix. On λαλοί young men among the myrrh, see also Pherecrates fr. 70.
56. Peppler (1910).

ΔΗΜ.
μὰ Δί' ἀλλ' ἀναγκάσω κυνηγετεῖν ἐγὼ
τούτους ἅπαντας, παυσαμένους ψηφισμάτων.

AGORACRITUS
So you're going to be fingerative up their talkative?
DEMOS
No, I'll make them go hunting
and keep them all from their propositions.

Finally, Demos welcomes in the Thirty-Year Peace Treaties, quite the opposite of Cleon keeping peace offers out of reach of deliberation, and terms which, in *Acharnians,* Dicaeopolis could negotiate only outside the Assembly. Where Dicaeopolis reaped the benefits of his peace negotiations individually, now the collective Demos will take them to the entire countryside (1394). A democratic deliberative process, clear speaking, and widespread peace: such are the benefits of the Demos asserting its proper judgment in the Assembly. And finally, in the last lines of the script as we have it, there is a final translocation: Cleon will be relegated to outside the city's gates in view of the foreigners he once tried to mutilate (1407–8).

GOING TO THE SOURCE: LANGUAGE AND SCHOOLING IN THE *CLOUDS*

Aristophanes devoted at least a fair share of the plays of the first five years of his career to the nature and purpose of civic language, especially in the deliberative process.[57] It is logical enough, then, that he should focus a play on the anterior processes that promoted such language and prepared speakers for deliberative occasions. Aristophanes lays claim to novelty in his play on the topic, *Clouds,* though not specifically for exploring language education. A number of plays from the same few years that seem to involve teachers

---

57. *Banqueters* of 427 certainly explored the issue (fr. 205). *Babylonians* of 426 may well have, but the fragments are too scanty and unclear to determine this. *Merchant Ships* cites the prosecutor Euathlos (fr. 424) and could come from this period. *Farmers,* which also seems to belong to these years, mentions Gorgias and Philippus (fr. 118). A bit of dialogue (fr. 101) reveals that singing (ᾄδειν) can mean a poor defense in court. Cf. Polyzelus fr. 13, "but a voice neither too bitter (τρυγερούς) or too sweet," which seems to have more to do with drama than with rhetoric. See Hall (2006, 328–35) on τρύξ in drama.

and students could suggest that education was in vogue as a topic among comic playwrights in the late 420s.[58]

The revised history of early rhetoric has meant reconfiguring the context of language training in fifth-century Athens.[59] First, the new history makes clear that there was no institutionalized training in formal speaking, whether called ῥητορική or not, nor was there an expectation or requirement of such training for elite public life.[60] Because of the lack of a more traditional aristocratic education, knowing art and letters (μουσική and γράμματα) was an issue, as it is for the Sausage-Seller in *Knights* (188–89), but adding the new wave of rational, clever speech techniques was a prompt for comic ridicule, not a reflection of the new expected or required training. In this sense, the depiction of Socrates' Phrontisterion in *Clouds* can be deceptive. It is a home and location for Socrates and his esoteric followers, but it is not an institution, any more than is the house of Callias, sponsor of itinerant intellectuals stopping over in Athens, in Eupolis' *Kolakes* or Plato's *Protagoras*. Typical instead is the specialized διδάσκαλος, such as Prodamus (Eupolis fr. 17 from *Aiges*; cf. the metaphor of the *grammatodidaskalon* at Eupolis fr. 192.13–15) or the unidentified διδάσκαλος in Aristophanes' *Banqueters* (frr. 206, 225). In the fourth century comedy will reflect recognized stereotypes of students of philosophical schools such as the Pythagoreans or Cynics, and institutions like the Academy and Lyceum.[61] In the meantime there are enough individual thinkers and teachers to form a chorus in Amipsias' *Konnos* (fr. 11), but the institutions where the emerging rhetoric appears on the comic stage remain those of the political arena. In *Clouds* in particular, Aristophanes explores language training en route to his full-fledged satire of the court system in *Wasps* of the following year.

While Aristophanes' claims to novelty should be interpreted with caution, some aspects of the creative novelty of *Clouds* have been underappreciated by scholars, especially when it comes to "rhetorical" language.[62] Already in *Knights* Aristophanes engaged in transforming terms for politically prominent speakers, with an end toward redefining them as ethically desirable or undesirable.[63] He engages in the same process in *Clouds* but on a larger

---

58. On Eupolis' *Aiges, Clouds*, and comedies about education at this time, see Storey (2003, 67–74).
59. Schiappa (2003, 157–71).
60. Morgan (2007, 304–8).
61. Olson (2007, 238–51).
62. See Major (2006) on Aristophanes' claims to novelty, among other things, in the revised portion of *Clouds*' parabasis (518–62). Cf. Platter (2007, 84–107) and Biles (2011, 167–210).
63. See discussion above of *prostates, epitropos*, etc.

scale and so thoroughly that it can seem as though he is straightforwardly dramatizing or reflecting established usage, when in fact he is reconstituting terminology and reevaluating people involved in the exploration of, and training in, language use.

Aristophanes' depiction of Socrates and the Sophists in *Clouds* is almost always treated as ancillary evidence for a characterization of the Older Sophists derived primarily from other sources, mostly Plato. Even in studies sympathetic to the Sophists' projects, the dynamic transformation in the play is underappreciated.[64] Since an overwhelming majority of the testimony about the Older Sophists derives from sources a generation later at the earliest, there is little to provide precise cultural context for the impact of the Sophists in the late 420s. Still, this is not sufficient reason to consider Aristophanes' depiction primarily as a mirror of popular perception or even of a widespread one. In fact, the internal dynamic of the play suggests that Aristophanes was working against a less hostile perception of them. At the very least, we should, with the benefit of hindsight, realize that *Clouds* is the earliest extant example of the perspective that the Sophists engaged in morally destructive projects.

In general, of course, Aristophanes is rarely restrained or subtle when introducing the ethical character of his targets. When his protagonist Strepsiades initially describes the activity of the residents of the "Thinkery of Wise Souls" (ψυχῶν σοφῶν τοῦτ' ... φροντιστήριον, 94), he does not refrain from including the moral dynamic of their vocation (97–99):

οὗτοι διδάσκουσ', ἀργύριον ἤν τις διδῷ,
λέγοντα νικᾶν καὶ δίκαια κἄδικα.

They teach, if you give them money,
how to win by speaking both justly and unjustly.

No teachers in Athens at the time, of course, baldly claimed to teach the ability to obtain victory by unjust means if a disciple spoke as taught, any more than Cleon would claim to be a successful thief (as his character does in *Knights*) or than real-world Prytaneis would fall victim to the blunt flattery and deception their stage counterparts do in *Acharnians* and *Knights*. Aristophanes is taking the trouble to spell out their moral deprav-

---

64. Cf. the Introduction, 7–18. For recent attempts to distinguish Socrates in *Clouds* from other sources, see Patzer (1994), Noël (2000) and Cavallero (2007). Mitscherling (2003) makes a rather too blunt attempt to recover Aristophanes' culpability for Socrates' trial. Whitehorne (2002) explores Aristophanes' visual representation of intellectuals.

ity, because he is engaged in persuasive characterization rather than using an established stereotype.[65] Only after the initial mold is set does Aristophanes permit debate. The ensuing dialogue between Strepsiades and Pheidippides contrasts these devious thinkers in terms of their respectability. Strepsiades tries to insist on their fundamental nobility and venerability (μεριμνοφροντισταὶ καλοί τε κἀγαθοί, 101). Pheidippides immediately identifies them as quite the opposite (πονηροί γ', . . . κακοδαίμων, 102–4), specifying them as verbal con artists (ἀλαζόνας, 102)[66] and naming names (Chaerephon and Socrates, 104).

Aristophanes stacks the deck in the same way when he introduces the primary intellectual project to be analyzed in the play. When Strepsiades insists his son go for an education at the Phrontisterion, he explains what he is to learn (112–18):

εἶναι παρ' αὐτοῖς φασιν ἄμφω τὼ λόγω,
τὸν κρείττον', ὅστις ἐστί, καὶ τὸν ἥττονα.
τούτοιν τὸν ἕτερον τοῖν λόγοιν, τὸν ἥττονα,
νικᾶν λέγοντά φασι τἀδικώτερα.
ἢν οὖν μάθῃς μοι τὸν ἄδικον τοῦτον λόγον,
ἃ νῦν ὀφείλω διὰ σέ, τούτων τῶν χρεῶν
οὐκ ἂν ἀποδοίην οὐδ' ἂν ὀβολὸν οὐδενί.

They say that both *logoi* are in there with them,
the stronger, no matter what that is, and the lesser.
This other of the two *logoi*, the lesser,
they say wins by speaking more unjustly.
If you'll learn this unjust *logos* for me,
then these debts I owe now because of you,
I wouldn't have to pay back an obol to anyone.

Aristophanes does not assume the spectators know what these *kreitton* and *hetton logoi* are, and does not so much explain them as define them. He does not provide a positive, or even neutral, definition that will then be revealed as masking an undesirable reality later in the play.[67] He quite forcefully

---

65. Of course, Aristophanes is otherwise willing to let characters show unforeseen characteristics, as he does with Demos in *Knights* and the chorus in *Clouds*. Compare the dynamic change Aristophanes engages in to transform Euripides into a villain in *Frogs* (see Chapter 6).
66. Cf. MacDowell (1990).
67. The use of φασι in 112 and 115 does not require that these are standard definitions in Athens at the time. Rather it sets up the fantastic fable quality of the *logoi* to come (cf. a similar use at *Kn*. 1300).

equates the *hetton logos* with injustice. This insistence makes sense insofar as Aristophanes needs to emphasize the immorality, because he cannot take for granted that the audience will recognize it. Strepsiades' statement unequivocally states that the two *logoi* are *kreitton* and *hetton* and then defines the *hetton logos* as unjust (only by implication is *kreitton logos* just, as no *logos* is described as just anywhere in the play).[68] That Aristophanes is defining the two *logoi* in terms of justice is crucial to what he is doing, yet the significance of it has been underplayed since antiquity, under the influence of a tradition hostile to the Sophists, which takes it as axiomatic that the idea of binary *logoi* is ethically perverse. The referent for these two *logoi* is certainly Protagoras' concept of binary *logoi*, but no source of the fifth century or earlier, except Aristophanes, treats *kreitton* and *hetton* as morally superior and inferior.[69] Indeed, *Clouds* features the earliest characterization of either of the two *logoi* as explicitly unjust. Such is the power of Aristophanes' characterization and its congruence with the later criticisms of Protagoras' idea by Plato, Aristotle and others that the novel dynamic in *Clouds* is overshadowed.

Indeed, the *logoi* in Strepsiades' introduction, and the personifications who come on stage for the *agon* later in the play, have been characterized ever since antiquity in moral terms. The scholarly equipment with the script (the hypotheses, scholia, etc.) refers to the two *logoi* in the *agon* as *Dikaios* and *Adikos Logos*, although the characters refer to each other explicitly only as *Kreitton* and *Hetton*.[70] Although a scholar like Kenneth J. Dover acknowledges the names *Dikaios* and *Adikos* do not go back to Aristophanes, he still translates their names in morally evaluative terms, "Right" and "Wrong." Translations of their names routinely work on this analogy, the most popular being "Better" and "Worse" Arguments, which frontloads Aristophanes' conclusion rather than reflecting the dynamic process by which Aristophanes takes the neutral terms and transforms them into moral adversaries.

While it is impossible to be certain that Aristophanes is the first or crucial figure to reinvent Protagoras' opposing *logoi* as moral adversaries, the

---

68. Cf. Euripides frr. 189 and 206 (*Antiope*) and *Suppliant Women* 487 for nearly contemporary deployment of these terms on stage. Cf. Chapter 6 for dating *Antiope* to the 420s rather than after 411.

69. Schiappa (2003, 103–10). Aristophanes also subtly implies that the *logoi* are mutually exclusive as well as opposed to each other. Whereas Protagoras seems to envision accounts of the same experience and bolstering one *logos* to the status of the other, Aristophanes begins with the embedded premise that the two represent opposite and irreconcilable descriptions of an objective (making it easy to conclude that one is true and one is false).

70. Limited scholia (Σ^{RVE} 889) are the only external ancient texts to call them *Kreitton* and *Hetton*. See Dover (1968, lvii–viii).

mechanism and steps he takes to facilitate the transformation are clear and recognizable. Aristophanes uses a distinctive literary technique to effect his translation of opposing *logoi,* from names that are devoid of moral terminology into a value-laden vision of subversion. This technique, first documented in detail by Hans-Joachim Newiger, consists of a three-stage series of transformations through metaphors.[71] First comes a commonplace expression containing a latent metaphor. Next, the metaphor takes concrete form on stage. Finally, the concrete form emerges in a new form that defines it ethically in the comic world. The classic example comes from *Acharnians,* in the sequence during which Dicaeopolis secures a peace with the Spartans. The key word here is *spondai,* simultaneously "libations" and "peace treaty."[72] This is the word containing the latent metaphor. Dicaeopolis sends Amphitheos to pursue terms with the Spartans, and he returns with the requested *spondai* (129–34, 175–86). Now the transformation into concrete form takes place, for Amphitheos has brought the *spondai* in the literal form of libations, that is, three samples of wine, each one representing a treaty of a certain number of years. Dicaeopolis tastes each sample and describes it with a mix of descriptions appropriate for the wine and for life under a peace treaty for the specified period of time (187–99). Dicaeopolis settles on the thirty-year *spondai* and then proceeds to usher in the third phase. Dicaeopolis settles in at his home in the country and uses the *spondai* as libations to celebrate the rural Dionysia (201–2). Now Aristophanes has the *spondai* right where he wants them. From an object of wrangling military negotiations, the *spondai* have become part of a morally desirable, peaceful, rural celebration.

The *logoi* in *Clouds* pass through these same three stages. The early conversation between Strespsiades and Pheidippides introduces the *logoi,* with the latent metaphor and moral coloring, but the transformation to concrete form and full moral explication comes later. When Socrates accepts the young Pheidippides as a student in place of the boy's befuddled father, he announces that Pheidippides will learn his lessons directly from two *logoi* (886). What Socrates means by this statement remains unclear until two characters step out onto the stage to initiate the play's formal *agon.* These two characters promptly introduce themselves to each other, and to the spectators, as Kreitton Logos and Hetton Logos (894). These introductions fit into a dynamic process running through the play, a process through which Aristophanes begins with *logoi* as little more than the colloquial equivalent of

---

71. Newiger (1957, esp. 119–22); cf. Edmunds (1980, 4).
72. On the dynamics of the stage properties used in this transformation and throughout *Acharnians,* see English (2007).

speeches or arguments, moves on to the concept of paired *logoi* as mutually opposing experiences—the basic concept associated with Protagoras—and during the course of the *agon* transforms the *logoi* into rival competitors for cultural supremacy. In doing so, Aristophanes charges that the basis for the novel language of the early Sophists is ethically deviant and a gateway to political subversion.

Further explication of Aristophanes' transformation requires looking back at Protagoras' concept of the two *logoi* and then following the path Aristophanes takes to set up and manipulate the concept in *Clouds*. Crucial again here is the work of Thomas Cole and Edward Schiappa, which reevaluates rhetoric as practiced and taught by the Sophists in the fifth century.[73] Both believe that rhetoric in the hands of the early Sophists was fundamentally a different pursuit from the formal discipline of *rhetorike* developed and refined in the hands of Plato, Aristotle and others during the course of the fourth century. Schiappa in particular groups this instruction with the philosophical speculation of the Sophists under the banner of inquiry into the fundamental concept of *logos, logos* as the object of thought and an elusive implement for communication. *Logos* in this environment, then, is not a static item but a point at which to begin framing questions and constructing definitions.

In this context, when Protagoras explains his philosophical system of the fundamental dichotomies of experience in the universe, he expresses it in terms of *logoi*. Schiappa has analyzed the details of several of Protagoras' key precepts and shown how later interpreters have colored, usually negatively, the essence of Protagoras' original statements. Two famous and notorious sayings of Protagoras especially concern us here. The first is the so-called "Two-*Logoi* fragment" (δύο λόγους εἶναι περὶ παντὸς πράγματος, fr. 80B6a). Scholars have often taken this as a statement applying to rhetoric, translating it to the effect that it is possible to debate both sides of any issue. Schiappa makes the case that the fragment is not fundamentally a statement about principles of debating, but a declaration about the relationship between the direct experience of external reality and the human capacity to communicate something about that reality. For every *pragma*, every experience, says Protagoras, there lie two *logoi*, attempts to communicate something about that *pragma* or experience, and these two *logoi* are mutually opposed to each other.[74]

---

73. See the Introduction, 1–12. For broad readings of *Clouds* with attention to the dynamics of *logos*, see O'Regan (1992) and Freydberg (2008, 11–54). For an application of Bakhtinian dialogics to the play, see Platter (2007, 42–62).

74. Schiappa (2003, 98–100).

Another fragment builds on this very model. This is the "Stronger and Weaker" *logoi* fragment (τὸ τὸν ἥττω δὲ λόγον κρείττω ποιεῖν τοῦτ' ἔστιν, fr. 80B6b). This is the fragment sometimes translated as "making the weaker argument appear the stronger" or the like. Protagoras speaks of making a *kreitton logos* into a *hetton logos*. As Schiappa again illustrates, this statement has a long history of pejorative interpretation when restricted to principles of rhetoric or debate. In this tradition, the saying refers to making a deficient argument prevail over a more sound argument. Without this negative overlay, the fragment again is a statement about the nature of experience. As Schiappa summarizes, the fragment advocates "the substitution of a preferred (but weaker) *logos* for a less preferable (but temporarily dominant) *logos* of the same experience."[75]

Protagoras thus does not advocate the promotion of a deficient, inferior, or unethical procedure at the expense of a superior action. But at least as early as Aristotle, Protagoras has suffered the charge that he advocates the devious use of inferior reasoning. In fifth-century comedy, Protagoras also was the object of mockery, such as when Eupolis caricatures him as a philosopher of humbug (fr. 157, from *Kolakes*).[76] Aristophanes takes Protagoras to task on a much grander scale. He manipulates and, as he sees it, exposes Protagoras' concepts of paired and opposing *logoi*, specifically the *kreitton* and *hetton*. After the resolution of the *agon*, the product of this training, Pheidippides, uses an ἀκατάβλητος λόγος, an "un-knock-downable *logos*" (1229), probably with reference to Protagoras' own Καταβάλλοντες Λόγοι, "Knock-down *Logoi*" (80 B1 DK).[77] In *Clouds* generally, Aristophanes charges Protagoras with being ethically irresponsible, much as later tradition does. Aristophanes makes his charges by framing questions and constructing definitions of *logos* in ways that evoke Protagoras, but he goes on to dramatize undesirable consequences resulting from Protagoras' concepts.

In this way, the three-stage transformation of *logoi* in *Clouds* is a progressive exposé of Protagoras' concepts of *kreitton logos* and *hetton logos*. The two *logoi* first appear in the script when Strepsiades characterizes them as just

---

75. Schiappa (2003, 113).
76. For the treatment of Protagoras and other intellectuals in Eupolis' *Kolakes*, see Storey (2003, 192–97).
77. Sutton (1987, 137–39) and Gallego (2005–6) recognize the Logoi as deriving from Protagoras' binary *logoi*, but Gallego tends to treat Protagoras' concept as flawed and thus exposed by Aristophanes, and neither sees Aristophanes' treatment as a new dynamic. Papageorgiou (2004b) argues that the moral dimension of the two *Logoi* is derived from Prodicus' parable of Virtue and Vice. He might be right that Aristophanes is conflating Prodicus' metaphor here, but the explicit, primary target is Protagoras.

and unjust (112–18). The unsophisticated Strepsiades mentions the *logoi* explicitly and by name but treats them more like "arguments" or "speeches." He vaguely gives them speaking ability and, more significantly, introduces a strong moral flavor by equating *hetton logos* with "an *unjust* argument." Strepsiades again mentions the two *logoi* when he meets Socrates, asking to learn the *logos* that never pays debts (245). So far the idea of *logoi* refers at most to a technique of debate, if an underhanded one. The mention of the paired *logoi* has the capacity to refer to the more broad-based sophistic concept of antithetical accounts of experience, but this identification takes the stage only later.

Further on in the play, when Pheidippides is entering Socrates' school, Strepsiades reviews the idea of the *logoi*. He asks Socrates to teach Pheidippides the two *logoi*, *kreitton* and *hetton*, or at least *hetton*, he says, the one that speaks injustice and trips up the *kreitton logos* (882–85):

ὅπως δ' ἐκείνω τὼ λόγω μαθήσεται,
τὸν κρείττον', ὅστις ἐστί, καὶ τὸν ἥττονα,
ὃς τἄδικα λέγων ἀνατρέπει τὸν κρείττονα

Just so he learns those two *logoi,*
the Stronger, no matter what it is, and the Lesser,
which speaks unjustly and trips up the Stronger one.

In response, Socrates ushers in the next transformation, that of the *logoi* into concrete form. Socrates declares that Pheidippides will learn directly from the *logoi* themselves, and promptly the two *logoi* walk out on stage, in as concrete and physical a form as the wine in the *spondai* metaphor.

The two newly personified *logoi* identify each other explicitly as *Kreitton Logos* and *Hetton Logos* (894; cf. 1338).[78] Despite all of Socrates' humbug so far in the play, it is only at this point that Aristophanes begins to demonstrate how education at the Phrontisterion, in the form of Hetton Logos, imbues its students with qualities of moral decadence. The *Logoi* are now far more than the debating techniques Strepsiades was seeking earlier. They become entire life experiences and incarnations of cultural perspectives. Just as Protagoras' conception of *logoi* embraces more than simply words, Aristophanes' conception expands to cover not just legal wrangling, but also a physical form and a model for responding to experience of the world. But Aristophanes finds the experiences encapsulated in the *Kreitton* and *Hetton*

---

78. Schiappa (2003, 110–13).

Logos quite different from those proposed by Protagoras. True to their identities as mutually opposing *logoi,* the two characters argue, counterargue, and contradict one another. As the *agon* proceeds, *Hetton Logos* stands revealed as a shameless pervert, a clown, a parricide and an adulterer. He openly preaches decadence and perversion. Where Protagoras speaks of changing a *hetton logos* into a *kreitton logos,* Aristophanes has *Hetton* overwhelm *Kreitton.* Hetton persuades Kreitton Logos, the upholder of Athens' glorious past, that Athens is indeed already composed of deviants (1088–1101).[79] In a sense, *Kreitton* does become *Hetton* (ἡττήμεθ' . . . , 1102–4) as he strips off his clothes and races out into the spectators to join his soon-to-be fellow perverts. This extended characterization goes beyond comic caricature. Aristophanes has recast Protagoras' notion of battling *logoi* entirely in the morally evaluative terms of the comic stage. A statement of the abstract principle of cosmic dynamics becomes a declaration of political and cultural values.

With this transformation complete, one more transformation is necessary, one that plays out the dramatic consequences of the cultural threat. Pheidippides, after his training with *Hetton Logos,* dramatizes this transformation. Strepsiades has Socrates confirm that Pheidippides learned the very *logos* that had been on stage. It soon becomes evident what a change to *hetton logos* really means. Pheidippides is capable of warding off debts, but he also listens to Euripides and righteously beats up his own father (1172–1201, 1321–1439). At the climax of the play, Pheidippides patently invokes the *hetton logos* (1444–45) to argue that beating his own mother is proper, the final outrage that leads Strepsiades to repent and burn Socrates' Phrontisterion to the ground.

With these developments, Aristophanes brings a stinging indictment. Protagoras' definition of the *logoi* may not be predicated on assigning ethical weight to one or the other of contradictory accounts of the world. The Sophists may provide instruction as a practical matter or as an intellectual pursuit. The comic stage, however, colors all human activity in terms of ethical and moral values. Make no mistake, warns Aristophanes, these *logoi* will lead to personal depravity and cultural subversion.

In the next century, Plato and Aristotle have similar anxieties about the practice and teaching of rhetorical ploys. Progressively they work to separate

---

79. Papageorgiou (2004a) emphasizes that *Kreitton* here stands up for aristocratic restraint, objecting to Dover's thesis that the character's sexual obsessions undercut his position. The sexual politics of the scene are surely not so simple as Papageorgiou attempts to make them, and he leaves little explanation for how or why *Hetton* dominates.

the tools of rhetoric from its distasteful moral baggage, and eventually these efforts culminate in the focalized discipline of *rhetorike,* which Aristotle can dissect, albeit with ambivalent concerns about its ethically undesirable side effects.

The critique presented in *Clouds* is therefore important both because it offers a rare explicit characterization of sophistic rhetoric from a contemporary source, and because it preserves one of the earliest criticisms of the very principles that eventually allowed classical rhetoric to emerge as an important discipline in its own right. Although the philosophical underpinnings and craft of rhetoric would change and become more complex, Aristophanes had already isolated the ethical conundrum that would haunt future philosophers and orators alike.

The series of transformations by metaphor does not override Aristophanes' other techniques for orienting education in language within the civic space of Athens, but one such technique is deployed in delayed fashion compared to other plays. Unlike in *Acharnians* and *Knights,* Aristophanes does not emphasize any translocation with respect to the proper venue for the debate between the two *logoi.* The location is nominally near Socrates' Phrontisterion, and initially, when the chorus sets the parameters of the debate, they do not point to any potential impact for public deliberation but characterize it as for the benefit of Pheidippides (934–38):

παύσασθε μάχης καὶ λοιδορίας.
ἀλλ' ἐπίδειξαι σύ τε τοὺς προτέρους
ἅττ' ἐδίδασκες, σύ τε τὴν καινὴν
παίδευσιν, ὅπως ἂν ἀκούσας σφῶν
ἀντιλεγόντοιν κρίνας φοιτᾷ.

Stop fighting and wrangling.[80]
Instead, you describe what you taught
in the old days, and you the new
education, so that he can hear both of you
debating and then decide to join.

In response, Hetton Logos declares he will overwhelm Kreitton Logos and leave him in helpless silence, a goal cited also by Dicaeopolis in *Acharnians* and the rivals in *Knights,* but here not yet applied to Athens more broadly (941–49):

---

80. On λοιδορία, see the Appendix.

κᾆτ' ἐκ τούτων ὧν ἂν λέξῃ
ῥηματίοισιν καινοῖς αὐτὸν
καὶ διανοίαις κατατοξεύσω,
τὸ τελευταῖον δ', ἢν ἀναγρύζῃ,
τὸ πρόσωπον ἅπαν καὶ τὠφθαλμὼ
κεντούμενος ὥσπερ ὑπ' ἀνθρηνῶν
ὑπὸ τῶν γνωμῶν ἀπολεῖται.

And then from what he says
with new phrases and ideas
I shoot him down.
In the end, if he makes so much as a grunt,
his whole face and eyes
will be like he was stung by hornets,
he'll die from the thoughts.

Aggressive as this description is, zero-sum debate is not undesirable in Aristophanes' conception of deliberation. He does not wish such debate short-circuited, but he trusts the judgment of the Demos and has no compunction about drumming out inferior and destructive ideas, in the appropriate place.[81] The chorus indeed announces the stakes and gives a favorable introduction to Kreitton Logos, but they do not disparage Hetton Logos' methods or goal (950–60):

νῦν δείξετον τὼ πισύνω
τοῖς περιδεξίοισιν
λόγοισι καὶ φροντίσι καὶ
γνωμοτύποις μερίμναις,
λέγων ἀμείνων πότερος
φανήσεται. νῦν γὰρ ἅπας
ἐνθάδε κίνδυνος ἀνεῖται σοφίας,
ἧς πέρι τοῖς ἐμοῖς φίλοις
ἐστὶν ἀγὼν μέγιστος.
ἀλλ' ὦ πολλοῖς τοὺς πρεσβυτέρους ἤθεσι χρηστοῖς στεφανώσας,
ῥῆξον φωνὴν ᾗτινι χαίρεις καὶ τὴν σαυτοῦ φύσιν εἰπέ.

Now both of them will rely on their roundly clever
speeches and thoughts and meticulous thought-strikes

---

81. Plato, *Prot.* 319b–c takes it as standard practice that the Athenian Assembly shouts down the testimony of some advisers.

and show which one can show off the better speech. For all
wisdom is at stake here.
For that, my friends, is what this contest is ultimately about.
But, you who crowned our ancestors with valuable character,
speak your voice, rejoice in it, and tell of your own nature.

The chorus gives a positive introduction to Kreitton Logos, invoking Athens' glorious ancestors and calling on him to use his φωνή, "voice," rather than his γλῶττα, "tongue" (cf. Chapter 2 and the Appendix). At the climax of the debate, however, Aristophanes elides the judging of the debate in the theater with the spectators' identity as the Demos in the Athenian democracy. When Hetton Logos is making his case that taking it up the ass is nothing bad (1085), he refers to those who play a leading role in the public deliberative process (συνηγοροῦσιν, 1089; δημηγοροῦσι, 1093) and the bulk of the spectators in the theater (τῶν θεατῶν ὁπότεροι πλείους, 1095–6). When Kreitton Logos concedes that these are all deviants (εὐρυπρώκτους, 1098) and runs to join them, the reason Aristophanes leaves the location general becomes evident. He wants to dramatize the effect and impact of the education on the deliberative process but without actually making it take place in the proper prescribed locations of the Assembly, Council or courts. Indeed, as it is, the revelation applies to any or all of them, but Aristophanes does not have to subject the Demos to the results directly.[82] Rather he shows the cause-and-effect dynamic and, at the fiery conclusion of the play, the proper location and action to be taken to prevent the undesirable results.

The subsequent debate between Pheidippides and Strepsiades gradually unleashes the consequences of Hetton Logos in ever-widening civic arenas.[83] This debate begins, like the contest between the Logoi, and despite Strepsiades' disbelief, as a healthy exchange, even if Pheidippides, like Hetton Logos, is bold in his prediction (1335–44). As the contest proceeds, however, Aristophanes pushes the consequences of Hetton Logos beyond domestic disputes. The chorus expects the younger generation in their babble (λαλῶν) will be energized in their abuse of their elders (1391–96), a contrast that implicitly parallels the young prosecutors who abuse older men (*Ach.* 676–702; *Wasps*). Pheidippides makes explicit how the energized younger generation can overhaul the political arena (1421–24):

---

82. See Roselli (2011, 19–62, esp. 31–32) for a strong analysis of the dynamic of Old Comedy in engaging and managing spectators.

83. For a detailed analysis of the way the terminology in this scene develops from that earlier in the play, see Kloss (2001, 116–31).

οὔκουν ἀνὴρ ὁ τὸν νόμον θεὶς τοῦτον ἦν τὸ πρῶτον,
ὥσπερ σὺ κἀγώ, καὶ λέγων ἔπειθε τοὺς παλαιούς;
ἧττόν τι δῆτ᾽ ἔξεστι κἀμοὶ καινὸν αὖ τὸ λοιπὸν
θεῖναι νόμον τοῖς υἱέσιν, τοὺς πατέρας ἀντιτύπτειν;

Wasn't it a man who made this law in the first place,
just like you or me, and spoke to persuade people in the old days?
Is it somehow less possible for me in the future
to make a new law for sons so they can beat up their fathers?

Strepsiades responds to these arguments and concedes the justice of them. Using language loaded with terms of moral evaluation, he concedes (1437–39):[84]

ἐμοὶ μέν, ὦνδρες ἥλικες, δοκεῖ λέγειν δίκαια,
κἀμοιγε συγχωρεῖν δοκεῖ τούτοισι τἀπιεικῆ·
κλάειν γὰρ ἡμᾶς εἰκός ἐστ᾽, ἢν μὴ δίκαια δρῶμεν.

Gentlemen of my generation, it seems to me he speaks justly,
and it seems to me right to agree with what is fair:
it's fair that we should suffer if we commit a wrong.

Crucial here is that Strepsiades respects the deliberative process as long it adheres to justice, even when he loses an argument and can suffer for his loss. Implicitly, it is as if, once again, the *logos* Pheidippides uses were not morally loaded, whether "worse," "bad" or "injust," but merely *hetton*, "lesser," and so Strepsiades submits to it. It is only when Pheidippides goes on to make a manifestly unjust claim, explicitly relying on *hetton logos* to do so, that the consequences become unacceptable for civic life. At this crucial juncture Aristophanes emphasizes that that Hetton Logos is the instrument that leads Strepsiades to change his mind (1444–51):

ΦΕ.
τί δ᾽ ἢν ἔχων τὸν ἥττω
λόγον σε νικήσω λέγων
τὴν μητέρ᾽ ὡς τύπτειν χρεών;

---

84. Editors have repeatedly noted the weakness of these lines, but N. G. Wilson goes too far in deleting them, for there is no plausible explanation for their addition by a later hand (unlike actors' interpolations in tragic scripts, and it cannot be based on a gloss). Among the more likely explanations are that it belongs elsewhere or that it is a consequence of the partially revised state of the script.

Στ.
Τί δ' ἄλλο γ' ἤ, ταῦτ' ἤν ποιῇς,
οὐδέν σε κωλύσει σεαυτὸν ἐμβαλεῖν εἰς τὸ βάραθρον
μετὰ Σωκράτους
καὶ τὸν λόγον τὸν ἥττω;

PHEIDIPPIDES
What if I use the *hetton*
logos to defeat you by saying
I must beat my mother?
STREPSIADES
The only thing that will happen if you do that
is I'll throw you into the pit
with Socrates
and the Hetton Logos.

To reset the deliberative process, Strepsiades takes Hermes on as an adviser in the deliberative process, rather than Hetton Logos (1478–85):

ἀλλ', ὦ φίλ' Ἑρμῆ, μηδαμῶς θύμαινέ μοι,
μηδέ μ' ἐπιτρίψῃς, ἀλλὰ συγγνώμην ἔχε
ἐμοῦ παρανοήσαντος ἀδολεσχίᾳ
καί μοι γενοῦ ξύμβουλος, εἴτ' αὐτοὺς γραφὴν
διωκάθω γραψάμενος, εἴθ' ὅ τι σοι δοκεῖ.
ὀρθῶς παραινεῖς οὐκ ἐῶν δικορραφεῖν
ἀλλ' ὡς τάχιστ' ἐμπιμπράναι τὴν οἰκίαν
τῶν ἀδολεσχῶν.

My beloved Hermes, don't be angry with me,
and don't crush me. Instead forgive
me my insane actions because of their blather.
And be my adviser about what you judge best.
You rightly recommend that I not stitch together a lawsuit,
but as soon as possible set fire to the home
of the blatherers.

In a way, Strepsiades stays true to the deliberative process by taking the advice of divine counsel, a culturally established, traditional and venerable way to come to judgment about the well-being of Athens. Furthermore, the debates in the play have taken place outside the civic areas for political deliberation, but the results threaten the processes in those areas, so Strepsiades and Aristophanes proceed to an extrapolitical solution to remove completely the source of the threat: physical destruction of the Phrontisterion.

A DAY IN COURT: THE DELIBERATIVE PROCESS IN *WASPS*

Aristophanes focused on the Assembly and Council in his first plays but also touched on the functioning of the courts in democratic Athens. In *Wasps* he puts the courts at the center of his focus but couches his analysis repeatedly in terms of the broader needs of democratic deliberation and in contrast to the needs of the Assembly and Council. Although *Acharnians*, *Knights* and *Clouds* focus on other arenas for public deliberation, each references the functioning of the courts. The elderly chorus of Acharnians sounds what is the most prevalent complaint (679–80, 685–86):

οἵτινες γέροντας ἄνδρας ἐμβαλόντες ἐς γραφὰς
ὑπὸ νεανίσκων ἐᾶτε καταγελᾶσθαι ῥητόρων,
. . .
ὁ δέ, νεανίας ἑαυτῷ σπουδάσας ξυνηγορεῖν,
ἐς τάχος παίει ξυνάπτων στρογγύλοις τοῖς ῥήμασιν

You throw old men into lawsuits
to be ridiculed by young *rhetores* . . .
The young man, eager to be the *synegoros* against him,
knocks him to the wall and beats him with rounded words.

In comedy generally, as in this passage, there seems to be little difference between a ῥήτωρ and a συνήγορος.[85] A fragment of *Banqueters* mentions both ῥήτορες and συνήγοροι, without any indication that they are meaningfully different groups (Aristophanes fr. 205.6–9; cf. Chapter 2).

---

85. See Connor (1971, 108–19) for the history of ῥήτωρ and related terms in the politics of Athens in the last third of the fifth century. For a similar account of συνήγορος, see Carter (1985, 120–25). The position of συνήγορος changed in the coming years, but a fragment from the third century suggests their reputation only worsened (Philemo Jr. fr. 3 dub.):

μόνῳ δ' ἰατρῷ τοῦτο καὶ συνηγόρῳ
ἔξεστιν, ἀποκτείνειν μέν, ἀποθνῄσκειν δὲ μή.

It's possible only for a doctor and a *synegoros*
to commit murder and not die for it.

More often than ῥήτωρ, however, a συνήγορος appears to refer to young, aggressive prosecutors, a group likely, as comedy depicts them, to use the new dubious style of speaking to achieve their ends.[86] One more fragment assumes the idea (Aristophanes fr. 424):[87]

ἔστι τις πονηρὸς ἡμῖν τοξότης συνήγορος
ὥσπερ Εὔαθλος παρ' ὑμῖν τοῖς νέοις.

We have a rascal archer prosecutor,
like you young ones have Euathlos.

The drive of young prosecutors against their venerable elders is not the only pernicious influence on the courts. The chorus of Knights cites the impact of Cleon among experienced prosecutors and the resulting turmoil in the courts and the city (973–84):[88]

ἥδιστον φάος ἡμέρας
ἔσται τοῖσι παροῦσι καὶ
τοῖσι δεῦρ' ἀφικνουμένοις,
ἢν Κλέων ἀπόληται.
καίτοι πρεσβυτέρων τινῶν
οἵων ἀργαλεωτάτων
ἐν τῷ δείγματι τῶν δικῶν
ἤκουσ' ἀντιλεγόντων,
ὡς εἰ μὴ 'γένεθ' οὗτος ἐν
τῇ πόλει μέγας, οὐκ ἂν ἤστην
σκεύη δύο χρησίμω,
δοῖδυξ οὐδὲ τορύνη.

For those here and traveling to here,
the light of day will be sweetest
if Cleon is destroyed.
Although some old men,
of the most painful sort,

---

86. This is not a rule, however. *Knights* 1358–61 uses συνήγορος where otherwise ῥήτωρ more often appears.

87. The fragment comes from *Merchant Ships*, which is usually, but not securely, dated to the year or two before *Wasps*. Euathlos is also named by the chorus of Acharnians as a young, vicious prosecutor (703–4).

88. Buis (2005) explores the role of aggressive litigiousness in *Knights* more broadly.

in the Lawsuit Bazaar,
I heard them talking back and forth,
that if the man hadn't become
so important in the city, there wouldn't be
two useful tools:
the pestle and ladle.

Cleon is thus means for stirring up troublesome forensic activity in the courts. Accordingly, when Cleon is at bay and Demos is restored to his proper judgment, Agoracritus announces the rejuvenated Demos by first calling for quiet in the courts (1316–18):

εὐφημεῖν χρὴ καὶ στόμα κλῄειν καὶ μαρτυριῶν ἀπέχεσθαι,
καὶ τὰ δικαστήρια συγκλῄειν οἷς ἡ πόλις ἥδε γέγηθεν,
ἐπὶ καιναῖσιν δ' εὐτυχίαισιν παιωνίζειν τὸ θέατρον.

It is required to maintain silence, close mouths and refrain from testimony,
to close up the courts, which the city enjoys,
and for the spectators to sing for new good fortune!

Closure of the courts and celebration by the spectators in a legitimate way summarize the goals of Aristophanes' last two plays of the 420s: *Wasps* and *Peace*.[89] Moreover, all the basic principles laid out in the brief statements in *Acharnians* and *Knights* play out on a large scale in *Wasps:* the abuse of elders by the young, the manipulation of the courts by Cleon, and the apparent lack of any significant role of the courts when the judgment of the Demos and the deliberative process are restored.

Aristophanes uses the prologue of *Wasps* to make the transition from his dramatizations of the Assembly to his upcoming analysis of the courts. The slave Sosias has a riddling dream that refers to the Assembly. The dream is a big, important one for the ship of state, says Sosias (28–29). He describes a whale presiding over sheep on the Pnyx (31–36), and once Xanthias interprets the monster as Cleon, Sosias adds Cleon's supporter Theorus as well as the lisping Alcibiades to the picture (42–45). With this oblique reminder of Aristophanes' past treatment of these issues, Xanthias immediately turns to explicating the current play to the spectators (54), although he says that Cleon will not be the subject of another slicing attack (62–63). It turns out,

---

89. Carrière (2004) argues that *Wasps* continues themes of education, politics and *nomos* vs. *phusis* from *Clouds*.

of course, that the issue this time is addiction to jury service. The problem is immediately set up as a conflict between the elderly Philocleon and his son Bdelycleon, and Aristophanes waits (other than the punning names on Cleon) until the *parodos* to broaden the political issues at stake.

After some shenanigans involving Philocleon trying to escape from his house, the chorus of elderly jurors arrives to rescue their besieged comrade. At this point, Aristophanes weaves in the political issues he will develop as the play unfolds. First, the chorus mentions their eagerness for a trial wherein Cleon will prosecute Laches, who was an opponent of Cleon as well as linked to the peace process, whereby Aristophanes foreshadows the trial he will put on stage later in the play. Aristophanes is more nuanced now in his manipulation of political terminology. He again obliquely refers to, but avoids, Cleon's epithet of προστάτης, "protector," by using κηδεμών of him instead (242). Thus the chorus simultaneously refers to him positively (as they should in character, since they are his supporters) but undercuts him as well, as they will do more than once. A short time later, in dialogue with Philocleon, the chorus disparagingly refers to Bdelycleon as Δημολογοκλέων (342), which on the one hand invokes Cleon as a "demagogue," not necessarily a negative term at this time, but also distorts the title.

When analyzing the dysfunction of the Assembly and Council in *Acharnians* and *Knights*, Aristophanes dramatized a faith in the deliberative process: if the Demos asserts its proper judgment in the processes in these venues, success and prosperity will result. He does not assert comparable faith in the courts. The problems with the courts in *Wasps* are the same as those he pointed out in earlier passages: aggressive prosecutors and Cleon using lawsuits to his own end, but whereas with the Assembly and Council, deliberation translocated elsewhere is successful and the Demos rendering its judgment in these institutions rectifies them, the best court seems to be no court at all.[90] The chorus of Wasps complains simply that Bdelycleon objects to trials at all (409–14):

... Κλέωνι ταῦτ' ἀγγέλλετε,
καὶ κελεύετ' αὐτὸν ἥκειν
ὡς ἐπ' ἄνδρα μισόπολιν
ὄντα κἀπολούμενον, ὅτι

---

[90]. Hansen (1978) demonstrates that the Demos was identified with the authority of the Assembly but not readily with that of the *dikasterion*, so perhaps the perspective in Aristophanes' plays reflects a viewpoint that the sovereignty of the Demos resides primarily in the Assembly and Council, while the Demos' role in the courts could be reckoned as something apart.

τόνδε λόγον ἐσφέρει,
μὴ δικάζειν δίκας.

... report this to Cleon,
and tell him to come,
to face a man who hates the city
and who's going to die, because
he's introducing this argument
not to judge cases!

When Bdelycleon arrives, he takes on the chorus as if he were already fighting Cleon. He asks them not to shout (Cleon's regular *modus operandi* in *Knights*) but to listen to the issue at stake (415). The chorus responds with shouting and charges of tyranny, as they invoke the city and Theorus again, as an ally of Cleon (417–19; cf. 42–43 for Theorus). This latest charge raises an issue Bdelycleon will address explicitly later in the play, but also marks another difference from Aristophanes' analysis of the Assembly and Council. In the context of the democratic process in those institutions, tyranny was not inherently a problem; it just had to be the political tyranny of the Athenian Demos. The chorus's hollow cries of generic tyranny ignore this possibility and put the problem in a separate category from the logjam in the other institutions. When the chorus repeats the charges of tyranny and monarchy a little later (463–70), Bdelycleon makes explicit that they are just shouting rather than deliberating and reaching reconciliation (471–72):

ἔσθ' ὅπως ἄνευ μάχης καὶ τῆς κατοξείας βοῆς
ἐς λόγους ἔλθοιμεν ἀλλήλοισι καὶ διαλλαγάς;

Isn't there some way we can enter into dialogue and reconciliation with
    each other,
without the fighting and shrilled-out shouting?

After the chorus invokes the charge of tyranny yet a third time, Bdelycleon makes clear that invoking tyranny is inimical to the deliberative process, and the problem of tyranny is not a part of Athens' greatness (488–90):

ὡς ἅπανθ' ὑμῖν τυραννίς ἐστι καὶ ξυνωμόται,
ἤν τε μεῖζον ἤν τ' ἔλαττον πρᾶγμά τις κατηγορῇ,
ἧς ἐγὼ οὐκ ἤκουσα τοὔνομ' οὐδὲ πεντήκοντ' ἐτῶν.

> All you have is "tyranny" and "conspiracy,"
> if anyone criticizes any issue big or small.
> I hadn't *heard* the word in fifty years!

Aristophanes refers to a past where the Athenians cast out the tyrants, and in the fifty years or so that followed, Athens grew into a rightly successful empire, but other than the Demos holding its rightful place as ruler of an Athenian empire, the charge of tyranny is meaningless and an obstacle to the proper deliberative process.[91] Aristophanes next layers on the issue of class, which becomes increasingly important in his plays.[92] Bdelycleon says he wants his father to live an aristocratic life (βίον γενναῖον, 506) but gets labeled a tyrant for the attempt. He puts Philocleon's lot as a juror on the same level as slavery (517). To set up the *agon,* Bdelycleon frames the issue in terms of what Philocleon gets from the empire out of this arrangement (520), setting up the basic antinomy: slavery vs. king of the world, where rightly members of the Athenian Demos should be rulers.[93] Lawsuits and courts really have no intrinsic role in this scenario. In practice, according to Aristophanes, courts only provide occasions for destructive self-serving individuals to enslave the Demos against its own interest.

Accordingly it makes sense that the ensuing *agon* debates mostly not the court system or tyranny, but whether Philocleon is in fact a king or not. There is no question that being king is good, only whether Philocleon as a representative of the Demos is in fact one. This is consistent with Aristophanes' support of a dominant Demos: the Demos should be a monarch, tyrant, king, whatever, and control Athens, Greece, and Athens' entire empire. The details of the court proceedings are all secondary to this commitment.

To highlight and make explicit the arguments in what follows, Aristophanes has Bdelycleon interrupt Philocleon's argument in order to highlight six crucial issues in his exposé:[94]

---

91. Aristophanes' characterizations of the threat of tyranny differ significantly in 411 and later, under the shadow of the oligarchic coup. See Chapters 5–6.
92. See Reinders (2001, 28–71) for a survey of the term δῆμος and related class terms in Greek literature as a context for Aristophanes' use.
93. The analysis by Brock (2009) of the principles that guided the empire provides a useful historical backdrop for this scene. He argues that the Athenians, other things being equal, preferred democracy, but pragmatism (according to three principles: capacity to interfere, money and security) guided policy more than ideology.
94. Papageorgiou (2004c) finds Bdelycleon's techniques in the *agon* comparable to rhetorical manipulation found in oratorical texts and concludes that a sinister ambiguity permeates his presentation. Papageorgiou's reasoning requires that a substantial portion of the spectators, and perhaps Aristophanes himself, must find Bdelycleon's mathematical calculations disarming and disagree with

1. The powerful supplicate the juror (559).
2. Jurors can mock wealth (576).
3. Jurors are not audited (587–88).
4. The Council and Demos hand difficult cases over to jurors (590–91).
5. No one wins with the Demos without reducing the jurors' workload (594–95).
6. Cleon guards them (596ff).

Each one of these points represents an obstacle to Aristophanes' preferred goal of the Demos deliberating, deciding and guiding Athens to peace, prosperity and control of its empire.

1. Supplication of the juror sidetracks the normal deliberative process.
2. The mocking of wealth turns out to be inverted and hollow, as Bdelycleon shows shortly.
3. The lack of accountability of jurors bypasses the process generally, and auditing is an important prerogative of the Demos in holding leaders accountable (see *Knights* 1145–50, where Demos will use auditing to rein in misbehaving leaders).
4. The Assembly and Council are actually abdicating their duties by sending cases to the courts.
5. Meanwhile, jurors place self-indulgent restrictions on proper proposals to the Assembly.
6. Finally, Cleon gets to wield undue influence and cloud the judgment of the masses (*plethos*).

Bdelycleon's interjections and follow-up arguments pertain more to the deliberative and political process generally than to the operation of the courts and juror behavior. After establishing that jury pay amounts to a paltry percentage of the income of the empire, Bdelycleon explains where the money goes and why (666–71):

ἐς τούτους τοὺς "οὐχὶ προδώσω τὸν Ἀθηναίων κολοσυρτόν,
ἀλλὰ μαχοῦμαι περὶ τοῦ πλήθους ἀεί." σὺ γάρ, ὦ πάτερ, αὐτοὺς
ἄρχειν αἱρεῖ σαυτοῦ τούτοις τοῖς ῥηματίοις περιπεφθείς.
κᾆθ' οὗτοι μὲν δωροδοκοῦσιν κατὰ πεντήκοντα τάλαντα

---

them. But there is no compelling reason to believe that they should have done so. Bdelycleon is not a character without ambiguity, of course, but there is nothing in the script to indicate that what he says in the debate is transparently weak, false, or cynically manipulative.

ἀπὸ τῶν πόλεων ἐπαπειλοῦντες τοιαυτὶ κἀναφοβοῦντες,
"δώσετε τὸν φόρον, ἢ βροντήσας τὴν πόλιν ὑμῶν ἀνατρέψω."

[The money goes] to those "I won't betray the rabble,
but I'll always fight for the masses" people. Because you, father,
choose them to rule you, since you've been cooked up by their catchphrases.
And then these same men take bribes on the order of fifty talents
from the subject cities, making threats like this and frightening you with
"Give up the tribute, or I'll thunder and knock down your city!"

Once again Aristophanes invokes, but twists, the language of Cleon in his role of protector of the Demos. With the thundering, his speech resembles the arrogant language of Pericles in his Zeus-like caricature from comedy.

Bdelycleon, and Aristophanes, maintain the argument in the *agon* in terms of the type of deliberation more in keeping with the Assembly and Council than the courts. Bdelycleon characterizes Philocleon as "gaping" (χασκάζεις, 695) uselessly as a juror, a metaphor Aristophanes uses repeatedly of useless spectators at the Assembly. Philocleon and his comrades are encircled by "Demos-izing" speakers (δημιζόντων, 699). Bdelycleon concludes with more general attacks on the administration of the Athenian empire at the expense of poor jurors, with again no particular comments on activity in the courts in particular. Even so, on these grounds, Philocleon and the chorus concede that Bdelycleon's reasoning is persuasive (743–49).

Now a full-scale translocation of the courts takes place (758ff). The translocation itself is not surprising, since Aristophanes had pointedly translocated the political process before, in *Acharnians* and *Knights,* and once again the translocation moves the process from its normal public space to the domestic realm. The translocation in *Wasps* differs in meaningful ways, however. First, the translocation is only a concession by Bdelycleon that the process continue at all (761–66). Philocleon has submitted himself to Bdelycleon's will and begs only that he be able to be a juror somehow. Unlike other translocations, where the deliberative process of the Assembly and Council is desirable and will have positive effects even when translocated, here the new trial process is a grudging concession, and there is no pressure anywhere in the play to have trials resume in the public courts. After the makeshift courtroom is set up, the chorus praises Bdelycleon's support of the Demos, in terms of this being the new and proper established system (885–90):

ξυνευχόμεσθα ταὐτά σοι κἀπᾴδομεν

νέαισιν ἀρχαῖς ἕνεκα τῶν προλελεγμένων.
εὖνοι γάρ ἐσμεν ἐξ οὗ
τὸν δῆμον ᾐσθόμεσθά σου
φιλοῦντος ὡς οὐδεὶς ἀνὴρ
τῶν γε νεωτέρων.

We pray with you and sing for you
for this new start, because of what you have stated.
For we are on your side since
we sense that you love the Demos
like no man
of the younger generation.

Thus the chorus declares resolution to one significant problem in the functioning of the courts: aggressive young prosecutors preying on the elderly. The solution is to stop these types of cases entirely, with not even a worry about the lack of court activity. Bdelycleon is pursuing prosperity for the Demos. The other major source of dysfunction in the courts is Cleon's drive to use lawsuits against his enemies, which the dramatization of Philocleon's domestic court will address. In the enactment of this court, Philocleon's persistence in convicting the defendant dramatizes again the dysfunction of the court system and the solution becomes simple trickery to force an acquittal. As with removing young prosecutors, once this solution has been reached (even by deceit and compulsion), the problem is solved. The remainder of the play moves on to other issues, and there is no suggestion that court cases will or should continue. They simply are not a factor.

The proceedings of the mock trial itself have provided the most persistent example for scholars who insist that the formal divisions of canonical rhetorical theory were operative in Aristophanes. Two speeches are at issue, the prosecution by the dog, a barely disguised Cleon (907–30), and Bdelycleon's defense on behalf of Labes, a barely disguised Laches, the opponent of Cleon cited earlier in the play (950–79; cf. 240 for the earlier reference to Laches). Both speeches are interrupted by other characters on stage, so the divisions identified do not reflect continuous line numbering. Murphy divides the prosecution speech as follows:[95]

---

95. Murphy (1938, 105–6). On the comic technique of interrupted speech (though not in this scene in particular), see Kloss (2001, 189–203).

1. Προοίμιον, 907–9
2. Διήγεσις, 910–14, statement of the crime.
3. Πίστεις, 915–16, "If criminals give me no share of their loot, I cannot benefit you jurors."
4. Ἐπίλογος, 922–30, a direct attack on the defendant and a demand for strict punishment

Sousa e Silva cites the speeches for various devices but not necessarily an overall scheme, but Hubbard updates Murphy's scheme:[96]

1. Προοίμιον, 907–9, summary of the charge and formulaic address to the jurors
2. Διήγεσις, 910–14, narration of the event
3. Πίστεις, 915–25, proofs, consisting of the prosecutor's self-described value as a citizen and an attack on the defendant's character and earlier behavior, which are consistent with the present crime
4. Ἐπίλογος, 927–30, reiteration of the prosecutor's plea for conviction and warning of future consequences of acquittal

As with Diceaopolis' speech in *Acharnians,* these divisions do not hold up under scrutiny. Both Murphy and Hubbard consider this the προοίμιον (907–9):

τῆς μὲν γραφῆς ἠκούσαθ' ἣν ἐγραψάμην
ἄνδρες δικασταὶ τουτονί. δεινότατα γὰρ
ἔργων δέδρακε κἀμὲ καὶ τὸ ῥυππαπαῖ.

You have the indictment that I entered
here, gentlemen of the jury. The most frightful
of deeds he committed against me and the "yo-ho"!

This is admittedly the beginning of a speech, but nothing makes it conform especially to the requirements of a classical προοίμιον. Indeed, of the two sentences, the second sentence could just as easily, but no more helpfully, be construed as part of a narrative, since it says the defendant committed an act. The narrative itself is minimal, but if Murphy or Hubbard moved the second sentence to the narrative, the *prooimion* would be reduced to a verse and a half. Even under Murphy's and Hubbard's division, the διήγεσις, ever

---

96. Sousa e Silva (1987–88, 64–68); Hubbard (2007, 500–501); cf. Harriott (1986, 37–43).

the most ephemeral section of precanonical oratory, is even shorter than the προοίμιον (910–11):⁹⁷

ἀποδρὰς γὰρ ἐς τὴν γωνίαν τυρὸν πολὺν
κατεσικέλιζε κἀνέπλητ' ἐν τῷ σκότῳ—

For he ran off to the corner, and Sicilied
off with a great cheese, and stuffed himself in the dark.

Murphy's section of proofs consists of this couplet (915–16):

καίτοι τίς ὑμᾶς εὖ ποιεῖν δυνήσεται,
ἢν μή τι κἀμοί τις προβάλλῃ, τῷ κυνί;

And so who will be able to take care of you,
unless someone tosses something to me, your dog?

Hubbard would add four more lines to this (922–25, i.e., those following the interruptions by Philocleon and Bdelycleon):

μή νυν ἀφῆτέ γ' αὐτόν, ὡς ὄντ' αὖ πολὺ
κυνῶν ἁπάντων ἄνδρα μονοφαγίστατον,
ὅστις περιπλεύσας τὴν θυείαν ἐν κύκλῳ
ἐκ τῶν πόλεων τὸ σκῖρον ἐξεδήδοκεν.

Don't let him go now, since by far he is
the most solitary-eating man of all dogs,
who sailed the kitchen island in a circle
and ate the rind off the cities.

Murphy and Hubbard reasonably split on assigning these lines. Murphy sees that Cleon is making a summary call and command to the jury.⁹⁸ Hubbard prefers to add this to the list of proofs. Were this sentence a few lines earlier,

---

97. Both Murphy and Hubbard paper over the minimal narrative in different ways. Each lists the section as covering lines 910–14, but line 912 to the middle of line 914 is an interruption by Philocleon. Hubbard further disguises the weakness of this section by presenting Cleon's speech (without Philocleon's interjections) in four parts, as if the parts corresponded to the canonical divisions he claims, but the first section, in Hubbard's own scheme, covers both the *prooimion* and *diegesis* and totals five continuous lines.

98. Murphy is in fact reluctant to label anything "proofs" at all, since the facts are admitted by both sides, and thinks βεβαίωσις, "confirmation," is a better characterization of this section.

however, they could just as easily assign it to the narrative, since it tells part of Labes' criminal activity. This sort of mix of narrative and argumentation is exactly what characterizes precanonical oratory, however.

After yet another interruption by Philocleon,[99] Murphy and Hubbard agree on the ἐπίλογος (927–30):

πρὸς ταῦτα τοῦτον κολάσατ'—οὐ γὰρ ἄν ποτε
τρέφειν δύναιτ' ἂν μία λόχμη κλέπτα δύο—
ἵνα μὴ κεκλάγγω διὰ κενῆς ἄλλως ἐγώ·
ἐὰν δὲ μή, τὸ λοιπὸν οὐ κεκλάγξομαι.

Accordingly, punish him! For a single bush
could never nourish two thieves,
so I won't be barking to no end.
But otherwise, I won't bark in the future.

Much like Dicaeopolis' speech in *Acharnians*, the speech here is more a cascading parody. Where Dicaeopolis' speech began and ended with direct tragic parody and sandwiched a pastiche of arguments in between, the speeches in *Wasps* consist of opening and closing lines knocking off court speeches, and probably Cleon's style in particular, with a heap of punning claims (which are themselves further interrupted by Philocleon) placed in between. Bdelycleon's defense speech has even less organization. After two lines of speaking (950–51), Philocleon again interrupts, and the two engage in dialogue (952–61), followed immediately by Bdelycleon calling up the cheese grater to testify (962–66). After a few lines calling for pity (967–72), the lines that Murphy and Hubbard cite as the end of Bdelycleon's speech in fact consist of his calling up the defendant's puppies (975–79). In response to this display, Philocleon begs Bdelycleon to stop, which he does, without adding to or concluding his speech (980–81).

The remainder of the scene consists of dialogue and debate between Philocleon and Bdelycleon about the verdict (982–89). Eventually, Bdelycleon tricks Philocleon into acquitting (990–94), and this forces another moment of desperation and reliance on Bdelycleon (995–1002). As he did after his successful speech about the false qualities of a juror's life, the son quickly announces the next activity in his father's life (1003–7):

---

99. Both Murphy and Hubbard gloss over these interruptions, but continuous speech making on a much larger scale is amply testified in drama. Cf. the discussion of *Thesmophoriazusae* in Chapter 5.

καὶ μηδὲν ἀγανάκτει γ'. ἐγὼ γάρ σ', ὦ πάτερ,
θρέψω καλῶς, ἄγων μετ' ἐμαυτοῦ πανταχοῖ,
ἐπὶ δεῖπνον, ἐς ξυμπόσιον, ἐπὶ θεωρίαν,
ὥσθ' ἡδέως διάγειν σε τὸν λοιπὸν χρόνον
κοὐκ ἐγχανεῖταί σ' ἐξαπατῶν Ὑπέρβολος.

Don't worry about anything. Father, I'm going to
take good care of you, take you everywhere with me:
to dinner, to parties, to shows,
so you'll lead a sweet life in the future,
and Hyperbolus won't trick and gape at you.

Scholars have wondered at times about the ensuing scenes wherein Bdelycleon attempts to groom his father for sophisticated life, but the progression is consistent with Aristophanes' political ideology.[100] In *Acharnians*, once Dicaeopolis found a way to make the deliberative process work, albeit outside the Pnyx, he enjoys success and prosperity. In *Knights*, when Demos regains control of the deliberative process in the Assembly, Athens enjoys success and prosperity. In *Clouds*, when Strepsiades has identified and neutralized the growing threat to the democracy, the play is over. Now in *Wasps*, the two reasons the courts obstruct the democracy, aggressive young prosecutors and the suits directed by Cleon against his enemies, are removed, so Philocleon can enjoy success and prosperity. Certainly by implication the Demos will receive full proper benefits from the administration of empire now, but the play does not dwell on that. Bdelycleon wants his father to join elite life, but success and prosperity for Philocleon really consist of food, drink, sex and the pleasure of the freedom to act as he wishes. That the elite life is not a desirable path for the Demos is confirmed in passing by Cleon's presence at an elite symposium (1220–24), but Bdelycleon, who has been loyal and a boon to his father in freeing him from two sets of evils, does not come in for censure for this attempt. The Demos is simply in for better pleasure than the hypocritical, stuffy and mismatched environment of the symposium. Bdelycleon's final project is a failure, but one with no losses or criticism. The chorus also makes clear, in their ode celebrating their waspishness, that the success and prosperity at the end of the play is analogous to the success of Athens and her empire in the "good old days" (1106–21).

---

100. Reinders (2001, 207–12) reviews political readings of the play. McGlew (2004) expresses a similar idea when he recognizes that *Wasps* problematizes the mechanisms of persuasion in public democratic institutions, but finds that Philocleon is restored to an unappealing political animal at the end, while I think Philocleon's failure to function in elite life is celebratory.

BRINGING IT ALL BACK HOME: *PEACE*

In *Wasps*, after Philocleon has conceded that the juror's life does not bring the benefits he thought and he has been bamboozled into rendering a judgment of acquittal, his son Bdelycleon offers him a new life (1003–7, quoted above).

The last episodes of *Wasps* make a mockery of Philocleon participating in banquets and symposia, but Bdelycleon's promise serves as a template for Aristophanes' play of the next year, *Peace*. Where *Clouds* and *Wasps* each have a darkness and even cynicism (neither expresses as much faith in the restoration of Athens as do *Acharnians* and *Knights*), as scholars have noted, with Athens buoyed by the death of Cleon and nearing treaty with Sparta, *Peace* is lyrical and giddy by comparison.[101] Aristophanes also takes the occasion to recapitulate his ideological stance on the war and the democracy's role in it, as well as make good on a promise that deliberation restored to its proper location means success and prosperity for Athens.

To this end, once Peace herself has been put on stage after an elaborate rescue, Aristophanes has Hermes discourse on the trajectory of the war and the future of Athens. This narrative may justly receive criticism as naïve or distorted, and the asides by Trygaeus and the chorus indicate it was unorthodox at the time (615–18), but it is a legitimate summary of Aristophanes' ideology as it pertains to the war, the functioning of the Athenian democracy and the path to future prosperity. Hermes begins with Phidias' troubles prompting Pericles' need to do something to divert the bite of the Demos (605–8). Aristophanes thus invokes again the negative portrayal of Pericles from comedy. Given that all extant testimony from comedy from this date and earlier attacks Pericles as a manipulative and capricious ruler placing his own needs above those of Athens, it is not surprising that Aristophanes maintains this stance toward Pericles. Pericles' use of the Megarian decree and fanning the flames of war with Sparta conflicts with Thucydides' favorable report of him, but it is a natural extension of comedy's take on the dominance of Pericles in Athens (cf. Chapter 2).

As Hermes continues to tell it, while the war destabilized the Athenian empire, corruption affected all sides and the destruction of crops inflamed farmers to the cause (619–31), orators (λέγοντες) in Athens fueled the war's momentum (632–37):

---

101. Harriott (1986, 119–38); Reckford (1987, 3–52, 93–104).

κἀνθάδ' ὡς ἐκ τῶν ἀγρῶν ξυνῆλθεν οὑργάτης λεώς,
τὸν τρόπον πωλούμενος τὸν αὐτὸν οὐκ ἐμάνθανεν,
ἀλλ' ἅτ' ὢν ἄνευ γιγάρτων καὶ φιλῶν τὰς ἰσχάδας
ἔβλεπεν πρὸς τοὺς λέγοντας· οἱ δὲ γιγνώσκοντες εὖ
τοὺς πένητας ἀσθενοῦντας κἀποροῦντας ἀλφίτων,
τήνδε μὲν δικροῖς ἐώθουν τὴν θεὸν κεκράγμασιν.

And then when working people gathered from the fields,
they didn't understand that they were being sold out the same way.
They just didn't have raisins and loved their figs,
so they looked to the orators: They understood that
the poor were weak and lacked barley grain,
so they shoved this goddess [Peace] away with forked shrieks.

While other comic references to politicians and public speakers refer to *rhetores* and such, who in practice plied their trade by delivering speeches, this is the only reference in Aristophanes to this group explicitly as λέγοντες, "speakers."[102] Even so, Aristophanes says nothing about the tricks of language, organization of speeches or their mechanics in any way, merely that they are manipulating the desperate poor and spreading corruption (635–47). The point man for this activity is, of course, Cleon, indicated by the shrieking (637) and then alluded to as a tanner (647). Central to the story, however, must remain the deliberative process, and Aristophanes has Peace, speaking through Hermes, express particular anger on this topic (659). Peace was denied three times when she made herself available after the events at Pylos (665–67), it is reported. As such, there was a complete failure of the deliberative process, and Trygaeus admits that this was wrong, blaming the influence of Cleon (668–69). Since Cleon is dead, Peace asks who now controls the Pnyx (680). Upon hearing it is Hyperbolus, she turns away in disgust (681–84), disapproving of this "protector" of the Demos (προστάτην, 684), the mantle that Cleon wore and which Aristophanes has alluded to in distorted form several times.[103] Trygaeus responds that the Demos is merely seeking an ἐπίτροπος, the more venerable and positive term, and uses Hyperbolus only as a temporary measure (just as Demos says he does with such leaders at *Knights* 1127–30). "We shall be better at deliberating" (εὐβουλότεροι γενησόμεθα, 689), Trygeus assures Peace, and after his return to earth, he does consider Hyperbolus dismissed (922 and

---

102. Other instances do not refer to public speakers. Only *Kn.* 1118 uses the participle of λέγω of someone speaking in a political context, but it does not refer to a class of speakers.

103. Cf. discussion of this title above, 70–72.

1319). With this assurance, Peace goes on to ask about playwrights rather than politics (694–705; cf. Chapter 6).

With this questioning finished, Hermes turns to the tasks that will enact the benefits of Peace. Trygaeus receives the personification of the harvest ('Οπώρα) for his sexual and digestive satisfaction (706–12). The other task is to take *Theoria* to the Council (713–18). "Theoria" seems to refer primarily to public spectacles (so scholia), although it can also refer to a delegation, but the key point here is that full restoration of peace means the Council will engage in its deliberative and administrative functions, but now focused on happy occasions for the Demos to participate in.[104] After the *parabasis*, Trygaeus arrives back on Earth, and, once he has explained his mission, his first act is indeed to return *Theoria* to the Council.

Here, once again, Aristophanes engages in an act of translocation, but for the first time he is not transferring deliberative activity *away* from its proper public institution and location but restoring deliberation *to* it. Such a restoration, like all proper deliberation, leads to success and prosperity, and Trygaeus enumerates explicitly and at length the many pleasures, sexual and otherwise, that will ensue upon *Theoria*'s return to the Council (894–908).

To dramatize this particular translocation, Aristophanes engages in unique staging.[105] Whereas previously he had transformed the space in the Theater of Dionysus into the Pnyx while the Assembly was being held (*Ach.*, *Kn.*), or turned the stage into a domestic version of a public court (*Wasps*), the actions of the Council had only been reported (*Kn.*). This time, rather than put the Council on stage, Aristophanes capitalizes on the fact that the theater includes the seating of the *Bouletikon*, where the real-life Prytaneis are seated. Trygaeus delivers the personified Theoria directly to the Prytaneis (887, 905). In a crucial way, then, the run of plays from *Acharnians* to *Peace* happens to form a unit, for *Acharnians* begins with the stage version of the Prytaneis being incompetent and corrupt at the Assembly, ignoring or refusing peace and its benefits, and *Peace* celebrates the real-life Prytaneis happily accepting peace and its responsibility for the prosperity of the Demos.

CONCLUSION

The comedies of the late 420s continue the vestiges of patterns and perspectives visible in the fragments of earlier comedies. The formal terminology

---

104. *Theoria* also appears in the list of activities to which Bdelycleon plans to take Philocleon, confirming its role in the happy life of the Demos (*Wasps* 1005).

105. Cassio (1985).

and rules for structuring speeches are still not yet in evidence. Rather, comic playwrights continue to satirize prominent individuals who use unorthodox language in the public arena and to combat the phenomenon with their own creative, comic discourse. The survival of complete scripts allows a much broader and deeper analysis of how Aristophanes tackled the issue. His plays reflect an abiding faith in deliberation presided over by a sovereign Demos, and his concern with language is focused on whether it facilitates or hinders the deliberative process and the ability of the Demos to render sound judgment. Aristophanes' faith in the deliberative process is such that he has his protagonist Diceaopolis in *Acharnians* still use the deliberative process, but translocated outside a dysfunctional Assembly, and garner astounding prosperity. In *Knights,* both the Council and the Assembly are crippled by Cleon's abuse of the deliberative process. Aristophanes' support of the Demos is so strong, however, that when Demos resumes proper judgment, Athens returns to its glory days of empire, with Demos as sovereign, before prominent individuals like Pericles or Cleon used their vigorous speech making to abuse the Demos. In *Clouds,* Aristophanes turns to the mechanisms that generate such speakers, focusing on Protagoras' model of binary *logoi* in particular. The play emerges as the earliest-known example of the charge that the scientific exploration of language blossoming at the time was in fact a movement toward cultural decadence. This time the protagonist does not translocate the deliberative process but cuts the phenomenon at the root by burning down the Phrontisterion wherein a deviant *logos* could otherwise corrupt the future generations of Athens. Having dramatized the deliberative processes in the Athenian Assembly and Council in *Acharnians* and *Knights,* Aristophanes next focuses on the courts in *Wasps.* The familiar patterns continue with regard to the details of language (no canonical strictures but continued comic satire of unorthodoxy), but Aristophanes expresses no vision for a corrected system of court trials. Whereas the Assembly and Council should continue to operate under the prudent guidance of the Demos, the best courts seem to be no courts at all. Finally, in *Peace,* Aristophanes returns the deliberative process, figuratively and literally, to the Athenian Council, and the city will prosper.

Aristophanes' five extant comedies from 425 to 421 provide the most thorough record of dramatic output for any five-year period in the whole of antiquity. The arc of these five comedies, from the war-torn dysfunctional Assembly that begins *Acharnians* to the restoration of prosperity to the members of the Council seated in the theater at the end of *Peace,* cannot be replicated anywhere else. Perhaps even if comparable plays survived for another five-year period, such an arc would never occur again anyway. After the performance of *Peace* in 421, the Peace of Nicias was signed, and, as it happens, our knowledge of both the history and the dramatic output of Athens plummets for the next several years. When more detailed sources emerge again, the twin specters of the Sicilian expedition and oligarchic revolution change the rules of public discourse. The pathway to these changes is the subject of the next chapter.

4

The Years of Confidence, 421–414 B.C.E.

ἀναγκαῖον δὲ καὶ πρὸς ταῦτα μὴ μόνον τοὺς οἰκείους πολέμους τεθεωρηκέναι ἀλλὰ καὶ τοὺς τῶν ἄλλων, πῶς ἀποβαίνουσιν· ἀπὸ γὰρ τῶν ὁμοίων τὰ ὅμοια γίγνεσθαι πέφυκεν.

And regarding this [war and peace], it is necessary to have watched not only how one's own wars have turned out, but also those of others, for similar results naturally come of similar causes.

—Aristotle, *Rhet.* 1.4.9.1360a3–6

THE LOST YEARS, 420–415 B.C.E.

When Thucydides concludes his account of the ten years of war from 431 to 421 B.C.E. and embarks on the next stage of his narrative, he argues briefly that the period of the armistice, lasting nearly seven years, in retrospect was not a period of peace but of low-level hostilities leading to renewed conflict (5.26). His compressed survey of events between the Peace of Nicias and the Sicilian expedition (5.27–116) thus focuses on the political and military events that provide evidence of his thesis, that the period should be reckoned an intermediate phase of the war. Consequently, even with other sources available, our knowledge of the *Zeitgeist* of Athens from the summer of 421 to the winter of 415 is patchy at best when compared to the previous decade and the following years.

Thucydides acknowledges that he is looking back from the perspective of the end of the war.[1] Playwrights writing comedies for the seasons of 420–415 did not have the benefit of hindsight and so simply kept producing plays in the environment as they knew it. Unfortunately, no complete comedy survives from this period, and the next extant one, *Birds*, was produced while the Sicilian expedition was ongoing. Still, this period covers the later years of Eupolis' career and the early years of Plato Comicus, and Aristophanes was still active, along with a range of lesser-known playwrights, so it is worth charting the evolving commentary of the remains of comedy from this period on politics, rhetoric and the trajectory of the Athenians.

Aristophanes' plays of the 420s display a consistent interest in the problem of leadership in the democracy. While Aristophanes in *Peace* attempts to dismiss the importance of Hyperbolus and other popular leaders in the wake of the Peace of Nicias, other comic playwrights continued to find the topic one of recurring interest. Aristophanes himself complains a few years later, in his revised *parabasis* of *Clouds*, that his attack on Cleon in *Knights* inspired a string of imitators attacking Hyperbolus (551–59).[2] A. H. Sommerstein rightly points out the exaggeration of Aristophanes' complaint, but it is fair to say that anyone perceived as a leader of the Demos or a commanding presence in Athens was likely to be a person of interest for a comic playwright. At a minimum, Hyperbolus was a substantial target in Eupolis' *Marikas*, Hermippus' *Artopolides* and Plato Comicus' *Hyperbolus*, in addition to being at least cited in other plays. Plato Comicus would go on to produce at least two more plays named for such individuals, *Pisander* and *Cleophon*. Alcibiades was prominent in Eupolis' *Baptai* and in other plays, noted for his distinctive style of speaking.[3]

Fragments of these so-called demagogue comedies and similar plays confirm only that some motifs found in Aristophanes' political plays were also to be found in other plays. A passage in Eupolis' *Marikas* gave an ancient commentator reason to reference Cleon sputtering in *Knights* (fr. 192.135–36). An unplaced fragment ridicules Cleon himself for the public greeting χαῖρε, "Hello! Rejoice!" while he was actually hurting the city (Eupolis fr. 331 = Olson E17). A vivid and economical sketch of Syracosius as an orator appears in Eupolis (fr. 220, from *Cities*):

---

1. See Strauss (1997) on the issue of periodization of the Peloponnesian War.
2. On this phenomenon generally, see Sommerstein (2000) and Storey (2003, 342–44). Note that Aristophanes does not use the term "demagogue" in this passage.
3. Cf. the Appendix. This leaves aside the cottage industry in hunting for allusions to Alcibiades in other plays. See Dover (2004) for a criticism of this approach.

Συρακόσιος δ' ἔοικεν, ἡνίκ' ἂν λέγῃ,
τοῖς κυνιδίοισι τοῖσιν ἐπὶ τῶν τειχίων·
ἀναβὰς γὰρ ἐπὶ τὸ βῆμ' ὑλακτεῖ περιτρέχων.

Whenever he speaks, Syracosius resembles
little dogs at the walls,
because he walks up to the *bema* and yaps as he runs around.

As is true of fifth-century comedy in general, terms for negative speech appear, but again none are technical terms, and no passage indicates or implies a formal system for instruction or rhetorical composition. More often, pejorative terms describe fancy or clever speaking. The harshest of these terms is ἀδολεσχεῖν, "blather," and connected forms.[4] Eupolis has a line addressing a σοφιστής, probably sarcastically or ironically, to teach ἀδολεσχεῖν (fr. 388). Eupolis also applies ἀδολέσχην to Socrates (fr. 386; cf. *Clouds* 1480, of Socrates' students when Strepsiades is attacking the Phrontisterion; on the term σοφιστής, see Chapter 2). Another fragment of Aristophanes (fr. 506) points to the corrupting influence of someone engaged in ἀδολεσχεῖν:

τοῦτον τὸν ἄνδρ' ἢ βιβλίον διέφθορεν
ἢ Πρόδικος ἢ τῶν ἀδολεσχῶν εἷς γέ τις.

A book has ruined this man,
or Prodicus, or some one of those blatherers.

Other common terms offer variations on this same theme. While in the next century λαλέω becomes an ordinary word for talking, in fifth-century comedy it retains its sense of empty chatter. Eupolis succinctly summarizes: λαλεῖν ἄριστος, ἀδυνώτατος λέγειν, "superb at chatter, incapable of speaking" (fr. 116, from *Demes*). A scholiast reports Aristophanes describing Gorgias and Philippus as λάλοι (fr. 118, but there is no certainty that the scholiast uses Aristophanes' exact wording). Since Euripides receives as much criticism for being a sophist (in the modern sense) as anyone in Greek comedy (see Chapter 6), it is unsurprising that his tragedies are not just λάλοι but "chatter around" (περιλαλούσας Aristophanes fr. 392) and elsewhere need more salt and less chatter (Aristophanes fr. 595; cf. fr. 158 for the salt

---

4. Cf. the entry in the Appendix.

metaphor). Aristophanes' use of other words based on the λαλ- stem is also recorded (frr. 151, 684, 949).⁵

These fragments overlap with a continued interest in education. A phrase in Eupolis' *Marikas* is a metaphor of a class dismissed by a teacher (*grammatodidaskalon*, fr. 192.13–15). As in Aristophanes, teaching, of language or anything else, is the province of an individual instructor with an individual or group, but not an institution. Thus there is the teacher Prodamos in *Aiges* who teaches grammar and music (fr. 17). For Eupolis, Socrates is again more a charlatan than a philosopher or teacher (fr. 386 = Olson F1 and 395 = Olson B2), as is Protagoras (frr. 157–58 from *Kolakes*). Eupolis' *Kolakes* of 421 places Protagoras and other visiting intellectuals in the home of Callias. Decades later, Plato also dramatizes such a gathering at the house of Callias but implies a setting in the 430s, when Pericles and his sons are alive, and Alcibiades and the playwright Agathon are quite young. In this dialogue, Plato includes a debate between Socrates and Protagoras about whether *aretē* can be taught, and he has Protagoras cite the chorus in Pherecrates' *Savages* (Ἄγριοι) of 420, which might imply the play dealt with educational issues (*Prot.* 327c–d). At a minimum, the play had to deal with what constituted civil society.

The fragmentary remains of these and similar plays reveal some overlapping motifs with Aristophanes' plays, but not enough material for productive speculation about the broader ideological stand of Eupolis or other comic playwrights, either as congruent or in contrast with Aristophanes, as regards rhetorical language and democratic deliberation.⁶ As the previous chapter has shown, much of what Aristophanes' comedies convey about public language and the democratic process unfolds over a number of episodes and requires context to discern the significance of translocation and revelations about characters' orientation on the ideological grid. No fragments of other fifth-century comedies permit analysis of these types of progressions or recovery of the necessary types of contexts.

The most important lost play of the 410s is undeniably Eupolis' *Demes*, although its famous fragments and papyrus remains raise more problems

---

5. Cf. the entry in the Appendix. For other instances of λαλέω where the context is unclear or at least there is no indication of political or philosophical content, see Pherecrates frr. 2, 70, 138; Strattis fr. 54; and adesp. 1005. Covering a similar semantic field is ληρέω, for which see Cratinus fr. 208 (= Olson B6) and adesp. fr. 174 dub. Pherecrates' Λῆροι seems to refer to women's accoutrements, not the verb of empty talk; cf. L. B. Carter (1985, 121).

6. Storey (2003, 338–48) is rightly cautious about characterizing Eupolis' political orientation, but he is a little eager to downplay Eupolis having an interest in political comedy at all, often trying to separate "satire," "personal attacks," or "military" jokes from political comedy, although it is not clear why there is a firm line between all these. Even Storey must admit at least four of Eupolis' plays engaged in "political comedy" (*Poleis, Marikas, Chrysoun Genos* and *Demes*).

than they solve in understanding the play. While the play has often been assigned to 412 B.C.E., Storey makes a compelling case for production ca. 417.[7] The date of 412 rests overwhelmingly on the idea that Eupolis composed the play subsequent to the disaster on Sicily and that the resurrection of the figures from Athens' past constituted a reflection, in a time of crisis, on what Athens had and now needed. In *Knights,* Aristophanes was already invoking the same figures Eupolis revives in *Demes* (Solon, Miltiades, Aristides) and was revivifying the Athens of the generation of Marathon, so there is no requirement that 412 be a necessary or distinct moment for such a play. The reference to controversy about the battle of Mantinea in 418 (fr. 99.30–32) and other *komoidoumenoi* fit a date ca. 417 far better than the date 412. Indeed, if comedy is still in part reeling off jokes about demagogues in the wake of Aristophanes' *Knights,* Eupolis' staging a play not with an individual representative of the Demos but with a whole chorus of "Demoi" is also a possibility.[8]

The section of the lengthy papyrus fragment (99.23–34) attacking some prominent speaker and political leader indicates the nexus of motifs found in Aristophanes' plays were also found in *Demes.* While there remain many viable candidates for the exact individual vilified here, the specifics of the attack find easy parallels elsewhere in comedy. This is someone whose suitability to lead the Demos is in question (ἄξιοὶ δημηγορεῖν, fr. 99.23; once again, the term is not yet pejorative, and it makes more sense for it to be positive here, since it emphasizes the contrast between the individual and what he strives for). His manner of speech is an issue, not because he speaks formally but because he does not speak proper Attic (ἡττίκιζεν, 25) and thunders like a god (τοῦ θεοῦ βροντῶντος, 31; reminiscent of attacks on Pericles). The issue of proper deliberation is embedded in the citation of the speaker threatening to lock up generals who object to some sort of motion to act at Mantinea (30–32). This action in the Assembly is the climactic example of why the individual should not be a leader (ἄρχειν, 33).

That Eupolis devoted part of a choral ode to criticizing the ambitions of a public, political speaker who was boisterous and advised the Demos badly does not mean he espouses a faith in the deliberative process and the sovereignty of the Demos that Aristophanes illustrates in his plays. The passage merely indicates that Eupolis engaged in some of the same issues of public language and leadership that Aristophanes does. Indeed, the plot and other

---

7. Storey (2003, 111–14). For support of a date as late as 410, see Telò (2007, 397–401).

8. Storey (2003, 391–94) makes a good case that *Demoi* refers to the outlying communities of Attica and that the chorus is made up of representatives from there. Even so, it is hard to imagine that Eupolis did not make some use of or play on the term corresponding to the Demos itself.

fragments of *Demes* suggest that Eupolis presented a significantly different view from Aristophanes of a crucial leader and speaker from Athens' past: Pericles.

The remains of *Demes* make clear Pericles was one of four figures from Athens' past (the others being Solon, Miltiades and Aristides) to reappear in some way. Plutarch says of Pericles' arrival in the play (Plut. *Per.* 3.7 = Eupolis fr. 115):

ὁ δ' Εὔπολις ἐν τοῖς Δήμοις πυνθανόμενος περὶ ἑκάστου τῶν ἀναβεβηκότων ἐξ Ἅιδου δημαγωγῶν, ὡς ὁ Περικλῆς ὠνομάσθη τελευταῖος:
"ὅ τι περ κεφάλαιον τῶν κάτωθεν ἤγαγες."

Eupolis in *Demes* inquires about each of the demagogues once they have come up from Hades and says, when Pericles is called out last:
"What you have brought is the headmost of those below."

The laudatory introduction of Pericles is probably undercut by yet another joke about Pericles' misshapen skull,[9] but Eupolis does seem to give pride of place to Pericles by putting him last among revered figures from the past. Thomas Braun has observed that this represents a shift in perspective on Pericles, since comic references during his lifetime and in Aristophanes' plays of the 420s are uniformly critical.[10] Braun further sets up a contrast with Themistocles, who would seem a logical candidate for resurrection but is absent. Braun argues that, in the case of Themistocles, his reputation remained tainted by charges of self-enrichment, and it would take until the fourth century for his name to be invoked in a consistently positive way. Pericles, by contrast, ultimately had a reputation for personal virtue and, once the war was seemingly concluded, became a viable candidate for lionization.

Braun's argument oversimplifies the situation and papers over testimony that does not favor his conclusion. For both Themistocles and Pericles, Braun does rightly acknowledge positive and negative testimony in the fifth century. Themistocles was undeniably a hero of the Persian Wars but his later reputation was hindered by his descendants in Asia Minor who were supporting the Persians. For Pericles, Braun acknowledges the criticisms leveled during his lifetime but, in analyzing the passages in *Acharnians*

---

9. Cf. fr. 325 from *Chrysoun Genos*, which says only that Eupolis referred to the Odeon in this play, but which might indicate a reference to Pericles (cf. Cratinus frr. 73, 118 for the image).

10. Braun (2000).

and *Peace* that fault Pericles posthumously for the war, Braun argues that Aristophanes was mostly finding an efficient way to lampoon and criticize the start of the war more than directing his attack against Pericles himself. Beyond that, Braun claims, fifth-century criticism of Pericles is consistent with Thucydides' praise in that all agree he was beyond personal corruption. Consequently, Pericles would be a good candidate for resurrection, while Themistocles remained a "hot potato."

Braun faces essentially the same bifurcated testimony about Pericles as Plutarch millennia earlier, with comic sources criticizing him, and Thucydides offering praise. And he reaches a conclusion much as Plutarch does, by preferring Thucydides' portrait of personal virtue over the derogatory claims of comic playwrights. To an extent, however, Braun simply misrepresents the comic critiques. Hermippus' characterization of Pericles as a do-nothing hypocrite does not imply agreement that Pericles was personally virtuous (fr. 47). Aristophanes is obviously satirizing the start of the war, but in the passages from both *Acharnians* and *Peace* he quite definitely says Pericles pursued war because of personal matters (whether his connection to Aspasia or Phidias), putting his tyrannical self above the needs of the Demos and Athens. These are not portraits that agree that Pericles was personally beyond corruption.

In the broader picture, Braun may simply be trying to make a much simpler conclusion and narrative than are possible or desirable. It does seem fair to say that by some point in the fourth century both Themistocles and Pericles were widely recognized as heroes of Athens' past.[11] Their reputations in the last decades of the fifth century seem to have been messier, however. Herodotus offers a Themistocles who deserves credit for his accomplishments in the Persian Wars, without hiding his questionable actions later, and his history was likely in circulation in some form by the 420s. Aristophanes has two passing references to him in *Knights,* both invoking him in somewhat heroic terms. Themistocles is cited in *Demes* as clever but thieving (σοφὸς γὰρ ἀνήρ, τῆς δὲ χειρὸς οὐ κρατῶν, fr. 126), so there was at least room for ambivalence. By contrast, all references to Pericles down to Aristophanes' *Peace* in 421 B.C.E. are negative. Thucydides is laudatory, but it is unclear when he puts forth his portrait. It is certainly after Pericles' death and could even be in the last years of the century. Eupolis' *Demes* offers the first and only positive comment in comedy, but, as it happens, no other reference in comedy to Pericles survives from the rest of the century, so

---

11. Isocrates, Aeschines and Lycurgus each cite them as model figures from the glorious past. See Braun (2000, 216) for specifics.

putting the play's fragmentary references in context is even more difficult.[12] Perhaps the positive portrayal of Pericles was novel and influential. Perhaps in the continuing difference of opinion about Pericles, *Demes* was the first to portray him positively on the comic stage. Perhaps Eupolis was out of step with the times, and only later, when Pericles' stock rose, did the play gain approval.[13] Perhaps with the Peace of Nicias, or even earlier, despite Aristophanes' protests in *Peace*, Pericles' role in the war was being reevaluated and his role in *Demes* reflected his new popularity.

Whatever the cause and whatever Pericles' exact role, his oratory was a critical part of his characterization (fr. 102 = Olson E10):

(Α.) κράτιστος οὗτος ἐγένετ' ἀνθρώπων λέγειν·
ὁπότε παρέλθοι δ,' ὥσπερ ἀγαθοὶ δρομῆς,
ἐκ δέκα ποδῶν ᾕρει λέγων τοὺς ῥήτορας.
(Β.) ταχὺν λέγεις γε.
    (Α.) πρὸς δέ γ' αὐτοῦ τῷ τάχει
πειθώ τις ἐπεκάθιζεν ἐπὶ τοῖς χείλεσιν·
οὕτως ἐκήλει καὶ μόνος τῶν ῥητόρων
τὸ κέντρον ἐγκατέλειπε τοῖς ἀκροωμένοις.

A. This man was so powerful a person at speaking.
Whenever he stepped up, just like good runners,
he caught up with *rhetores* from ten feet back when he spoke.
B. You're talking about fast there!
A. As well as his speed,
a certain persuasiveness sat upon his lips.
He was charming that way and the only *rhetor*
who left a sting in those who heard him.

Other fragments of *Demes* testify that oratory was a concern not limited to this passage. The thundering speech of the demagogue (fr. 99.31), the effective but criticized speaker nicknamed "Bouzyges" (fr. 103),[14] the dismissal of Phaeax's speech (fr. 116), and someone's "circular talk" (fr. 108) point to an interest in public oratory. Again at this point we hit the limits of our evidence, for without contexts such as we have for Aristophanes' plays, the ultimate evaluation of such speakers and the role more generally of oratory

---

12. On the supposed allusion to Pericles in the character of Aeschylus in *Frogs*, see Chapter 6.
13. See Storey (2003, 111) on the reputation of *Demes*.
14. Although a scholiast identifies Bouzyges in Eupolis fr. 103 as Pericles, the point of the comment is the speaker's inferiority to Pericles; cf. Storey (2003, 134–36).

in the democracy are beyond recovery. In any case, nothing contradicts the broader picture that speakers and speech making did not conform to the formal precepts of classical rhetoric from the next century.

Other potential factors in the production and reception of *Demes* are two areas of tension Thucydides discusses obliquely and cautiously: the fear of tyranny among the Demos and the growing influence of Alcibiades. Aristophanes highlights paranoia about tyrants and speakers' use of this bogeyman as far back as *Wasps* in 422, but Thucydides highlights it as productive in the interrogations into the scandal over the Mysteries (6.53.3 and 6.60). As modern scholars have noted, despite Thucydides' ridicule of the Demos' ignorance and paranoia, Alcibiades' influence was at least a legitimate concern for supporters of democracy, and the oligarchic coup four years later indicates that the specter of the overthrow of the democracy was not abstract fantasy. It is possible, and it would seem logical, that Eupolis incorporated these tensions into his *Baptai*, likely produced within a few years of *Demes*, but the confused and unreliable testimony about the play and Alcibiades' role in it do not allow for much sober discussion. One fragment involves reelection (fr. 98), and another mentions a proposal significant for the city (προβούλευμα βαστάζουσι τῆς πόλεως μέγα, fr. 76), but otherwise only Alcibiades' supposedly homicidally angry reaction to the play gives any hint of the stakes raised in the play.[15]

Aristophanes' output during these same years is even more vestigial. Of plays for which there is some reason to date around this period, *Seasons* reportedly put some unorthodox gods on trial and expelled them (Cic. *De leg.* 2.37) and contains some expression of cynicism about utopia (fr. 581), foreshadowing the debate about poverty in *Wealth* at the end of Aristophanes' career. *Heroes* mentions part of a *klepsydra* (fr. 328), so some reference to a trial may be involved. *Amphiareus* from the Lenaea of 414 used the proverb "Deliberation is sacred" (ἱερὸν συμβουλή, fr. 32), appropriate enough for Aristophanes, but by this year a complete play provides direct evidence for how Aristophanes portrayed the fears and ambitions of the Athenian Demos.

BIRDS: DELIBERATION AND UNIVERSAL EMPIRE

The long, rollicking ride that is *Birds* incorporates a number of lines, passages and scenes similar to the isolated fragments of comedies from the

---

15. See Storey (2003, 101–10) and the entry for Alcibiades in the Appendix.

period. The obsession with tyrants of the distant past, harshly ridiculed by Thucydides, finds a quick gibe in the parody of public declamations, offering a substantial reward, "if anyone kills one of the dead tyrants" (ἤν τε τῶν τυράννων τίς τινα / τῶν τεθνηκότων ἀποκτείνῃ, 1074–75). If Storey is right that Eupolis' *Demes* began with an episode in which the protagonist raises the legendary figures of Athens' past glory from the dead, Aristophanes might be offering a deflated version of such a scene (1553–64):

πρὸς δὲ τοῖς Σκιάποσιν λίμνη
τις ἔστ᾽ ἄλουτος οὗ
ψυχαγωγεῖ Σωκράτης·
ἔνθα καὶ Πείσανδρος ἦλθε
δεόμενος ψυχὴν ἰδεῖν ἣ
ζῶντ᾽ ἐκεῖνον προΰλιπε,
σφάγι᾽ ἔχων κάμηλον ἀμνόν
τιν᾽, ἧς λαιμοὺς τεμὼν ὥσπερ
ποθ᾽ οὑδυσσεὺς ἀπῆλθε,
κᾆτ᾽ ἀνῆλθ᾽ αὐτῷ κάτωθεν
πρὸς τὸ λαῖτμα τῆς καμήλου
Χαιρεφῶν ἡ νυκτερίς.

Near the Shade Feet there
is a lake, where unwashed
Socrates makes souls uplifted.
There came Pisander,
asking to see the soul
that abandoned him in life.
With a camel-lamb for a sacrifice,
he cut its throat and,
just like Odysseus, he ran away.
Then toward him from below
toward the gushing of the camel came
Chaerephon the bat!

Whether it is Odysseus interrogating the figures of the mythological past on his epic quest or the convention of resurrecting heroic Athenians, here the process is reduced to a bogus intellectual, a cowardly politician, and an eccentric local character. The responding ode also fills in an established heroic ritual with contemporary low-grade troublemakers (1694–1705):

ἔστι δ' ἐν Φάναισι πρὸς τῇ
Κλεψύδρᾳ πανοῦργον
Ἐγγλωττογαστόρων γένος,
οἳ θερίζουσίν τε καὶ σπείρουσι
καὶ τρυγῶσι ταῖς γλώτταισι
συκάζουσί τε·
βάρβαροι δ' εἰσὶν γένος,
Γοργίαι τε καὶ Φίλιπποι.
κἀπὸ τῶν Ἐγγλωττογαστόρων
ἐκείνων τῶν Φιλίππων
πανταχοῦ τῆς Ἀττικῆς ἡ
γλῶττα χωρὶς τέμνεται.

There is in the Accusa-nation near the
court clock: the evil race of
Tongue Bellies!
Who sow and gather fruit and with their tongues
reap havoc.
They are barbarians by race,
like Gorgias and Philip.
And because of those Tongue Belly
Philippines,
everywhere in Attica,
the tongue is cut out separately.

As always in comedy, the tongue is the vocal tool of malfeasance (see Chapter 2 and the Appendix), here imported from outside Greece to feed bellies and be linked vaguely with the practice of cutting tongues out separately and prominently at sacrifices.

These motifs offer little but consistency with other such terms and images in comedy. The broader context of *Birds* has catapulted the play to the first tier of disputation among scholars. The leading issue has been what to make of parallels between the fundamental plot (and then how details square with these broader parallels) and the grand undertaking of the expedition against Sicily.[16] Broadly speaking, critics have attempted to map some sort of allegory between the characters in the plot and the historical actors in

---

16. Konstan (1998, 3–6) offers a helpful survey of scholarly trends regarding this problem; see also note 19 below on other contributions in the same volume.

the real-life drama of the Sicilian expedition and/or to map the new Cloudcuckooland onto Athens. Allegorists have generally struggled because Aristophanes simply does not seem to employ prolonged and detailed allegories. A character may have an allegorical dream (e.g., *Wasps* 13–53), and Aristophanes is not subtle about pointing out thinly veiled allegorical attacks on historical figures, but systematic understated allegories either fail to hold up at all or are so vague as to command little independent assent. Furthermore, allegorists most often seek a narrative parallel to that found in Thucydides, which would also require the awareness of *hybris* and the expectation of failure, but such dark tones are difficult to lay claim to in a play that is the most joyous of Aristophanes' extant plays, perhaps excluding *Peace*. The requirement, or at least preference, for a sense of impending doom will be an issue revisited later. Allegorizing the bird *polis* onto historical Athens fares little better. The new world is neither consistently a utopia nor consistently a dystopia. It parallels, inverts, subverts and emulates Athens without a coherent sense of purpose and little more than suits the dynamic of a scene or even a one-off joke.

At the risk of oversimplifying a profoundly ramshackle play, I would like to suggest that once again tracing the dynamic of deliberation and translocation provides a more coherent and productive focus both for analyzing the unfolding of the plot against its historical backdrop and for mental peregrinations through Cloudcuckooland. Such a focus will allow for the generally aggressive and victorious trajectory of events in the play, along with the loose and discursive panorama of the birds' *polis*, but it will raise a potentially disturbing conclusion about Aristophanes' depictions of Athens and the Demos' imperial ambitions.

No deliberative process in any of Aristophanes' fifth-century plays proceeds without conflict, but the process in *Birds* proceeds smoothly in one remarkable way. Whereas in *Acharnians, Knights* and *Wasps* the process utterly fails in its proper civic location and must translocate to become successful, in *Birds* a speaker meets initial hostility, but the deliberative process is quickly successful, so prosperity and victory results for all parties involved.[17] In this sense, the resistance Peisetaerus meets initially from the birds (310–405) is no more than Dicaeopolis must overcome to persuade the Acharnian chorus of his position. In both cases, prosperity ensues, but Dicaeopolis has to endure a failed Assembly before demonstrating the benefits of deliberation. In *Birds*, when the arriving birds attack the visiting

---

17. Peisetaerus and Euelpides do leave Athens, and thus the deliberative process is translocated, but they do not flee a failed site of deliberation, as protagonists do in *Acharnians, Knights* and *Wasps*.

humans for what they perceive as betrayal to their enemy, Tereus is able to reason with them about the principles of deliberation. Of the human intruders, he poses the question (371–72):

> εἰ δὲ τὴν φύσιν μὲν ἐχθροί, τὸν δὲ νοῦν εἰσιν φίλοι,
> καὶ διδάξοντές τι δεῦρ' ἥκουσιν ὑμᾶς χρήσιμον;

> What if they are enemies by nature but friendly by intention,
> and have come here to teach us something useful?

The chorus of birds is skeptical, yet they do not cut off the prospect of a productive assembly but inquire further (373–74):

> πῶς δ' ἂν οἵδ' ἡμᾶς τι χρήσιμον διδάξειάν ποτε
> ἢ φράσειαν, ὄντες ἐχθροὶ τοῖσι πάπποις τοῖς ἐμοῖς;

> How could they ever teach or tell us anything useful,
> when they are enemies of our ancestors?

Tereus now sounds a note about the value of open discussion (375–80):

> ἀλλ' ἀπ' ἐχθρῶν δὴ τὰ πολλὰ μανθάνουσιν οἱ σοφοί.
> ἡ γὰρ εὐλάβεια σῴζει πάντα. παρὰ μὲν οὖν φίλου
> οὐ μάθοις ἂν τοῦθ', ὁ δ' ἐχθρὸς εὐθὺς ἐξηνάγκασεν.
> αὐτίχ' αἱ πόλεις παρ' ἀνδρῶν γ' ἔμαθον ἐχθρῶν κοὐ φίλων
> ἐκπονεῖν θ' ὑψηλὰ τείχη ναῦς τε κεκτῆσθαι μακράς·
> τὸ δὲ μάθημα τοῦτο σῴζει παῖδας, οἶκον, χρήματα.

> But the wise actually learn a lot from their enemies,
> for caution keeps everything safe, and from a friend
> you wouldn't learn that, but your enemy immediately makes it necessary.
> For example, cities learn from enemy men and not from friends
> to build high walls and acquire long ships,
> a lesson that keeps children, home and property safe.

It is neither the first nor the last time Aristophanes promotes the idea that Athenians should heed advice from those outside the traditional deliberative process. The chorus responds in an approving and open-minded way (381–82):

ἔστι μὲν λόγων ἀκοῦσαι πρῶτον, ὡς ἡμῖν δοκεῖ,
χρήσιμον· μάθοι γὰρ ἄν τις κἀπὸ τῶν ἐχθρῶν σοφός.

Listening to arguments first, it seems to us,
is useful, because someone wise can learn from their enemies.

And when everyone is ready for Peisetaerus' speech, the birds indicate that they will negotiate in good faith (460–61):

ἀλλ' ἐφ' ὅτῳπερ πράγματι τὴν σὴν ἥκεις γνώμην ἀναπείσων,
λέγε θαρρήσας· ὡς τὰς σπονδὰς οὐ μὴ πρότεροι παραβῶμεν.

But of the affair about which you have come to persuade us of your view,
speak confidently: We won't break the treaty first.

Confidence is hardly Peisetaerus' problem, for he is in fact eager to impress the birds (465–66):

μὰ Δί', ἀλλὰ λέγειν ζητῶ τι πάλαι, μέγα καὶ λαρινὸν ἔπος τι,
ὅ τι τὴν τούτων θραύσει ψυχήν.

By God, I've been ready so long to deliver a long speech with some fat verbiage,
that will shatter their souls.

As with the speeches in *Wasps*, scholars have at this point summarized Peisetaerus' persuasion of the birds as a formal rhetorical speech, but the specifics bely the characterization. Murphy's *prooimion* (467–70), for example, consists of three rapid-fire claims by Peisetaurus, each interrupted by the chorus leader. The structure is no different from the "proofs" that follow (471–521), except that Euelpides now adds his own asides. The *epilogos* consists mostly of Peisetaerus' *pnigos*, as he rounds out his presentation with a flourish. Murphy does not even attempt to analyze the remainder of the speech (550–626). His description in fact makes the scene seem less like a formally organized rhetorical specimen than debate at an assembly, which in fact it better resembles.[18]

---

18. Murphy (1938, 107) shows his scheme for the passage, and Sousa e Silva (1987–88, 86–87) supports it. Murphy concludes: "What follows is a series of concrete proposals (550–570), and a group of refutations. The chorus and Hoopoe offer objections, which Peisthetaerus [*sic*] answers (571–585), and the speech ends with a list of the various advantages which men will enjoy if they accept

More than seeing a political assembly, however, scholars have noted the echoes of the thought and reasoning of the Sophists in the arguments to the birds, used by Tereus and Peisetaerus himself. Employment of such ideas can seem paradoxical, sinister or at a minimum satirical given Aristophanes' hostility to such thinking elsewhere in his plays. Once again, however, location and purpose are the ultimate criteria. Tereus calls an open assembly of the birds, and Peisetaerus makes his case. In terms of cause and effect, the closest parallel to Peisetaerus' accomplishments as far as the deliberative process is concerned is Dicaeopolis' venture in *Acharnians*. Both meet parties hostile to them at first sight, but once they make their arguments, their opponents concede the superiority of the speakers. Wild success and prosperity ensue. The biggest difference is that Diceaopolis had already failed in the Assembly even to air his ideas, so the benefits of his plan accrue to him almost alone. In *Birds,* since the Assembly allows Peisetaerus to air his ideas, and he implements them, the benefits accrue to them all, including the Athenian spectators of the play.

Scholars have explored in detail various ways that Cloudcuckooland reconfigures Athens, but the key point here is that, in contrast to Diceaopolis' individual success, in *Birds* prosperity extends to the Athenian Demos. On top of the various intruders Peisetaerus deals with, scenes that redesign the *polis* physically and politically, some passages make the inclusiveness explicit. Peisetaerus receives a crown for the benefits he has brought, a rite of recognition in Athens done in the name of the Demos. A herald describes part of the change (1280–84):

πρὶν μὲν γὰρ οἰκίσαι σε τήνδε τὴν πόλιν,
ἐλακωνομάνουν ἅπαντες ἄνθρωποι τότε,
ἐκόμων ἐπείνων ἐρρύπων ἐσωκράτουν
σκυτάλι᾽ ἐφόρουν, νυνὶ δ᾽ ὑποστρέψαντες αὖ
ὀρνιθομανοῦσι, . . .

Before you founded this *polis,*
all the humans were going Spartan,
with long hair, hungry, dirty, going Socrates,
and carrying little clubs. But now they've completely turned around
and gone *bird!*

---

the birds as gods (586–626). A more precise division than this need not be given." He concedes: "The many interruptions during Peisthetaerus' argument in some measure destroy the rhetorical nature of the speech."

If the Athenians, and other Greeks, had been looking elsewhere to find themselves, the new *polis* of *Birds* has everyone flocking, literally, back to Athens. The extent of this accomplishment reaches its climax when the gods send an embassy to negotiate terms. In this sequence, Aristophanes makes explicit that the new *polis* is a victory for democracy over tyranny. The most recalcitrant of the divine ambassadors, Poseidon, complains about his Triballian companion and makes a sideswipe at democracy in the process (1570–71):

ὦ δημοκρατία, ποῖ προβιβᾷς ἡμᾶς ποτε,
εἰ τουτονί γ᾽ κεχειροτονήκασ᾽ οἱ θεοί;

O Democracy, where are you taking us now,
if the gods elected *this!*

When the embassy meets Peisetaerus, he makes explicit that the new *polis* is a democracy, when he explains what he is cooking (1583–85):

ὄρνιθές τινες
ἐπανιστάμενοι τοῖς δημοτικοῖσιν ὀρνέοις
ἔδοξαν ἀδικεῖν.

Some birds
were rebelling against the birds' democracy
and have been convicted.

Critics have often found this a satirical or sinister image, but in its historical context it should have been reassuring.[19] Poseidon has just disparaged democracy, but Peisetaerus, who has been keeping out troublemakers, who has been crowned for the benefits he has showered on everyone, makes clear that this new city is a democracy safe from elements who would overthrow it. Finding anything sinister here requires speculating that the conviction of the birds in question somehow was not the product of due process or that Peisetaerus in cooking them is somehow suppressing dissent tyrannically, but there is absolutely nothing in the play from any character to support such fears. Rather, he is safeguarding the democracy at a time that the Demos

---

19. Hubbard (1998) finds this scene and the play in general a reflection of popular outrage against mounting tyranny. For a perspective diametrically opposed to Hubbard, and closer to what I propose here, see Dunbar (1997). Romer (1998) leans toward a dark reading but is more sensitive to the problems of interpretation.

was worried about insurrection. It is the power of the gods, meanwhile, that resides with Zeus that takes the form of τυραννίς (1605, 1643). The dispute between Poseidon and Heracles' inheritance only reinforces the closed, elite nature of the gods' power.

After Peisetaerus secures power from the gods, the play closes with a celebration of his marriage and status as τύραννος (1708). The title can seem jarring and has again led critics to spy sinister, underhanded commentary on Peisetaerus' achievement. In more charitable moments, interpretations suggest a Periclean democracy, where an elite citizen guides the Demos, but such a model is without parallel in Aristophanes. Inevitably, however, scholars have had to acknowledge there is nothing in Aristophanes that remotely allows reading this final celebration, a scene that has no hint of irony or criticism in an author never shy about either, as cynical. A more coherent and consistent interpretation is simply that Peisetaerus is now fully identified with the Demos. He has been crowned in a way that reflects the prerogative of the Demos, he protects the democracy and has brought success and prosperity to all. The scene in this way reenacts the rejuvenation of Demos from *Knights* ten years earlier. Peisetaerus can thus be τύραννος and marry Βασίλεια, and rule all the Greeks, just as the titles of *tyrannos, basileus* and *monarchos* are positive when applied to Demos in *Knights* (τύραννον, 1114; τὸν τῆς Ἑλλάδος ὑμῖν καὶ τῆς γῆς τῆσδε μόναρχον, 1330; ὦ βασιλεῦ τῶν Ἑλλήνων, 1333).

There are, of course, major reasons critics and scholars have been reluctant to make an equation between Peisetaerus' imperial success and the imperial ambitions of the Athenian Demos at the time. One is the persistent idea that Aristophanes is fundamentally a critic of the democracy, and so any model he holds up must somehow reflect that fundamental criticism. Nevertheless, I hope I have made a case so far that Aristophanes consistently dramatizes a faith in the core processes of the Athenian democracy, even as he sharply attacks its institutions when they fail to function properly. A more serious problem is the implication for Aristophanes' treatment of these imperial ambitions in the concrete form of the Sicilian expedition. Thucydides narrates the deliberations about the expedition as a process of lunacy compounded by ignorance and incompetence. Euripides had used a harsh trilogy to rail against the Athenians for their inhumanity the year before *Birds*.[20] It is natural to want to see this awareness reflected in Aristophanes. Even Jeffrey Henderson, who promotes Aristophanes as voice of

---

20. Cf. Chapter 6, but note that Erp Taalman Kip (1987) argues against this reading of the tetralogy of 415.

the deliberative Demos and who comes closest to acknowledging the cheerleading for the Demos in this play, prefers to see some caution here.[21] But the Sicilian venture was approved with enthusiasm by its supporters, however foolish and disastrous it became in hindsight, and as problematic as it seemed even to some parties at the time. It is an unpalatable idea to say that Aristophanes, at least as far as what he projects in *Birds*, belonged to the uncritical supporters and was thus on the wrong side of history. But that it is unpalatable does not make it less true, on the best evidence available.

Three years later, Aristophanes has his protagonist obliquely begin to address the staggering losses that did in fact ensue. "Shut up. Don't bring up past trouble" (σίγα, μὴ μνησικακήσῃς, *Lys.* 590), says the official in response, a man charged with bringing better guidance to the Demos. And indeed, by the spring of 411 Aristophanes had many other problems he wanted to address about the health of the democracy.

---

21. Henderson (1998a, 145): "It seems to me that *Birds* is at once critical and hopeful, with the emphasis on hopeful. . . . *Birds* would certainly chide the spectators about their shortcomings, including their errors of 415, while still anticipating victory in the West." Slater (1998), wittily, but in parallel, feels obligated to eye fledgling criticisms of the costs of war and democracy.

5

Crawling from the Wreckage, 411 B.C.E.

δημοκρατία οὐ μόνον ἀνιεμένη ἀσθενεστέρα γίνεται ὥστε τέλος ἥξει εἰς ὀλιγαρχίαν, ἀλλὰ καὶ ἐπιτεινομένη σφόδρα.

Democracy will weaken and finally become oligarchy, not only when it is too loose, but also when it is stretched too much.

—Aristotle, *Rhet.* 1.4.12.1360a25–27

After the celebration of *Peace* in 421 and the ebullient confidence of *Birds* in 414, Aristophanes' next extant play, *Lysistrata,* of 411, finds Aristophanes back in attack mode, and the situation in Athens at the time leaves little doubt about why. Externally Athens was engaged again in war operations against Sparta, now allied with Persia, and internally major changes were taking place. Although Thucydides would in retrospect reckon the years between the Peace of Nicias and the Sicilian expedition as a period of low-level hostilities, and the expedition itself as the resumption of the war, for Aristophanes most likely it was only with the battles of the summer of 412 that he considered Athens once again at war.[1] From this perspective, Aristophanes wasted no time in launching a play critical of the war. While nothing in *Lysistrata* even hints that Aristophanes presages the oligarchic coup that

---

1. See Strauss (1997) on the problem of periodization and the Peloponnesian War.

ensued months after the play's production, the internal changes in Athens were sufficient to disturb and inspire him. Aristophanes is no less pointed or specific about the times than in any other play.

While Thucydides devotes most of his history of 413–412 B.C.E. to political and military movements, he does comment on other developments. When he summarizes the reception in Athens of the news that the expedition to Sicily was a catastrophe, he says that the first reaction was disbelief, then (8.1.1):

ἐπειδὴ δὲ ἔγνωσαν, χαλεποὶ μὲν ἦσαν τοῖς ξυμπροθυμηθεῖσι τῶν ῥητόρων τὸν ἔκπλουν, ὥσπερ οὐκ αὐτοὶ ψηφισάμενοι, ὠργίζοντο δὲ καὶ τοῖς χρησμολόγοις τε καὶ μάντεσι καὶ ὁπόσοι τι τότε αὐτοὺς θειάσαντες ἐπήλπισαν ὡς λήψονται Σικελίαν.

Once they realized, they were hard on those of the *rhetores* who had encouraged the expedition, as if they had not voted for it themselves, and angry with the oracle-readers and prophets who had used divination to inspire hope in them to take Sicily.

The Athenians begin planning what to do next, and Thucydides includes this somewhat sardonic account (8.1.3–4):

τῶν τε κατὰ τὴν πόλιν τι ἐς εὐτέλειαν σωφρονίσαι, καὶ ἀρχήν τινα πρεσβυτέρων ἀνδρῶν ἑλέσθαι, οἵτινες περὶ τῶν παρόντων ὡς ἂν καιρὸς ᾖ προβουλεύσουσιν. πάντα τε πρὸς τὸ παραχρῆμα περιδεές, ὅπερ φιλεῖ δῆμος ποιεῖν, ἑτοῖμοι ἦσαν εὐτακτεῖν.

In order to bring some economical restraint to the city's business, they also empowered a board of elders to enable proposals about the situation as circumstance called for it. As the Demos is inclined to do, at the moment of terror, they were ready to put all their affairs in order.

For a playwright always interested in the role of *rhetores* in the democracy, the importance of deliberation, the folly of oracles and the benefits of peace, it was only a matter of how to dramatize his response. Only one passage in *Lysistrata* refers specifically to the deliberations that resulted in the Sicilian expedition, wherein one of the venture's strongest proponents, Demostratus, advocates proposals in the Assembly, while women shriek inauspiciously during a celebration of the Adonia (388–97). Thus for the first time since the 420s, we have a play with a vignette of failed deliberations in the

Athenian Assembly, so it should be no surprise that the deliberative process will once again be crucial to a play and that it is translocated. The topic plays itself out at length in the *agon* and focuses squarely on the very character who actually referred to Demostratus but who embodies the bottleneck in democratic deliberation: the Proboulos.

The office of Proboulos has left little trace in the historical record. Thucydides comments on the creation of the board and later mentions how an enlarged board cleared the legal hurdles to permit the oligarchic revolution (8.67), a process described more fully in Aristotle (*Ath. Pol.* 29). Other than the names of two of the members (Hagnon at Lysias 12.65 and Sophocles at Arist. *Rhet.* 1419a26–30), nothing more is recorded, and it is no surprise that the office did not survive when democracy was restored in 410. Still, it is evident from even the sparse evidence that the Probouloi represented a significant concession on the part of the Demos. In *Lysistrata*, the Proboulos seems to have independent authority to negotiate and pay for war supplies. The very title of the office suggests they have powers to make proposals to or set the agenda for the Council. Their later activity indicates they were empowered, or at least entrusted, to consider the power structures of the democracy at a deep level. In any case, a representative of these elders was important enough in 411 for Aristophanes to make him the primary antagonist to his heroine in her plot to bring peace to Greece.

IDENTITY AND INCLUSION: *LYSISTRATA*

The *Lysistrata* is sufficiently rich that, in spite of this prominent choice of an immediately topical figure, scholars have mostly focused on other areas, from its nearly coherent plot to its play on gender dynamics.[2] As with Aristophanes' politics generally, scholars have debated whether there is much seriousness in the play, to the point that H. D. Westlake (1980) had to take pains to observe that, while the play's protest against the war is broad and fantastic, Aristophanes embeds sharply focused criticism of Athenian leaders. More recently, James McGlew examines the *Lysistrata* against the background of rising oligarchic power.[3] He argues that Aristophanes offers up two models of citizens, a negative one in the Proboulos and a positive one in

---

2. On gender dynamics, for example, see Byl (1991), Taaffe (1994), Mastromarco (1997), Andò (2004) and Faraone (2006), all of which at least touch on the limits gender identities put on Aristophanes' depiction of political success. See Henderson (1980) on what nearly constitutes a plot in the play.
3. McGlew (2002, 139–48).

Kinesias, to show the audience that, by grounding their sense of purpose in the *oikos* and restoring their passion for participation in politics, the city will prosper through their renewed involvement. Both Westlake and McGlew take steps in the right direction. Westlake demonstrates there is pointed and trenchant political commentary in the play, and McGlew rightly views the Proboulos as an embodiment of a certain trend in civic political behavior.

The episode of the Proboulos, which consists mostly of the play's *agon*, is the longest sequence in the play (nearly double the length of the next longest episode) and constitutes the central exploration of the current political circumstances. The Proboulos tends to be characterized by scholars, implicitly and explicitly, as a generalized authority figure, but such a figure would be without parallel in Aristophanes. Major political antagonists in his plays are attacked either as themselves (Lamachus in *Acharnians*, Cleon in *Knights* and *Wasps*) or as personified abstracts (Polemos in *Peace*, Poverty in *Wealth*). Neither scholiasts in antiquity nor scholars today have access to sufficient information to determine whether the Proboulos character in fact represents an individual historical holder of the office. Without such information, the Proboulos most resembles a certain class of political operatives, along the lines of the sycophant in *Acharnians*, the arms dealer of *Peace*, or the various con artists who visit Peisetaerus in *Birds*. At a minimum, though, the Proboulos represents a more specific political entity than the government in general or the supporters of the war. Since the Probouloi had the authority to present legislation directly to the Assembly, bypassing one bulwark of the democracy, the Council, they effectively set the agenda for the democracy. Given Aristophanes' demonstrated faith in the Demos retaining ultimate judgment over the deliberative process, the Proboulos is a natural antagonist.

It is precisely as a figure inimical to the democratic process that Aristophanes portrays his Proboulos. It is customary today, when describing the Athenian democracy, to point out that it was less democratic than many modern democracies in that it accorded citizenship to a comparatively restricted subset of the resident populace, excluding women, metics, and slaves. In late fifth-century Greece, of course, the Athenian democracy was on the more inclusive end of the political spectrum. The bulk of the ideological, indeed political and military, tension was not over how much more inclusive the democracy could or should be, but whether franchise should be restricted to fewer citizens. Democrats invoked the fear of tyranny, should such restrictions be put in place. Oligarchs invoked the fear of irresponsible mob rule. The vote of the Proubouloi to pave the way for the oligarchic Five Thousand clearly places them in the oligarchic camp in favor of further restricting the size of the functional deliberating body of Athens' government. The traumatic news of the failure of the Sicilian expedition provided political ammunition for the oligarchs to criticize the judgment of the popular democracy. Aristophanes invokes just this scenario when he introduces the Proboulos. He has the Proboulos, upon entering the stage, discuss the deliberations over the Sicilian expedition and emphasize the need to control the war effort, when he first arrives to confront the obstructionist actions of the women (387ff.).[4]

In order to highlight the contrast between the oligarchic movement toward restriction, represented and articulated by the Proboulos, versus the democratic principle of inclusion, Aristophanes places the moral and religious authority for successful political leadership in a group currently excluded from deliberations: the women of Greece. Thus Aristophanes uses the episode involving the Proboulos to dramatize his criticism of the oligarchic agenda. Even as the Proboulos tries repeatedly to silence the women, Aristophanes has Lysistrata demonstrate throughout the *agon* that the women possess superior experience and leadership. Lysistrata's forces twice rout the Proboulos's Scythian archers. After the women dominate militarily, the formal *agon* begins. In debate, Lysistrata quickly declares that the women will control the finances, because they can do a better job (486–501). Questioned further by the Proboulos, Lysistrata cites the failure of men's earlier deliberations, but her solution is quite the opposite of that of the Proboulos and the oligarchic factions. In the past, when the women heard about the men failing in deliberation about important business (κακῶς ὑμᾶς βουλευσαμένους μέγα πρᾶγμα, 511) before the Demos (ἐν τῷ δήμῳ, 514), their husbands shut them out of the process (514–22). In the tradition of Aristophanes' protagonists, Lysistrata translocates the deliberative process by gathering the women to save Greece (524–25).[5] Even the men themselves are aware of their own failure, Lysistrata says (522–24). So now, much as Dicaeopolis and other comic protagonists before her, she and the women are taking control of the deliberative process (527–28):

ἢν οὖν ἡμῶν χρηστὰ λεγουσῶν ἐθελήσητ' ἀντακροᾶσθαι
κἀντισιωπᾶν ὥσπερ χἠμεῖς, ἐπανορθώσαιμεν ἂν ὑμᾶς.

---

4. On the significance of the Proboulos' invocation of the Adonia at his entrance here, see Reitzammer (2008). Cf. O'Higgins (2003, 160–68).

5. Murphy (1938, 107–8) proposes an analysis of lines 507–97 as an organized rhetorical speech but concedes: "The dialogue form nearly obliterates the speech of Lysistrata which underlies the whole." I argue that debate and deliberation provide a much more important structure or reference point than a single speech.

So if you'll be willing to listen back to us while we give useful advice,
And keep silent as we did, we can straighten you out.

Through Lysistrata's prescriptions, Aristophanes attempts to swing the pendulum away from oligarchic restriction, by calling for broader, not narrower, participation in the deliberative process. The call for listening to and embracing the broadest possible coalition climaxes in Lysistrata's speech on wool working as a metaphor for governance (574–86). Lysistrata first describes removing the dirty and corrupt factions in the city, via the metaphor of culling dirt and knots from raw wool (574–78), along with cutting off the "heads" (κεφαλάς, 578). She then calls for *metics*, allied foreigners, debtors and colonists to participate (580–85; cf. Chapter 3 on the treatment of foreigners in *Knights*). The result will be harmonious prosperity, in the form of a cloak for the Demos (τῷ δήμῳ χλαῖναν, 586). The thrust of her proposal is clear: reject the oligarchic special interests and involve more people, not fewer, in the political process. Prosperity of the Demos should be the goal and will be the result.

The ode that follows the dismissal of the Proboulos appears where, in other plays, a *parabasis* appears. In place of a *parabasis* come rival odes between the men's and women's semichoruses, but, as would be characteristic of a *parabasis*, Aristophanes reiterates the political point Lysistrata has just made. In their odes, the women continue sounding the theme that advice from a broader coalition will save Athens. The women establish their own civic credentials by citing their participation in the city's religious festivals (638–47). They go on to declare that they have the right and authority to advise the *polis* because they contribute sons to the citizen body and because the men have squandered the city's finances (648–57). In conclusion, the women declare that they, unlike the men, have support throughout the Hellenic world, invoking in particular their allies in Sparta and Thebes (696–705). Where Lysistrata earlier had demonstrated their commitment to bringing Athens' allies under the political umbrella, the women now assert that they can unite even Athens' enemies in a common cause.

The resolution of the play's conflict validates the women's claims and advice. Later in the play, Kinesias meets up with a Spartan ambassador, and, after discerning the extent of the women's plot, they decide to pursue a treaty together. Kinesias declares that he will have his companions on the Council choose the representative for the negotiations (ἐγὼ δ' ἑτέρους ἐνθένδε τῇ βουλῇ φράσω/ πρέσβεις ἑλέσθαι 1011–12), in the process bypassing or ignoring the authority of the Probouloi. In the negotiation scene that follows, the men, of their own accord, request that Lysistrata provide guidance.

Lysistrata takes on the role, informed by her experience as a woman, and insists on a Panhellenic spirit throughout the proceedings.[6]

Familiar principles thus gird the play's events. No one uses canonical rhetorical structures or events in their speeches, but Lysistrata engages in persuasive advocacy in support of the Demos. She knows the disastrous results of incompetence at the Assembly, so she translocates the deliberative process. Spatially she moves it to the Acropolis, but the more important movement is one of identity. Unlike previous plays, in this play a protagonist who is not a member of the Demos, insofar as she does not have the right to speak or vote in the deliberative process of the *polis*, takes over the process. Crucially, Aristophanes' long-standing point remains: sound deliberation in service to the Demos yields success and prosperity. In this play more than in any previous ones, the action during the play directly dramatizes this prosperity for Athenians and other Greeks. Dicaeopolis was prosperous in *Acharnians*, Demos was rejuvenated in *Knights*, Philocleon was happy in *Wasps*, the fruits of peace were promised in *Peace* and the benefits of empire were reported and implied for the Demos in *Birds*, but in *Lysistrata*, citizens like Kinesias, the representatives of the Council and the husbands of all the women involved in the strike, along with a Panhellenic coalition, all celebrate happiness and prosperity by the play's finale. Thus translocation of the deliberative process to marginalized identities becomes the most inclusive and promising mechanism for widespread success and prosperity. In his next play, Aristophanes uses this same translocation by identity, but on a still larger scale.

STANDING UP IN THE ASSEMBLY: *THESMOPHORIAZUSAE*

In rebuffing the Proboulos and referring authority to negotiate peace to the Council in *Lysistrata*, Aristophanes defends the role of the Council in leading Athens back to success and prosperity. The other play of 411 effectively does the same for the Assembly in ways that are both less and more direct. The two plays were first produced within months of each other, and it is reasonable to expect that their composition overlapped somewhat. There are some basic similarities to the two plays. Both make women central and prominent. Both begin with a problem and set up a proposed resolution to it. Central to each is a lengthy, formal debate, the *agon* between the Proboulos and

---

6. The finale of the play spotlights two songs sung by a Spartan, underlining in yet another way the principle of giving voice to those outside of the current deliberative process. On the uncertainty about the end of the script as we have it, see Revermann (2006, 254–60).

Lysistrata in *Lysistrata* and the Assembly of women in *Thesmophoriazusae*. Following an ode analogous to a *parabasis* in each play comes a series of episodes prolonging the conflict in a lighthearted way (the escaping women and the thwarting of Kinesias in *Lysistrata*, the series of Euripidean parodies in *Thesmophoriazusae*), before the principal character returns and resolves the conflict (Lysistrata and Euripides). Within this comparison, certainly, *Thesmophoriazusae* comes across as the less engaged with the political tremors shaking Athens at the time. It might be, however, the more subversive of the two plays.

Scholars have agreed that some pointed lines in *Thesmophoriazusae*, where Athena is invoked to make an appearance as a hater of tyrants (φάνηθ', ὦ τυράννους/στυγοῦσ', ὥσπερ εἰκός, 1143–44), were intended to reverberate strongly with spectators in Athens while the movement toward oligarchy was ongoing.[7] It is the lengthy and detailed staging of the Assembly, however, that presents the most sustained challenge to the looming oligarchy. Aristophanes is quite willing to dramatize or report a dysfunctional Assembly, but neither play of 411 does so.[8] The scene of the Assembly does experience a translocation, to the women's festival of the Thesmophoria, and it is a parody insofar as it devotes the occasion to deliberation about Euripides' defamation of the women's *demos,* but it hews closer to the actual proceedings of a public institution than any other scene in fifth-century comedy.[9] J. A. Haldane finds the scene "one of the most elaborately planned and carefully written passages in ancient drama" and details how Aristophanes merges language and procedure from the Athenian Assembly into this scene and moves from splitting the language evenly between actual usage and comic additions to suit the translocation to the Thesmophoria to "almost wholly a debating society."[10] Aristophanes also explicitly makes the Assembly the one remaining operating body of the democracy. Inlaw, by way of explaining how Euripides should have nothing to fear, says: ἐπεὶ νῦν

---

7. Much inevitable uncertainty clings to any sober attempt to match up *Lysistrata* and *Thesmophoriazusae* to the developments that culminated in the oligarchic coup in the summer of 411. See Shear (2011, 22–41) for an overview of events and sources and Austin and Olson (2004, xxxiii–xliv) for a solid overview of the issues pertaining to *Thesmophoriazusae*.

8. *Lys.* 390ff. refers to the Assembly in an unflattering manner, but this reflects the character of the Proboulos, who makes the reference and who is being introduced here. The occasion he describes also predates the Sicilian expedition and was well before the oligarchic threat became so serious and immediate.

9. Translocation of the area for deliberation was to become a historical reality in Athens shortly after the play's performance, as over the course of the revolution of 411, oligarchs and democrats jousted for control and the authority to govern in different locations. See Shear (2011, 36–40).

10. Haldane (1965, 39, 44). Cf. Chapter 3 and Rhodes (2010) for a similar documentation of the references to the Assembly embedded in *Knights*.

γ' οὔτε τὰ δικαστήρια/ μέλλει δικάζειν οὔτε βουλῆς ἐσθ' ἕδρα, "since the courts are not in session now and the Council is not meeting" (78–79). Thus of the three principal political institutions of the Athenian democracy, only the Assembly remains open and active.

When formal proceedings begin, the prose announcement comically mixes in some material to suit the women (295–311), but the passage is more remarkable for staying on topic and not undercutting the business of the Assembly than for satirizing it. A simple invocation for successful deliberation and success now seems to bear the weight of the occasion (301–11):

ἐκκλησίαν τήνδε καὶ σύνοδον τὴν νῦν κάλλιστα καὶ ἄριστα ποιῆσαι, πολυωφελῶς μὲν τῇ πόλει τῇ Ἀθηναίων, τυχηρῶς δ' ἡμῖν αὐταῖς. καὶ τὴν δρῶσαν καὶ ἀγορεύουσαν τὰ βέλτιστα περὶ τὸν δῆμον τὸν Ἀθηναίων καὶ τὸν τῶν γυναικῶν ταύτην νικᾶν. ταῦτ' εὔχεσθε, καὶ ὑμῖν αὐταῖς τἀγαθά.

[Pray] to make this current Assembly and meeting most right and good, both very beneficial to the city of the Athenians and fortunate for us, and she who provides the best counsel for the Demos of the Athenians and of the women, that she prevail. For this we pray, and for blessings for you.

This is not a satire to distort the proceedings but rather a nearly entirely straightforward reminder that the mission and activity of the Assembly, as it normally runs, are what is needed, and under attack, if not already missing in action. Similarly the group of prayers that follows reinforces the proper ritual of the Assembly, only with additions specific to the women's occasion (335–39):[11]

εἴ τις ἐπιβουλεύει τι τῷ δήμῳ κακὸν
τῷ τῶν γυναικῶν, ἢ 'πικηρυκεύεται
Εὐριπίδῃ Μήδοις τ' ἐπὶ βλάβῃ τινὶ
τῇ τῶν γυναικῶν, ἢ τυραννεῖν ἐπινοεῖ
ἢ τὸν τύραννον συγκατάγειν, . . .

If anyone plots any evil against the Demos
of the women, or makes overtures
to Euripides or the Persians to cause any harm to

---

11. On this passage in the context of constitutional debate just prior to the oligarch coup, see Shear (2011, 43–44).

the women, or intends to be a tyrant,
or cooperates in restoring a tyrant . . .

Where little over a decade earlier Aristophanes had mocked the Demos' paranoia about tyrants, and even three years earlier had used a similar parody to make such prayers against tyranny seem silly (*Birds* 1074–75), now the Demos seems to need a reminder that they are sworn to oppose tyranny. After more prayers specific to the women, the chorus emphasizes the point (352–67):

ξυνευχόμεσθα τέλεα μὲν
πόλει τέλεά τε δήμῳ
τάδ' εὔγματα ἀποτελεῖσθαι,
τὰ δ' ἄρισθ' ὅσαις προσήκει
νικᾶν λεγούσαις. ὁπόσαι δ'
ἐξαπατῶσιν παραβαίνουσί τε τοὺς
ὅρκους τοὺς νενομισμένους
κερδῶν οὕνεκ' ἐπὶ βλάβῃ,[12]
ἢ ψηφίσματα καὶ νόμους
ζητοῦσ' ἀντιμεθιστάναι,
τἀπόρρητά τε τοῖσιν ἐχθροῖς
τοῖς ἡμετέροις λέγουσ',
ἢ Μήδους ἐπάγουσι τῆς
ἀρχῆς οὕνεκ' ἐπὶ βλάβῃ,
ἀσεβοῦσ' ἀδικοῦσί τε τὴν πόλιν.

We pray together that this
may be well fulfilled
for the *polis* and the Demos.
All who deserve the best,
may they prevail in their speeches. And all who
deceive and transgress the
oaths established by tradition,
for profit or to cause harm,
or seek to invert
the laws and legislation
and tell secrets to our enemies,
or invite the Persians in the name of empire

---

12. N. G. Wilson deletes this line, but see Austin and Olson (2004, 169 *ad loc.*) for parallels.

to cause harm,[13]
they commit sins and wrong the city!

The entire meeting proceeds efficiently and effectively, and in a traditional manner as if to emphasize that the democracy need not, should not, be overhauled or dismissed. The Assembly receives its proposal from the Council (372–75), and the motion is read. At the open invitation for someone to speak on the proposal, Mica puts on a crown and prepares. The chorus is at once respectful and quips (381–82):

σίγα, σιώπα, πρόσεχε τὸν νοῦν· χρέμπτεται γὰρ ἤδη
ὅπερ ποιοῦσ' οἱ ῥήτορες. μακρὰν ἔοικε λέξειν.

Shut up and be quiet. Pay attention! She's clearing her throat now
just like *rhetores* do. Looks like it'll be a long one.

Mica and, in response, the hapless Inlaw give the two longest uninterrupted speeches anywhere in the extant plays, forty lines for Mica (383–432) and fifty-four for Inlaw (466–519), and, with the addition of a brief second bit of support for the prosecution by the Garland-Seller (a mere sixteen lines, 443–58), both sides get roughly equal time. While these are indeed the longest, most sustained speeches in the plays, and do reflect some parody of speech construction, they do not conform to fourth-century standards of rhetorical speech structure.[14] Even with the comic content (joke after joke at the women's expense), the speeches are a display of continued airing of issues in the Assembly, and the ability of the meeting to deliberate is crucial. At the conclusion of Inlaw's ill-conceived defense of Euripides, the chorus is stunned and offers (528–30):

τὴν παροιμίαν δ' ἐπαινῶ τὴν παλαιάν·
ὑπὸ λίθῳ γὰρ παντί που χρὴ
μὴ δάκῃ ῥήτωρ ἀθρεῖν.

I like the old proverb:

---

13. The text is problematic, and its sense is uncertain. See Austin and Olson (2004, 170–71 *ad loc.*) for details.
14. See Murphy (1938, 108–9) for his scheme of these two speeches. To compensate for the lack of a *diegesis*, he substitutes *prostheses* in his analyses of both speeches, as he does for the speech of Dicaeopolis in *Acharnians* (see Chapter 3, 56–60). Cf. Sousa e Silva (1987–88, 96–103) for a discussion of *Ach.* and *Thesm.* together, focusing mostly on the parodies of *Telephus*.

you have to look under every rock
so a *rhetor* doesn't bite!

As the women turn hostile, Inlaw invokes his right of free speech to defend his stance (εἰ γὰρ οὔσης/παρρησίας, 540–41). Aristophanes has long established that the ability to deliberate is crucial and central to success and prosperity. He has also been willing for protagonists to take the position sharply opposed to the majority, so there is legitimate suspense about what will happen. Is the Assembly dysfunctional? Mica and Inlaw debate (533–66) and prepare to come to blows (567–70), which would indicate a breakdown in the process, before the *prytanis* of this assembly, Critylla, orders them to stop brawling (λοιδορούμεναι, 571), a regular term for failed deliberation (cf. the entry in the Appendix). At this moment, Cleisthenes arrives, and the debate takes a different turn. When he reports that a man has infiltrated the meeting to defend Euripides, the women turn to inspecting Inlaw. Once he is exposed, rather than resume the threat of violence, they prepare to hand him over to the Prytaneis (654). After a search by the chorus (655–87), the parodies of Euripides' plays begin. With Inlaw ensconced on the altar playing Telephus (688–764), the women again prepare to report his actions to the Prytaneis (764). As the parodies continue (*Palamedes* 765–84, then *Helen* 850–928), the women continue to wait for the Prytaneis (854). A Prytanis does in fact arrive, scaring off Euripides and giving orders for how to detain Inlaw (923–48), for which he explicitly says he acts on the authority of the Council (943). It is following the climactic parody (*Andromeda* 1001–1135), with Inlaw still bound by the rightful authority of the Demos, that Aristophanes has the chorus utter its ode invoking Athena as protectress of the *polis* (1140–42) and hater of tyrants (1143–44).

Now Euripides returns and makes a formal proposal to the women, which gives them exactly what they want: cessation of the slander against them. Euripides and the chorus negotiate in formal terms (1163–64). Euripides uses the terminology for making an offer (ταῦτ' ἐπικηρυκεύομαι, 1163) that was used in the invocation at the start of the Assembly ([ἐ]πικηρυκεύεται, 336). That passage invoked death on anyone who made such an offer to Euripides or the Persians, overtures undeniably parallel to contemporary negotiations between Pisander and the Persians. In the play, however, the Assembly has held its debates, stuck with the established authority of the Council, and the enemy Euripides has come with his own proposal, conceding to the women. A parallel action outside the theater would have the Persians making a proposal of concession to the Athenian Demos, rather than the Demos conceding authority to tyrants whom the patron goddess of the city despises. The chorus agrees to accept Euripides' proposal, and the conflict is resolved (1170–71). In other plays, Aristophanes displayed his faith in the deliberative process by dramatizing it outside the Assembly and showing how the process still yielded success and prosperity. Here he demonstrates his faith in the democratic deliberative process by having it succeed in the Assembly, at a time when the Demos' reliability for making judgments to lead Athens to success and prosperity was under extreme pressure. At no time does Aristophanes ever concede with anything less than confidence that the Demos' judgment will lead Athens to maximize its potential. Whether it is the demagogues of the 420s or the oligarchs of 411, they are impediments to Athens' greatness by obstructing the deliberative process and collective judgment of the Demos. The only change Aristophanes ever promotes for configuring who should participate in the process is to expand the range of those advising and deliberating, whether it be the allies, metics or women, rather than shrinking the number of voices.

Thesmophoriazusae suffuses its political commentary with probing depictions of dynamics of gender and tragedy, both in the figure of Agathon who simultaneously adopts fully the character and gender of his creation, while defying any category himself, and more so in Euripides, who is made parallel to the Persian threat, hostile to the citizen body of the play, but ultimately reconciled. Six years later, however, in his last play of the era, Aristophanes revisits the problems of politics and tragedy, their relation to the Demos, and much more besides, but with irreconcilable results.

6

Tongues, *Frogs*, and the Last Stand

> That's the basis of some humor: tragedy plus time.
> —Lenny Bruce, ca. 1959[1]

Aristophanes' plays being ever topical, the breakneck pace of change in Athens after 411 B.C.E. is crucial for understanding the drive behind, context for and reception of *Frogs*. From 411 to the first production of *Frogs*, in 405, the stability of the democracy and role of tragedy for democracy became increasingly critical topics, with the survival of each at stake in very real ways. Despite the surreptitious advice Aristophanes dramatized in his plays of 411, over the ensuing months, an oligarchic revolution unfolded. Although democracy was restored the next spring, the dramatic festivals of the winter of 410 were held under the auspices of the oligarchy. What impact this had on the program is far from clear. No known play, tragic or comic, can be assigned securely to the schedule for this season. One bit of evidence, however, does suggest that the proceedings retained a lingering taint of the oligarchy. The litigant (unnamed) of Lysias 21 some twenty-one years later is defending himself in a democratic court. He epitomizes the balancing act that more than a few families tried to pull off in the years when Athens

---

1. Recorded as part of his appearance on KPIX TV, San Francisco; available on *Let the Buyer Beware* (2004) CD 1, track 3. Carol Burnett is credited with later saying more exactly that comedy equals tragedy plus time, but the general truism seems to have been established already when Bruce makes passing use of the idea.

lurched from democracy to oligarchy and back again.[2] Like a typical wealthy litigant, he lists his liturgies and service to the democracy, but he has to be cautious about referring to his contributions under the oligarchy of 411/10 and the tyranny of the Thirty in 403. He begins his litany of liturgies (21.1), ἐγὼ γὰρ ἐδοκιμάσθην μὲν ἐπὶ Θεοπόμπου ἄρχοντος, καταστὰς δὲ χορηγὸς τραγῳδοῖς ἀνήλωσα τριάκοντα μνᾶς, "I passed my audit in the archonship of Theopompus and, assigned as *choregus* for tragedy, I spent thirty minas." He dodges the oligarchic associations of the timing of his liturgy by saying only the amount he spent, although he must have been assigned the liturgy under the oligarchy, whether it was in the form of the Four Hundred or the Five Thousand at the time.[3] He is more expansive when describing his efforts the next year under the restored democracy (21.1–2): ἐπὶ δὲ Γλαυκίππου ἄρχοντος εἰς πυρριχιστὰς Παναθηναίοις τοῖς μεγάλοις ὀκτακοσίας. ἔτι δ' ἀνδράσι χορηγῶν εἰς Διονύσια ἐπὶ τοῦ αὐτοῦ ἄρχοντος ἐνίκησα, καὶ ἀνήλωσα σὺν τῇ τοῦ τρίποδος ἀναθέσει πεντακισχιλίας δραχμάς, "And under the archonship of Glaucippus [411, I was victorious] in the Pyrrhic dancing at the Greater Panathenaea, spending eight hundred drachmas and then in the men's chorus at the City Dionysia, under the same archon, and I spent, including the tripod, five thousand drachmas." He emphasizes his two liturgies in this year, his victories in both (whereas he is silent on this point about his tragic liturgy in 410), and the amounts he spent make it clear he spent more during the democratic year than the previous year (5,000 plus 800 drachmas versus 3,000 in the competitions of 410).

He had good reason to associate himself with the City Dionysia of 409, for it was more than just another festival under the democracy. Peter Wilson makes the case that this City Dionysia, and the tragic competition in particular, was a crucial ritual signaling the newly restored democracy at Athens.[4] Prior to the tragic competition that year, Thrasybulus, assassin of the oligarch Phrynichus, was prominently honored with a golden civic crown

---

2. See *Lys.* 25 for a pragmatic or cynical (depending on one's perspective) presentation of this sort of maneuvering from a litigant, tainted by involvement with oligarchy, now undergoing a *dokimasia*.

3. He names Theopompus, appointed by the Five Thousand but later reckoned as legitimate by the democracy, as the archon associated with his audit, rather than Mnasilochus, who was eponymous archon under the Four Hundred (Arist. *Ath. Pol.* 33.1). He similarly dodges naming the archon Pythodorus for his service in 404/3 (21.2), and in this he conforms to the democratic practice of not naming the archon of that year (Xen. *Hell.* 3.1.1).

4. P. Wilson (2009). Rhodes (2011b) challenges many of Wilson's conclusions but agrees broadly that the City Dionysia of 409 was distinctive for the restored democracy. Shear (2011, 141–54) surveys the importance of this Dionysia for the newly reempowered *Demos*.

by the Demos (*IG* 1³ 102). There could well have been a mass swearing of the oath of Demophantus, which called on citizens to kill those attempting to subvert the democracy.⁵ Two years earlier, in the same theater, Aristophanes had dramatized the Assembly urgently invoking curses on would-be tyrants, and it takes little imagination to see the actions of the Demos in the spring of 409 as an embodiment of the reminder embedded in Aristophanes' *Thesmophoriazusae* (see Chapter 5). Aristophanes' involvement in the festivals of 410 and 409, if any, is unknown now, but he must have been aware of how crucial tragedy was to the restored democracy. As Wilson further observes, the crowning of Thrasybulus is the earliest in an important tradition of the Demos recognizing civic benefactors, and the specific selection of the tragic performances at the City Dionysia as the occasion for this presentation emphasizes the importance of tragedy as symbolic of the democracy's civic identity and return to power. By the time of *Frogs*, then, tragedy was established as of central civic importance for the Demos in this critical, tumultuous time, so questions of tragedy's civic value were of immediate relevance. That Aristophanes himself would be awarded a civic crown for service connected with a play on this very topic should also be interpreted in this ideological environment.

At that crucial tragic competition in 409, Sophocles took first place with a tetralogy that included *Philoctetes*, which points to another potentially remarkable feature of the proceedings. If Sophocles was in fact one of the Probouloi who had made the vote that enabled the oligarchic constitution two years earlier, his presence and prominence on this occasion are striking.⁶ This, along with the litigant of Lysias 21 spending lavishly on a volunteer liturgy at the same festival, suggests there were options for at least some of those wishing to redeem themselves in the eyes of the democracy. In this context, *Philoctetes*' story of a diseased exile, broken oaths, betrayal and the struggles of a heroic war orphan may have resonated broadly, deeply and personally with the spectators.⁷ Scholars have also looked to *Oedipus at Colonus* a few years later for Sophocles' reflection on his troubled experience at this time.⁸ Sophocles' mournful presentation of wounded and morally compromised characters seeking redemption may well have contributed to his reputation for being affable, including the charitable references to him in *Frogs*.

---

5. For text of the oath, see Andoc. 1.97. Cf. Shear (2011, 136–41), who argues for the oath being sworn in the Agora.

6. Aristotle, *Rhet.* 1419a26–30.

7. Shear (2011, 154–59).

8. Markantonatos (2007, 30–40). Compton-Engle (2013) argues that Aristophanes incorporates the staging of the old, blind Oedipus in *Oedipus at Colonus* into *Wealth* in 388 B.C.E.

However *Philoctetes* fit into the precise ideological environment of 409, scholars have analyzed how Sophocles here explores issues associated with the construal of knowledge, democracy, the intellectual precepts fostered by the Sophists and the problematic role of speech and language in a community.[9] In the play, Odysseus relies on his "tongue" (96–99, 407–9; cf. 440, of Thersites; see Chapter 2 and the Appendix for the term's use in comedy), and his character embodies the means a manipulative speaker uses to lead a well-intentioned audience to destructive action. Such a character easily has parallels with individuals criticized by Aristophanes for swaying the Demos away from its intrinsic better judgment. For his last play before the democracy is again supplanted, this time by external forces, for oligarchy in the form of the Thirty Tyrants, Aristophanes again makes this issue central, as well as how tragedy itself approaches these same issues. But it is not Sophocles so much as another playwright who becomes the flashpoint for this controversy. If Sophocles went from being an instrument that supported the oligarchic insurgency to a prominent figure publicly wrestling with his conscience, simultaneously defending his decision and acknowledging the rueful consequences, Euripides seems to have gone down quite a different path, from a beloved supporter of the democracy to someone unworthy of the trust of the Demos.

Aristophanes had long bundled Euripides with issues of tragedy, speech and democracy.[10] Twenty years earlier, Euripides is the resource for Dicaeopolis as he prepares for his speech to the Acharnians, but this support consists of dramaturgical tools, and the scene is silent about the tragedian's ideological or political orientation. That Dicaeopolis can appropriate the style without the substance of Euripides is consistent with other passages where Aristophanes distinguishes the two. When Pheidippides sings a passage from Euripides, Strepsiades complains about its scandalous content, not its aesthetic quality (*Clouds* 1371–72). *Peace* sounds a further note of ambivalence. Trygaeus says that Peace herself is redolent of songs of Sophocles and "wordies of Euripides" (ἐπυλλίων Εὐριπίδου, 532), but Hermes reports that Peace objects to the association with Euripides (532–34)[11]:

---

9. Rose (1976); Carlevale (2000); Goldhill (2009).

10. The bibliography on Aristophanes' treatment of Euripides is large. Schwinge (2002) probes the cultural tensions and contradictions embedded in Aristophanes' criticism of Euripides. Hunzinger (2000), Voelke (2004) and Foley (2008, with helpful references) focus more on literary or genre appropriation. For tragedy incorporating comedy, see the survey in Seidensticker (1982) and then Schwinge (1997), and on Euripides in particular, Gregory (1999/2000).

11. For another contrast between the two playwrights, see fr. 682, where Euripides' skill is στρεψιμάλλος, "wool-tangled," and fr. 598, where beeswax sits on Sophocles' lips. For the range of associations of the stem στρεψ-, see Marzullo (1953, 110–24).

κλαύσάρα σὺ
ταύτης καταψευδόμενος· οὐ γὰρ ἥδεται
αὕτη ποιητῇ ῥηματίων δικανικῶν.

Oh, you'll regret
lying about her that way: she doesn't enjoy
a poet of forensic speeches.

In a very compressed form, Aristophanes sets Euripides and litigation in opposition to peace but acknowledges the appeal of Euripides' style. The courts are the democratic institution for which Aristophanes shows the least support (cf. Chapter 3), and aligning Euripides with language there is consistent with the idea that the courts are inevitably sites of discontent and wrangling.[12] On the other hand, the words or style of Euripides is sufficiently consistent with peace that Trygaeus can make the association. Along these lines, an undatable fragment has Aristophanes, apparently in his own voice, characterize his relationship to Euripides this way (fr. 488):

χρῶμαι γὰρ αὐτοῦ τοῦ στόματος τῷ στρογγύλῳ,
τοὺς νοῦς δ' ἀγοραίους ἧττον ἢ 'κεῖνος ποιῶ.

I use the round smoothness of his mouth,
But I create cheap ideas less than he does.[13]

Another fragment might rely on a similar contrast. A passage on papyrus from Satyrus' biography of Euripides draws on a lost comic scene where someone wants to measure Euripides' tongue which generated speeches (ῥήματ') in some fashion (fr. 656). The implied scenario indicates recognition of the effectiveness of Euripides' speech but resistance to it as well.[14]

In 411, *Thesmophoriazusae* found Aristophanes engaging in a much more extensive reflection on Euripides, taking appraisal of his plays from his

---

12. On Aristophanes' *Wasps*, courts and democracy, with reference to Euripides' *Suppliants*, see Mirhady (2009).

13. Note the use of στόμα, "mouth," rather than γλῶττα, "tongue," on which see Chapter 2 and the Appendix.

14. Wilamowitz' supplement, <ἐξεσ>μήχετο, followed by K-A, would make the metaphor "polishing" speeches, which fits well. Friedrich Leo (1960, 2.370) suggests that the imperfect tense implies Euripides is dead by the time of this statement, but such a conclusion is unwarranted. A variety of scenarios could explain the tense. For example, a character could be reporting an incident where someone used a quote from Euripides, and now the speaker says he wanted to measure out and cut Euripides' tongue for supplying it.

poorly received tetralogy of 415, *Palamedes* in particular, to his subsequent more romantic fare.¹⁵ As in the brief reference in *Peace*, legal trouble and the effectiveness of Euripides' speech drive the plot of *Thesmophoriazusae*, and Aristophanes puts him at the nexus of democratic speech and tragedy, for his plays get him into legal trouble and prompt the women's Assembly to convene in the play. While the content of Euripides' plays, specifically their misogyny, spawns trouble, his style, as presented in the series of parodies, is entertaining. Aristophanes' other play of 411, *Lysistrata*, while mentioning Euripides only in passing, may have set up the triangle that is central to *Frogs*. Elizabeth W. Scharffenberger finds Euripides recasting the reconciliation scene from *Lysistrata* into his own scene of negotiation in *Phoenician Women*, between Polynices and Eteocles under the presiding Jocasta.¹⁶ In turn, T. Davina McClain finds Aristophanes in *Lysistrata* engaging repeatedly with Aeschylus' *Seven against Thebes*.¹⁷ If Aristophanes is invoking Aeschylus here, the specter of the venerable playwright would provide extra grist for Euripides' mill in his reaction in *Phoenician Women*.

Still, none of this, especially the silly but ultimately innocuous role in *Thesmophoriazusae*, accounts for Euripides as the villainous antagonist of *Frogs* who is entirely unworthy to make a grab for the throne of tragedy, who must be routed by Aeschylus (and is to be stomped by Sophocles should somehow Aeschylus not succeed, 792–94), and condemned to popularity among only the criminal deviants of the underworld. Given this sharp contrast between the portrayal of Euripides in *Thesmsophoriazusae* of 411 and in *Frogs* of 405, it is reasonable to believe that Aristophanes was prompted to reappraise Euripides during the intervening years, and it is worth exploring what might have motivated Aristophanes to depict him as a villain. My particular answer to this problem will see it as a natural continuation of Aristophanes' abiding interest in rhetoric, public speech, and his support for the deliberative power and sovereignty of the Demos. My argument develops in three stages: (1) a reconstruction, within the limits of the evidence, of the plays Euripides produced since *Thesmophoriazusae* to which

---

15. The parody of *Telephus* (438 B.C.E.) might be the exceptional "golden oldie" in the set, but I wonder if *Auge*, which, on the basis of its metrical characteristics and content, belongs to Euripides' late period, dates to 414–412 and could have made the story of Telephus seem more recent, since the infant Telephus was a focus of the plot of *Auge*. *Auge* might even belong to the season of 411, and then Aristophanes might be parodying *Telephus* to match Euripides' then-current output, since he could not have parodied *Auge* itself. A fragment of *Auge* against tyranny (fr. 275, and see below) would be especially striking at this same time and parallel with Aristophanes' stance.

16. Scharffenberger (1995). On the date of *Phoenician Women* and political language in this scene, see discussion in the next section.

17. McClain (1998).

Aristophanes could have reacted; (2) an exploration of what, in terms of rhetoric and the democratic politics of 411–406, could have piqued Aristophanes' interest in what Euripides says about these matters in the plays since *Thesmophoriazusae*; (3) the conclusion that, while there can be no guaranteed simple answer for what prompted Aristophanes' harsh appraisal of Euripides in 405, evidence from *Frogs* and Euripides' late production is entirely consistent with Aristophanes now looking at Euripides as someone who had been appealing in his language but has betrayed the support of the Athenian democracy, just when tragedy was of paramount importance to the Demos. In this sense, in Aristophanes' estimation, Euripides is a figure comparable to Cleon or any other despicable demagogue.

EURIPIDES AND THE RHETORIC OF DEMOCRATIC ATHENS, 411–406

In *Thesmophoriazusae*, Aristophanes parodies two of Euripides' plays from the previous year (412 B.C.E.), *Helen* and *Andromeda*. With Euripides dead by the season of 405, there were, at the absolute maximum, six seasons (411, 410, 409, 408, 407, 406) during which new plays could have been performed, plays that Aristophanes could not have known when he composed *Thesmophoriazusae* but could have had access to when he composed *Frogs*. Only one play has a precise date within this interval, *Orestes* in 408. This at least confirms that Euripides put on a trilogy during this period. The other plays of 408 are a matter of speculation. A scholiast on *Frogs* 52 seems to list three plays "produced more recently" (τῶν πρὸ ὀλίγου διδαχθέντων), that is, later than *Andromeda* of 412, and so these should fall into the period 411–406: *Hypsipyle, Phoenician Women* and *Antiope*. Given that the scholiast had access to records with dates to be able to give the year of the *Andromeda* and was also able to cite three subsequent tragedies (not satyr plays), this note suggests that, adding in *Orestes,* Euripides had at least two tetralogies during this time frame, which is not unreasonable. Three tetralogies would have to represent an outside limit of Euripides' productivity during this time frame, since it would entail nine new tragedies and three new satyr plays, averaging a production every other year, which, while not impossible, is a formidable number. In any case, there seems to be no particular reason to doubt that *Phoenician Women* and *Hypsipyle* belong to this period, whatever the number and makeup of the tetralogies.[18] *Frogs* suggests familiarity with

---

18. Cropp and Fick (1985, 74–76) show that metrical criteria point to *Antiope* dating to earlier than 418, and some plot elements like the lurid revenge are familiar from the 420s. The characteriza-

three of these late tragedies. Aristophanes mocks the poor actor Hegelochos (*Frogs* 304), who mispronounced a line of *Orestes* (279) at its performance, and part of Aeschylus' parody of Euripidean lyric invokes lines from the Phrygian's bizarre song (1347–49; cf. *Or.* 1431–33). Independently, Scharffenberger and Ann C. Suter further argue that Aristophanes drew extensively on *Orestes* in composing *Frogs*.[19] E. K. Borthwick picks through the mashed-up references to Euripides' *Hypsipyle* embedded in *Frogs* 1320–28.[20] Dover notes that, although the play under debate is Euripides' *Oedipus* (*Frogs* 1184f.), there are similarities between Aeschylus' characterization of Oedipus and that in Euripides' *Phoenician Women* (1595–1614, delivered by Oedipus of himself).[21] Taken together, these references give some sense of which among the recent plays were available to Aristophanes.

Euripides' late plays have marked metrical features and repeated motifs, so several fragmentary plays are legitimate candidates for these final years as well. Of these, only *Antigone* and *Polyidus* can be securely identified as cited in *Frogs* (1182–87 ~ frr. 157–58, from *Antigone*, 1391 < fr. 170 from *Antigone*; 1476–78 allude to fr. 638 from *Polyidus*).[22] In terms of topicality, Christiane Zimmerman suggests that issues of exile and lack of burial would resonate in the years following 411. Thucydides associates the recall of exiles with the Five Thousand, the best Athenian government in his view (8.97.3), and recall of exiles remained a lively enough issue for Aristophanes to address it in *Frogs*. Zimmerman further points to provisions regarding the treatment of the oligarchic conspirators Archeptolemus and Antiphon for the controversy about burial.[23] Although she raises the issue with regard to

---

tions of speech come closest to what Aristophanes does in *Clouds* (see discussion of frr. 189 and 206 in Chapter 3), and the instances of political rallying are similar to those of *Suppliant Women*. I suspect that the routine confusion of *Antiope* and *Antigone* is at work here. Cf. note 22 below.

19. Scharffenberger (1998) and Suter (1997–98).

20. Borthwick (1994, 29–37). Cf. the half-line quote from the *Hypsipyle* (fr. 763) at *Frogs* 64. A fragment of Aristophanes' *Lemnian Women* (fr. 373) mentions Thoas, father of Hypsipyle, and seems to allude to Euripides' *Iphigenia among the Taurians* 30–33, and so could easily belong to this late period. For recent discussion of the date of *IT*, see Marshall (2009).

21. Dover (1993, 336). Compare also Dionysus' addled quotation of Euripides at *Frogs* 105 with *Phoen.* 602. If the fragments of Aristophanes' *Phoenician Women* (frr. 570–76) were more helpful, we might be able to chart his response to Euripides' play better. Similarly, while it is also easy to imagine, given the relative rarity of treatments of the title character, that Aristophanes' own *Polyidus* (frr. 468–76) parodied or at least referenced Euripides' play (frr. 634–45), the remains are even sparser and of little help.

22. I believe that *Antigone* is in fact the play named in Σ *Fr.* 52, noted above, following the frequent confusion of the two plays. The fragments of *Antiope* point to a play in the 420s (see note 18 above and Chapter 3), and the fragments of *Antigone* point to a late play.

23. Zimmerman (1993, 189–90). [Plut.] *Mor.* 833a (*Lives of Ten Orators*) says that they were executed and denied burial.

Polynices in Sophocles' *Oedipus at Colonus*, certainly Euripides' *Phoenician Women* and *Antigone* would be stronger candidates as plays that address the issues, and closer in time. The fragments of Euripides' *Antigone* do not provide any evidence for what the play may have said about Polynices' exile or burial, but one passage does testify, unsurprisingly, that tyranny was a topic (fr. 172):[24]

οὔτ' εἰκὸς ἄρχειν οὔτ' ἐχρῆν ἄνευ νόμου
τύραννον εἶναι· μωρία δὲ καὶ θέλειν
< . . . >
ὃς τῶν ὁμοίων βούλεται κρατεῖν μόνος.

It's not appropriate to rule, nor without laws should
there be a *tyrannos*. It's stupid even to want
< . . . >
who wishes to have power alone over his peers.

How this fragment fit into Euripides' play is unrecoverable, although it likely refers to Creon. For commentary within *Phoenician Women*, however, context is available for a story about this same family and from this time period, although interpretation is still fraught with difficulty. Nevertheless, I will argue that, despite many inevitable uncertainties, on the core tenets of the Athenian democracy as Aristophanes defends it against the looming oligarchy, Euripides' *Phoenician Women* is easily and reasonably read as supportive. At key points in the play, Euripides promotes sagacious deliberation as good and tyranny as bad. These stances should not be taken for granted, for Euripides' subsequent plays are not reticent about criticizing democratic deliberation.[25]

Phoenician Women does not provide anything like a simple allegory of the Demos versus tyrants, but all the uses in the play cast the term *tyrannos* in a decidedly unfavorable light.[26] In the prologue, when Jocasta narrates the family's troubles, Laius is invoked among *tyrannoi* (40), when Laius' chariot runs over Oedipus' feet, leading to the patricide. The context certainly does not suggest that the appellation reflects well on the doomed ruler. Jocasta

---

24. I adopt Badham's emendation at the end of the first line, for εἶναι νόμον in the MSS.

25. For purposes of my thesis, of course, I posit this only from the ideological perspective projected in Aristophanes' plays, whether Euripides and his audiences, ancient and modern, intend or agree with this perspective.

26. On *Phoenician Women* against the backdrop of terms associated with tyranny in tragedy more broadly, see Seaford (2003, 110–11).

later uses the term of Oedipus taking power at Thebes (51).²⁷ Later the chorus of Phoenician women refers to the "tyrannical" line of Agenor as both their own ancestors and of the ruling house of Thebes (291–92).²⁸ The remaining (much more pointed) uses come in the debate between Polynices and Eteocles. As Scharffenberger has observed, Euripides here invokes the victorious reconciliation (διαλλαγή) scene from Aristophanes' *Lysistrata*. Although the meeting will turn out to be acrimonious and unsuccessful, the chorus calls on Jocasta to preside, as over an occasion of reconciliation between the two (καὶ μὴν Ἐτεοκλῆς ἐς διαλλαγὰς ὅδε / χωρεῖ . . . διαλλάξεις τέκνα, 443–45; invoked again by the chorus at 468).²⁹ The attempt at reconciliation plays out in terms of Eteocles' tyrannical rule versus Polynices. When Polynices registers his complaint that Eteocles has not handed over power as they agreed, he says Eteocles is holding onto his tyranny (τυρρανίδ[α], 483). Polynices refers to his own turn at governing with the comparatively unmarked term ἀνάττειν (477; cf. *Suppliants* 406, where it refers positively to governance by the Demos). By contrast, Eteocles is blunt in defending his desire for tyranny, saying he will pursue it high and low and considering it a very great benefit (503–8). He concludes by saying that he will hold onto his tyranny and is quite willing to do so by unjust means (523–25). Whereas Polynices' speech garners praise from the chorus (497–98), Eteocles' rant earns their condemnation (526–27) and a reproach from Jocasta that he should not pursue tyranny at the risk of his city (560–61). Instead he should pursue equality (ἰσότης), since it fosters lawfulness (535–42; cf. *Suppliant Women* 430–37).³⁰ Such sentiments would surely play well with a resurgent democracy.³¹

---

27. Diggle, like many editors, deletes this line, but the case against it is not very strong. See Mastronarde (1995, 157–59). Deleting the line does not alter my broader argument.
28. Diggle, like many editors, deletes these lines, and I am inclined to follow them. Nonetheless, Mastronarde (1995, 231–32) makes a case for retaining the couplet, so I include the lines here. As with line 51, deleting the line does not alter my broader argument.
29. Scharffenberger (1995). Eteocles later refers to the negotiations as a failed reconciliation (515, 701). Line 375 would have Polynices also refer to reconciliation, but the line is certainly spurious.
30. On the Sophistic intellectual currents in Jocasta's speech, see Egli (2003, 198–202).
31. For a survey of the history of how scholars have characterized Euripides' relationship to the Athenian democracy throughout his career, see Michelini's (1987, 28–30) overview of the topic prior to 1987; the work surveyed by Michelini is the relevant backdrop for Holzhausen (2003). The topic of Euripides' and tragedy's place in the sociopolitical environment of fifth-century Athens has produced lively debate. Gregory (2002) provides useful perspective on Goldhill (1990, revised from 1987), Griffin (1998) and Seaford (2000). Michael Mendelson (2002, 1–49) focuses on ways that gender permeates Euripides' depiction of political issues and how it impinges on modern debates. Versnel (1995), Rhodes (2003) and David Carter (2004) each critique Goldhill along similar lines, that the institution of the City Dionysia was bound to the *polis* but not necessarily to a democratic *polis*.

Polynices also comes in for criticism, but in terms amenable to patriotic Athenian democrats. Jocasta questions the sanctity of Polynices attacking his native land (568–85), hoping to avert such "glory" among the Greeks (576–77). The problem of Polynices' awkward alliance with another city is earlier muted by his laments. It was only the gods or luck that brought him to Argos (413), he says. He is miserable and poor in exile (388–407; contrast the cowardly and wealthy Eteocles in 597) and misses free speech most of all (παρρησία, 391).

Ultimately, the attempt at reconciliation fails (443–637), so disasters result. In a sense this is a tragic inverse of the dynamic that Aristophanes dramatizes. In comedy, successful deliberation or reconciliation leads to success and prosperity. In *Phoenician Women,* failed deliberation and reconciliation lead to death and destruction. While tyranny fades from the play as an explicit point of discussion, deliberation does not. Creon says victory consists entirely in good deliberation (καὶ μὴν τὸ νικᾶν ἐστι πᾶν εὐβουλία, 721), and pushes to get a skeptical Eteocles to consider all his options (722–23), but with limited success, and soon Creon again implores him to deliberate (βουλεύου δ', ἐπείπερ εἶ σοφός, 735). The subsequent scene with Tiresias underscores that the tyrannical Eteocles, who would not deliberate, is not fit to rule. Tiresias has just assisted Athens to victory against the Thracians (852–57), but he does not consider Eteocles worth helping (865–66). Ultimately, he finds that the tyrannical line of Oedipus should not rule and does not even merit citizenship (τῶν Οἰδίπου/ μηδένα πολίτην μηδ' ἄνακτ' εἶναι χθονός, 886–87).[32]

Such hostility to tyranny is not unique here in Euripides. A passage from the *Auge,* another late play, would also fit well in an environment of the democracy under pressure from the looming oligarchy or under the restored democracy (fr. 275):[33]

κακῶς δ' ὄλοιντο πάντες, οἳ μοναρχίᾳ
χαίρουσιν ὀλίγων τ' ἐν πόλει τυραννίδι·
τοὐλεύθερον γὰρ ὄνομα παντὸς ἄξιον,
κἂν σμίκρ' ἔχῃ τις, μεγάλ' ἔχειν νομιζέτω.

Burian (2011) and David Carter favor the broad engagement of tragedy with political issues, although Carter (2007, 82–83) partitions Euripides' late plays from discussion. All agree that Aristophanes in *Frogs* takes it for granted that Euripides' tragedy was a cultural force. It is the specifics of Euripides' impact that Aristophanes takes to task.

32. Diggle and many editors delete these lines, but the grounds are ultimately weak. See Mastronarde (1995, 400–406).

33. See above, note 15, on *Auge* possibly belonging to 414–411.

Everyone should die cruelly who enjoys
monarchy or a tyranny of the few over the city.
The word "freedom" is worth everything.
Even if someone has little, let them believe they have much.

Anthemic crowd-pleasing passages like these are in evidence for Euripides' career at least as far back as the 420s (e.g., *Suppliants*),[34] so they are not distinctive enough criteria for dating or assessing Euripides' reaction to the particular environment after 411. Nor is there any evidence that Aristophanes highlighted such material. While *Frogs* does have a decidedly explicit political component in assessing Euripides, nowhere does Aristophanes seize on such political cheerleading. He does seize on statements that came across as morally outrageous (on which, more in the next section), but not ones patently for or against democracy.

Conversely, Euripides was experienced in offending the sensibilities of Athenian audiences. The revision of *Hippolytus* in the early 420s is perhaps the earliest documented example, but the best-attested case is his tetralogy of 415. While best documented today for its one surviving play, the closing tragedy, *Trojan Women*,[35] it is *Palamedes* that receives the only direct comment of evaluation of any single play by Aristophanes, and it is negative, for in *Thesmophoriazusae* Inlaw refers to it as tedious and shameful (848).[36] When Dionysus sarcastically calls Euripides a Palamedes in *Frogs* (1451), he characterizes Euripides' ideas as clever but useless. While the fragments of *Palamedes* are few, the reception of the play in antiquity suggests that Euripides construed Palamedes much as the character is found among intellectual and "Sophistic" writings. Gorgias' defense speech of Palamedes, Alcidamas' complementary prosecution speech by Odysseus, and other references treat him as an intelligent benefactor who did not suffer fools, was framed by a ruthless Odysseus and convicted by the duped masses.[37] The ancient account (introduction to Isocrates' *Busiris* 24–30) that the death of Palamedes recalled the execution of Socrates is historically impossible, but it does reflect the sense of ancient readers that the character of Palamedes in the play came across as a persecuted intellectual. The few surviving lines

---

34. Seaford (2003). Cf. Sophocles frr. 14 (sometimes attributed to Euripides), 201b, 873.

35. For a full treatment of *Trojan Women* in this context, see Croally (1994) and David Carter (2007, 130–39).

36. For comparison and context of this sort of insult toward tragedians, see Kaimio and Nykopp (1997, 26–31).

37. See Scodel (1980, 43–63, 90–93) on Euripides' *Palamedes* within the tradition of Palamedes as intellectual and Sophist. Cf. Sutton (1987, 111–13, 133–42), who sees the play as supportive of Protagoras.

cannot indicate how justified the designation of "frigid" was for the play (although the heavy-handedness of *Trojan Women,* for all its other merits, perhaps gives some idea what a chore the experience of the entire trilogy might have been), but it is not self-evident what could be "shameful" except the most noted travesty: that his death resulted from the vote, the collective judgment, of the foolish masses. For Aristophanes certainly, vigorous debate was one thing, but dramatizing the unfit collective judgment of the Demos would be quite another.

It can seem facile to say that Euripides reacted to the poor reception of his tetralogy of 415 with a series of crowd-pleasing lighthearted dramas, but it is a characterization congruent with the plays, extant and fragmentary, as we know them and with Aristophanes' reaction. If, after 415 and before 411, Euripides produced just one tetralogy, that of 412 including *Helen* and *Andromeda* (and more so if he produced two tetralogies during these years, both dominated by similar fare), it is easy to read *Thesmophoriazusae* as celebrating the rehabilitation of one of Athens' favorite sons. After years of harsh dramas, Aristophanes and the rest of the Athenian audience will forgive his misogyny, he has put the ugliness of 415 behind him, and now everyone can enjoy his light touch, which Aristophanes had always acknowledged, without the ickiness. It may not speak well of Aristophanes as a literary critic, but there is no sense of irony in *Thesmophoriazusae* in this regard. But it does bring our search full circle back to the problem of why his portrayal of Euripides in *Frogs* is so different.

If for Aristophanes and some substantial contingent of the Athenian theater-going public, with its heavy overlap with the constituency of the Athenian Demos, Euripides was enjoying a vogue by 412 and still some celebrity in 411, with the restoration of the democracy and its coming-out party in 409, it would be surprising if there was not expectation and hope of Euripides turning up with another set of crowd-pleasing hits. And he may have done so. The presentation in *Phoenician Women* of the plain-spoken Polynices driven to arms to cast out the tyrranical Eteocles would be a welcome pat on the back to the democratic forces, even as it acknowledges the pain of fighting kin. The play as a whole, while modern scholars are right to explore its intricacy and sophistication, can be enjoyed as a creative wild ride. The extensive remains of *Hypsipyle* seem comparably innocuous.

But not all of Euripides' late output is so appealing. *Orestes* has a quick line where Orestes praises Pylades' loyalty over tyranny (1156),[38] but, while the tragedy can again play as a fun romp, the curmudgeonly Euripides is evi-

---

38. The Phrygian's celebrated report refers to "tyrants'" homes (1456), which may or may not be especially marked, but at the very least there is nothing positive in the designation.

dent. Scholars have rightly been frustrated in making sense of the demented *deus ex machina* by Apollo, the de-heroicizing of most of the characters and the simple nastiness and brutality of the action. Fred Naiden puts the trial of Orestes in this play in the context of Assembly trials in Athens.[39] Such trials were extraordinary, but the decade prior to *Orestes* included high-profile Assembly trials following the mutilation of the herms and the coup of 411. Thus the brutal and dysfunctional proceedings in Orestes' trial spill over into critique of the Athenian Demos' handling of such trials. Such a depiction of public deliberation and the mass judgment of the Demos (only nominally of Argos) once again would cross Aristophanes' sensibilities. In the play, Tyndareus bluntly plans, before the "assembled mob of Argives" (εἰς ἔκκλητον Ἀργείων ὄχλον, 612), to provoke them to stone Orestes and Electra to death. Menelaus is himself morally compromised, but he offers a characterization of the Demos that is not refuted in the play (696–701):[40]

> ὅταν γὰρ ἡβᾷ δῆμος εἰς ὀργὴν πεσών,
> ὅμοιον ὥστε πῦρ κατασβέσαι λάβρον·
> εἰ δ᾽ ἡσύχως τις αὐτὸν ἐντείνοντι μὲν
> χαλῶν ὑπείκοι καιρὸν εὐλαβούμενος,
> ἴσως ἂν ἐκπνεύσειεν· ἢν δ᾽ ἀνῇ πνοάς,
> τύχοις ἂν αὐτοῦ ῥᾳδίως ὅσον θέλεις.

> When the Demos feel their vim and vigor but fall into a rage,
> it is like a raging fire to quench.
> But if someone, when it stretches out,
> relaxes and yields, they can seize the moment,
> and he might be able to blow on it.
> Then, when you approach the blasts,
> you can easily get whatever you want.

Aristophanes had long acknowledged the volatile temper of the Demos, but he always dramatizes the judgment of the Demos as ultimately sound and a path to success and prosperity. Worse yet, Menelaus' characterization is

---

39. Naiden (2010). Silva (2010) offers more general thoughts on the tensions in the trial. Barker (2011) analyzes the play in terms of political free speech and dissent in democratic deliberation.

40. References to the δῆμος in Euripides are certain only here and in the political debate between Theseus and the Theban herald in *Suppliant Women* (351, 406, 425 and 442). The passage in which δῆμος appears in *Andromache* (700) is deleted by Diggle and most editors since Busche. The appearance of the word at *IA* 450 is uncertain (against the MS reading, Diggle and most editors follow a version quoted in Plutarch with ὄγκον instead). The two sententious fragments where it appears (frr. 92, 626) come from Stobaeus without context.

flattering compared to what happens when the Demos actually meets. The messenger reporting the proceedings portrays the assembly as a mob (884) initially divided about what was proper to do, but ultimately manipulated and subject to irrationality (866–956). Along the way, the messenger discourses, with no sense of hope or optimism, on what a leader of the Demos should be like.[41] The messenger is explicit that, at the Assembly, the sensible speaker (εὖ δοκῶν λέγειν, 943) failed to persuade, and the evil speaker won (νικᾷ δ' ἐκεῖνος ὁ κακὸς ἐν πλήθει λέγων, 944).[42] At no point in the play does Euripides follow up with a corrective or counterbalance to this characterization and account. Nothing in *Phoenician Women* matches this decidedly cynical depiction, and there is not enough in the remains of the fragmentary plays, but such cynicism is not without parallel in Euripides' late plays. *Iphigenia at Aulis* dramatizes a similarly grim view of collective decision making in action.[43] Although this play would not have been known or available to Aristophanes, it confirms that Euripides' thought was leaning in this direction, so it is quite possible other plays staged with *Orestes*, or in this interval, contained similar affronts to the Demos.

I have deferred the most problematic and controversial matter to the last: Euripides' connection to Macedon and his composition for its monarch, *Archelaus*. The notoriously unreliable biographical tradition from antiquity says Euripides left Athens, discouraged after the tetralogy of 408, and spent his last years in the court of Archelaus, producing a play that boosted the king's genealogical credentials. Although modern scholars have mostly accepted the core of the narrative, S. Scullion has developed the argument that the story is bald fiction.[44] Moreover, he argues that *Archelaus* was performed in Athens and recognizably quoted in *Frogs* (1206–8). Scullion considers it crucial for demolishing the story of Euripides leaving Athens and dying in Macedon that Aristophanes is silent about any such turn of events

---

41. From this passage, Hartung deleted lines 904–13 entirely, and in this he is followed by Diggle. Willink deprecates the whole passage but deletes only 907–13. The passage is old enough for 907–10 to end up quoted in Stobaeus, although this is of scarcely any value for determining authenticity. The decision to excise the lines is purely aesthetic, and while editors have legitimate reason to feel that the lines are a bloated addition, I am ambivalent and undecided about whether they are genuine Euripides. A discourse on the proper role and characteristics of a προστάτης (911) is not out of place here. This and the reference to the unrestrained tongue (903; cf. the reference to Tantalus in line 10) make it feel just close enough to fifth-century usage that I do not feel confident that the passage is a later interpolation.

42. Diggle adopts Wecklein's χερῶν here, but, with Willink, I retain the MSS λέγων.

43. See Michelakis (2006, 73–82) for a survey of the issues.

44. Scullion (2003). Cf. Scullion (2006), where he argues further that the play was produced in a trilogy with *Temenus* and *Temenidae;* and Lefkowitz (2012, 99–100).

in *Frogs*. If, however, as Scullion envisions, Euripides was commissioned by the Macedonian king to produce a laudatory trilogy, to be staged in Macedonia, and Euripides also had it staged in Athens, one could just as reasonably expect some jab in *Frogs* about such a move. Indeed, there are many questions about how and why Aristophanes presents Euripides just as he does in *Frogs*. The argument from silence is not as strong as Scullion insists, and his scenario, while possible, is not necessarily any better a fit for the evidence than the traditional one.

The remains of *Archelaus* itself do seem to confirm that Euripides made an effort to manipulate mythological genealogy to benefit the Macedonian monarch. Some sort of commission and performance in Macedonia seems logical even to Scullion. As for political content, extant fragments do include sententious comments mentioning the evils of poverty and tyranny on a level with the gods (frr. 248 and 250; cf. Sophocles fr. 88 on godlike tyranny and the corruption brought on by money), as well as the potential dangers of clever speaking (fr. 253).[45] Without context, however, it is impossible to determine if these sentiments belong to a sequence favorable to the Demos, as in *Phoenician Women* (where Eteocles also says tyranny is godlike, 506) or unfavorable, as in *Orestes* (where clever speaking brings victory to the evil man).[46] I posit, however, that whether Scullion is right or not about his scenario, Euripides by this time represented something hostile ideologically for Aristophanes. If Euripides left for Macedon and wrote a tragedy celebrating the aristocratic genealogy of a monarch, when for the last several years he had been a celebrated favorite son and, at least looked upon as, a cheerleader for the democracy, such a move would certainly ring of a stinging reversal and betrayal. If Scullion is right, Euripides staged a play, maybe a trilogy, before the Athenians themselves, with this positive portrayal of a monarch, and the play was familiar enough for Aristophanes to make its opening lines the first to be demolished by the "little bottle of oil" (*Frogs* 1206–8). The combination of the cynical portrayal of the Demos in *Orestes*, favoritism toward a Macedonian monarch and inference from *Iphigenia in Aulis* that Euripides' bitterness toward democratic rule still held in his last days all suggest that in the years when the Athenian Demos ramped up its civic identification with tragedy, Euripides unpalatably turned on the Demos. Thus Euripides would have gone from hero to traitor in these years, and, to compound matters, the younger star of *Thesmophoriazusae*, Agathon, also

---

45. Duncan (2011, 78–82).
46. Frr. 643–44 from *Polyidus*, on bad leadership of the city, present a similar problem, but the similarity makes me inclined to suspect it is a strong candidate to be parallel to the *Orestes* scenario.

had departed Athens for Macedon (*Frogs* 83–84). This chronological progression explains one of most vexed problems of *Frogs* as well as the perplexing emotional dynamic at the play's climax.

EURIPIDES IN *FROGS*

> τὰ μὲν οὖν μνημονευτὰ ἡδέα ἐστὶν οὐ μόνον ὅσα ἐν τῷ παρόντι, ὅτε παρῆν, ἡδέα ἦν, ἀλλ' ἔνια καὶ οὐχ ἡδέα, ἂν ᾖ ὕστερον καλὸν καὶ ἀγαθὸν τὸ μετὰ τοῦτο· ὅθεν καὶ τοῦτ' εἴρηται, "ἀλλ' ἡδύ τοι σωθέντα μεμνῆσθαι πόνων."

> Memories are sweet not only of things that were sweet when they happened, but also some things that were not sweet, if later, after the fact, it is beautiful and good. Whence it is said, "As you know, it's truly sweet to remember pain after escaping it." Aristotle, *Rhet.* 1.11.8.1370b1–4, quoting Euripides' *Andromeda* (fr. 133)

In *Frogs,* Aristophanes seems to be taking a fresh account of Euripides' career with, I will argue, more topicality and immediacy than has usually been granted.

Early in the play, Aristophanes establishes the time frame for the progressive emotional dynamic he is going to present with regard to Euripides. Dionysus, in order to explain to Hercules why he is heading to the underworld, speaks of his intense desire for Euripides, prompted by his reading Euripides' *Andromeda* (52–54). The passage led a scholiast to ask, "Why not another of the more recently produced beautiful dramas, *Hypsipyle, Phoenician Women, Antiope?*" (διὰ τί μὴ ἄλλο τι τῶν πρὸ ὀλίγου διδαχθέντων καὶ καλῶν Ὑψιπύλην, Φοινίσσας, Ἀντιόπην;), since *Andromeda* was produced six years earlier. The question encapsulates what has become the most regularly debated problem of *Frogs:* why and how does Dionysus go from being an ardent admirer of Euripides to presiding ineffectually over a debate between Euripides and Aeschylus to finally choosing Aeschylus and rejecting Euripides? This transformation is the central movement of the entire play, so discussion most often embraces the idea of the unity of the play as a whole.[47] Most scholars have sought this unity in the character of Dionysus himself, both as the character in Aristophanes' play, usually merged with the ideal of comedy as a genre, and the broader multivalent

---
47. Segal (1961).

associations of the god in Athenian cultural and religious life.[48] Others have responded to the scholiast's query by finding the story and drama of Andromeda an integral part of the unfolding of *Frogs*.[49] Such readings expose much richness in the play and provide valuable observations about the interface between Aristophanes' comedy and the vibrant emotional and political life of the Athenian *polis*.

What I propose here does not supplant what Pavlos Sfyroeras and others have contributed to our understanding of *Frogs*. Rather I argue that the fecundity of Aristophanes' intertextuality with Euripides, tragedy more broadly and the ideology of the Athenian *polis* both broadly and deeply is anchored in a straightforward emotional trajectory, from carefree pleasure to confused disappointment to rejection, a trajectory with which the Athenian Demos would already have been familiar on account of Euripides. Aristophanes' dramatization extends beyond reenacting this emotional trajectory, for he sanctions the Demos' rejection of Euripides in favor of reviving a playwright associated with Athens' greatness, and does so in such a way that the resurrection of Aeschylus is not resorting to a figure from the remote past, but to a contemporary assertion of the Demos' judgment about Athens' civic identity. Aristophanes' democratic credentials prime him to chart the Demos' emotional progress in this way. Moreover, the political capital Aristophanes has established over the decades with the Demos means that he can also address the vexed problem of the Athenians exiled for their involvement in the coup of 411. Aristophanes can appeal for their recall, and he will be crowned by the Demos for this, but in the context also of validating and reassuring the Demos of their judgment.

As in nearly every reference by Aristophanes to Euripides, in *Frogs* there is a disjunction between the appeal of Euripides' words and the icky content of what he says. The *Andromeda* prompts a desire in Dionysus' heart (52–54, 66–67), but Hercules insists that the Euripides that Dionysyus praises (in the form of references to *Alexander, Melanippe the Wise* and *Hippolytus*) is dreck (100–106). Dionysus even acknowledges that Euripides is bereft of moral reasoning (πανοῦργος, 80), in contrast to Sophocles, who is associated with good humor (εὔκολος, 82).[50] So far, this is the Euripides of days past. If Euripides had betrayed the Demos before his recent death, the desire for Euripides from the days of *Andromeda* makes sense. The *Andromeda*

---

48. Lada-Richards (1999); Habash (2002); Silva (2007).

49. Sfyroeras (2008) finds *Andromeda* providing a tragic counterpoint to comedy in the play and also bound up with the crucial issue of desire (πόθος) both in drama and in Athenian civic life.

50. Bonanno (2005) suggests that adesp. 480 (Μουσῶν εὐκόλων ἀνθρήνιον), also of Sophocles, is in fact a quotation from Aristophanes.

belonged to a period of Euripides' popularity and before the horrific upheavals of 411–410. Hercules represents the perspective that Euripides was just terrible. Dionysus does not deny this, but he represents the appeal Euripides had, especially at the spike of his popularity ca. 412.

After this initial exchange, there is much other comic business before Euripides again becomes the focus of attention, but once he is, the *agon* between him and Aeschylus consumes the remainder of the play (755–1533).[51] What topical political commentary there is in the play apart from the *agon*, then, comes in these intermediate acts. Two politicians stand out for the attention they receive in this part of the play: Archedemus and Cleophon. In a section of the second *parodos*, the chorus of initiates mocks Archedemus (416–21), who was prominent politically at the time (Xen. *HG* 1.7.2) and noted here as leading the Demos (νυνὶ δὲ δημαγωγεῖ, 419). The attack is brief and general. Archedemus is "premiere in rottenness" (κἄστιν τὰ πρῶτα τῆς ἐκεῖ μοχθηρίας, 421), but this is far from the harshest comment Aristophanes makes about political leaders.[52] Archedemus had prosecuted the general Erasinides after the battle of Arginusae (for embezzlement, before the scandal over the aftermath of the battle arose). Opposition to Erasinides, who had solid democratic credentials, would alone categorize Archedemus as someone who did not have the best interests of the Demos at heart, so the swipe here is not surprising.[53] If Archedemus also participated in the prosecution of the generals, Aristophanes might have had additional motivation to swipe at him, given the positive references to the battle elsewhere in the play (693–96).

The *parabasis* begins with a difficult passage satirizing another prominent political leader, Cleophon. The chorus invokes a Muse to attend (676–85):

τὸν πολὺν ὀψομένη λαῶν ὄχλον, οὗ σοφίαι
μυρίαι κάθηνται
φιλοτιμότεραι Κλεοφῶντος, ἐφ' οὗ δὴ χείλεσιν ἀμφιλάλοις
δεινὸν ἐπιβρέμεται
Θρηκία χελιδὼν
ἐπὶ βάρβαρον ἑζομένη πέταλον,
κελαδεῖ δ' ἐπίκλαυτον ἀηδόνιον νόμον, ὡς ἀπολεῖται,
κἂν ἴσαι γένωνται.[54]

---

51. Arai (2004) reads the intervening scene of Dionysus and the Frog chorus (209–68) as an analogy for Athenian spectators in the Theater of Dionysus acting as judges.

52. See, for example, *Lys.* 1160, where μοχθηρία means pathetic, obstructionist behavior, which would suit Archedemus as well.

53. Cf. the brief swipe at Cleon and Hyperbolus in 569–70.

54. I follow Dover, Sommerstein and others in printing κελαδεῖ from V et al. in 683, rather than

> . . . to see the great mob of folks whose wisdom
> sits numbering in the thousands,
> more worthy of honor than Cleophon, on whose double-babbling lips now
> a Thracian swallow
> rages fearsomely,
> perched on a foreign leaf,
> and cries a tearful nightingale's tune, that he will die,
> even if it's a tie.

In part, the image incorporates the comic abuse that Cleophon's mother was Thracian (cf. Plato Comicus fr. 61, from *Cleophon;* and Aeschines 2.76). Despite some uncertainties, the imagery certainly suggests Cleophon speaking before the judgment of the collected Demos. Euripides and others use ὄχλος pejoratively of a mob not using intelligent judgment (see on *Orestes* above), but in Aristophanes the word can range from unmarked or neutral to implicitly negative. In this instance, however, Aristophanes expands the expression by explicitly filling his ὄχλος with wisdom, not just collectively but distributively, and superior to that of Cleophon, so he insures the term ὄχλος does not carry negative connotation here. Indeed, this is part of the point of the expression, using a term otherwise used disparagingly of the Demos, but casting it as part of a characterization that articulates the intelligence of its members and its civic identity as a whole. By contrast, Cleophon fits the mold of many who influence the Demos in a bad way. The incongruity of a bold noise from a swallow (δεινὸν ἐπιβρέμεται) is comic, but the image of an abrasive speaker is a familiar one from comic attacks on Pericles, Cleon, Hyperbolus (also with non-Greek speech) and others. In the climactic line, ἴσαι seems certain to refer to equal votes, but the context of the voting is not certain. Since Plato Comicus was competing against *Frogs* with his own demagogue comedy on Cleophon (frr. 57–64), a reference to the voting for comedies cannot be discounted. The statement that he will die in the event of a tie, if it is an ultimatum, also has parallels, such as Cleon's threat not to speak anymore if the jury does not vote with him (*Wasps* 926–30), so perhaps the image plays on a sort of threat Cleophon would make in his public delivery. Such a threat would fit an address either before the Assembly or in a court trial. If the reference is to the Council, a rather different scenario may be intended.

Sommerstein has argued that the encore performance of *Frogs* in 404 was near in time to Cleophon's trial before the Council and subsequent

---

Fritzsche's τρύζει, adopted by Wilson.

execution.⁵⁵ He further suggests that calls for Cleophon's death in this passage and at the end of the play (1504) were at a minimum congruent with the desires of oligarchic activists to have Cleophon killed on the path to the next oligarchy and that it is worth considering whether Aristophanes could have been complicit in this movement. Sommerstein does give good reasons to suspect that the references to Cleophon in *Frogs*, especially the image of Aeschylus returning to Athens and insuring Cleophon's execution (1504), fit the cultural moment when Cleophon was on or near trial, or convicted and awaiting execution. The cry for Cleophon's death was not, though, as Sommerstein characterizes it, an exclusively oligarchic one. Two accounts survive of the machinations leading to Cleophon's trial and execution, both from speeches ca. 399 regarding the prosecution of offenders for their role in the atrocities under the Thirty. One speech attempts to lay out a case against an informant named Agoratus, a prosecution that requires making as tight a connection as possible between the defendant and the oligarchs. The prosecutor is at pains to argue that the Council of 405/4 was not a democratic body but dominated by oligarchs plotting the overthrow of the democracy (Lys. 13.20). To make this argument, the prosecutor describes the actions of the Council in that year in terms of their contrasting responses to Cleophon and Theramenes.⁵⁶ In this version of events, Theramenes was abroad plotting to bring home peace terms that would lead to the undermining of the democratic government. Cleophon opposed the peace, and so the oligarchic conspirators framed him and, after convicting him by irregular means, had him executed in order to remove one of the prominent advocates for the Demos (τοὺς τοῦ δήμου προεστηκότας, Lys. 13.7). On the basis of this narrative, it is easy to see Aristophanes' hostile characterization in *Frogs* as an oligarchic shill. The other speech of 399 to narrate these events muddies the waters considerably, however. Another speech (Lys. 30) prosecutes a certain Nicomachus, another oligarchic activist. According to this speech, Nicomachus crafted the legal language that enabled the oligarchic Council to judge Cleophon jointly with a jury and thus insure Cleophon's conviction (30.11). To a reader of *Frogs*, this is surprising, because Aristophanes calls for death for both Cleophon and Nicomachus in the same passage (1504–6). If Aristophanes' smears of Cleophon reflect oligarchic motivations, it is not evident why he simultaneously condemns one of their key operatives. The speech against Nicomachus also provides a broader perspective on Cleophon. The speaker says there is universal agreement that Cleophon was

---

55. Sommerstein (2009, revised from 1993).
56. On Theramenes in *Frogs*, see below.

targeted by oligarchic forces for removal to further their own ends (30.12). The speaker is also aware, however, that members of the democratic jury still may not have a favorable opinion of Cleophon and so argues that, even if Cleophon was rightly condemned, the complicity of Nicomachus should not be forgiven (30.13):

εἰκὸς τοίνυν, ὦ ἄνδρες δικασταί, ἐνθυμεῖσθαι καὶ ὁπόσοι ὑμῶν ἐνόμι-
ζον Κλεοφῶντα κακὸν πολίτην εἶναι, ὅτι καὶ τῶν ἐν τῇ ὀλιγαρχίᾳ
ἀποθανόντων ἴσως τις ἦν πονηρός, ἀλλ' ὅμως καὶ διὰ τοὺς τοιού-
τους ὠργίζεσθε τοῖς τριάκοντα, ὅτι οὐ τῶν ἀδικημάτων ἕνεκα ἀλλὰ
κατὰ στάσιν αὐτοὺς ἀπέκτειναν.

It is proper, gentlemen of the jury, to take this to heart, all of you who thought Cleophon was a bad citizen: that, although among those who perished under the oligarchy there was perhaps a criminal, nevertheless on account of even these sorts of men, you were angry at the Thirty, because they performed executions not on account of any crimes, but in the interests of their faction.

The prosecutor here is acutely aware of the ambivalence of Cleophon's reputation in 399.[57] On the one hand, as democratic Athenians tried to make sense of the rise of the Thirty, they recognized Cleophon as their last staunch defender and a victim of the machinations of the oligarchs. On the other hand, even with this rehabilitation of his reputation, some still reckoned him as deserving of his fate. He seems to have been in the unfortunate position of having been reckoned better off dead by both oligarchs and democrats. Later references indicate his reputation did not improve. A speech from a decade later or so cites him for his influence, and because his heirs inherited nothing of his estate (Lys. 19.48), but there is no attempt to invoke his heroic defense of democracy or his victimization. Decades later Aeschines cites him as someone who led Athens to destruction at a time of crisis (2.76).

Aristophanes composed *Frogs* without the benefit of hindsight, of course. As with the Sicilian expedition, Aristophanes was on the wrong side of history but consistent in his own position.[58] The abuse of Cleophon could still

---

57. On Nicomachus' career, see Shear (2011, 73–74, 79–84). Cf. Carawan (2010) on details of the charge in Lys. 30 against Nicomachus, esp. 89–93, which indicate that he was involved only with the oligarchy of the Thirty, not the oligarchic governments of 411.

58. As it happens, Aeschines (2.76) pairs just these two failings (the Sicilian expedition and Cleophon) in Athenian history. Both mistakes would require broad-enough democratic support and also be ones the democracy acknowledged in retrospect. This would make Aristophanes a fairly typical democrat, though still an utterly singular author of comedy.

in fact belong to *Frogs*' initial performance in 405, rather than the revival in 404, as Sommerstein argues, and simply be ironically prescient in retrospect. Plato Comicus' play *Cleophon,* in the same cohort with *Frogs* in 405, although the fragments are too meager for any meaningful reconstruction of its content, at least indicates there were grounds for ridicule and abuse already. If the comments about Cleophon do date to the encore of *Frogs* in 404, when Cleophon was facing imminent execution, the simple fact of the Council being aligned against him may have been enough for Aristophanes. As I hope I have shown, Aristophanes is unwavering in his faith in the Council, and even if he was on the wrong side of history this time, it is not surprising that he would be aligned with the Council's position.

A swell of resentment against Cleophon would also make the passage satirizing him rhetorically effective in its place. Since Aristophanes' bold advice in the *parabasis* immediately follows, the satire on Cleophon serves, not in any technical, formal way, but in function, as a *captatio benevolentiae* for the spectating Demos.[59] Aristophanes sides with the Demos' anger toward Cleophon, establishing that he recognizes the proper punishment of those who do not serve the Demos' best interest. Then he can most effectively launch into advice that the Demos might at first not find readily acceptable.

To begin his case in the *parabasis,* Aristophanes sounds the refrain in favor of good advice (686–87):

τὸν ἱερὸν χορὸν δίκαιόν ἐστι χρηστὰ τῇ πόλει
ξυμπαραινεῖν καὶ διδάσκειν.

It is just that a sacred chorus offer recommendations and
useful instruction to the *polis.*

Aristophanes itemizes his central recommendations in two sections (πρῶτον οὖν 687 . . . εἶτ', 692). First he calls for the removal of "fears" (δείματα, 688), presumably of prosecution and punishment for those under the stigma of the oligarchic coup of 411. Aristophanes shrewdly characterizes these men as those who slipped up because of the tricks of Phrynichus, who was a prominent democrat prior to his sudden prominent role with the

---

59. With good reason, no scholar has argued that the *parabasis* here conforms to canonical rhetorical practice. Neither Murphy (1938) nor Sousa e Silva (1987–88) even attempts to place any speech from *Frogs* into a schema, and Hubbard (2007) limits *Frogs* to claims about technical vocabulary (on which, see the Introduction). That said, in technique this *parabasis* does exemplify how Aristophanes can employ methods of persuasion that were later catalogued and systematized. Lines 686–87 below also follow a general principle the substance of which would suit a formal *prooimion.*

oligarchy. Hence it is easy to envision these men as those who were lured by Phrynichus' democratic credentials to participate in the oligarchy. Their allegiances could thus more easily appear to have been to the democracy at heart.[60] The slipperiness of political allegiance is a constant theme among prominent Athenians between 411 and 405 and then in the aftermath of the Thirty. The wrath of the Demos against those perceived as disloyal could be lethal. Aristophanes had been aware of, and had commented on, the destructive anger of the Demos as far back as *Acharnians*, and he carefully calibrates his comments on complicated issues throughout *Frogs*. He satirizes Cleophon, touches on Theramenes, who perhaps more than anyone played both sides of the fence during these years (533–41), and, even with these acknowledgments, praises inclusiveness. He praises the decision to grant slaves citizenship for fighting in the navy and asks that Athenians who could serve the *polis* at least as well have the opportunity to do so (692–96). The chorus calls on the Demos to cast aside its anger, in the name of its sage nature (ἀλλὰ τῆς ὀργῆς ἀνέντες, ὦ σοφώτατοι φύσει, 700), and says shared struggle should be enough to recognize mutual kinship and citizenship (701–2; cf. *Lys.* 1129–34 for another statement of shared kinship among adversaries).[61] The judgment of the Demos is wiser than Cleophon or any other popular leader, after all, and should be able to distinguish good citizens (τῶν πολιτῶν τοὺς καλούς τε κἀγαθοὺς, 719) from the rotten (τοῖς πονηροῖς, 725) as they do coins, and posterity will recognize the Demos' sanity (705), and the wise will recognize even the Demos' suffering accordingly (735–37).

This *parabasis* has received much attention ever since antiquity because of the notice that it garnered Aristophanes a civic crown bestowed upon

---

60. See Shear (2011, 64) for the use of Phrynichus as a posthumous scapegoat for the oligarchy of 411.

61. The antode (706–17) makes an attack, the understanding of which is hampered by uncertain identification of its target. The verses mock a certain Cleigenes as a disgusting bath attendant, doomed to meet a bad end. The rareness of this name increases the likelihood that this man is to be identified with the Cleigenes of Halae (*PA* 8488; *LGPN* 1), who served as secretary on the Council in 410/9 (*IG* I³ 375.1). In this capacity, his name appears at Andocides 1.96, in the quotation of a law that made legal the killing of officeholders under an oligarchic regime at Athens. Circumstantially this would associate him with the harsher elements of the restored democracy. In addition, Schwartz and others have emended the name "Cleisthenes" (MSS) to Cleigenes at Lysias 25.25. The defendant in this speech cites Cleisthenes/Cleigenes as an opportunistic prosecutor, i.e., a sycophant, who enriched himself in the aftermath of 411. On the context for such statements, see Christ (1998, 72–117). If these plausible, but not certain, identifications are correct, Aristophanes singles out a notorious sycophant who took advantage of the Demos' pain and anger in the aftermath of 411. In this way, the attack on Cleigenes would be a logical interlude between *epirrhema* (686–705) and *antepirrhema* (718–37), both of which advise the Demos to follow its better instincts rather than an aggressive manipulator like Cleigenes.

him by the Athenian Demos. One of the strands of this notice is preserved in the *Life*, and while there are many reasons for suspecting the content of the *Life*, Sommerstein has shown that the notice all but certainly goes back to an authentic Athenian decree.[62] The passage specifically quotes the lines from the *parabasis* about advising the city and says Aristophanes received the crown for support for the Demos against tyranny (32–35). The *Life* routinely extrapolates material from the plays to create biographical narrative, but the words of the *parabasis* and the play in general are hardly so blunt as to prompt this sort of statement, so it must rely on either the text of the decree or statements elsewhere in lost plays. At a minimum, it vitiates claims that Aristophanes reads like a supporter of oligarchy.[63]

As noted, *Frogs*, and the *parabasis* in particular, acknowledge the slipperiness of political allegiances and the anger of the Demos, as well as its capacity for making a sound judgment over the long run. Issues of betrayal and the need for the Demos to make a sound judgment about its future direction bring us back to the central conundrum of the play, reintroduced in the scene immediately following the *parabasis:* what is one to make of Euripides?

Immediately following the *parabasis,* and after some banter between Xanthias and another slave, comes the setup for the *agon*.[64] When bustle, shouting and verbal wrangling are heard (θόρυβος καὶ βοὴ / χὠ λοιδορησμός, 757–58), the cause turns out to be Aeschylus and Euripides. There is factional strife (στάσις, 760) among the dead. All these terms are consistent with the image of verbal wrangling in the political arena (see the Appendix), so the description paves the way for the ensuing debate to be one of central significance for the Demos. It turns out that there is a throne for tragedy in the underworld, and its resident is supported in the Prytaneum (764), the latter component a direct parallel to an honor a living citizen of Athens can receive. Aeschylus holds this honor, and Sophocles, when he arrives, graciously acknowledges Aeschylus' place there (788–89). Euripides, however, stakes a claim, but the narrative reflects the ambivalent response to Euripides everywhere in Aristophanes. The criminal element in the underworld (a crowd, πλῆθος, 774, not the Demos) is taken in by Euripides'

---

62. Sommerstein (2009, revised from 1993) suspects it is awarded by the oligarchic Council for comments against Cleophon, and on balance he finds Aristophanes' portrayal of the *polis* as inimical to the democracy. Cf. Sommerstein (2005) and Lefkowitz (2012, 104–10).

63. Sidwell (2009, 41–44) argues that the decree was not prompted by the *parabasis* in particular but in recognition of Aristophanes' longtime service to the democracy, and prefers the recognition of Aristophanes and the encore of *Frogs* to have taken place in 403. Cf. Pritchard (2012, 24–26).

64. On the identity of Xanthias' interlocutor here, see Dover (1993, 50–55).

verbal gymnastics (τῶν ἀντιλογιῶν καὶ λυγισμῶν καὶ στροφῶν, 775) and in their madness (ὑπερεμάνησαν) reckons him very wise (κἀνόμισαν σοφώτατον, 776). Now bolstered in this way, Euripides makes for the throne, as if somehow he did not initially consider himself so worthy but was motivated by the reaction of his fans.

The political terminology resumes. Xanthias immediately expects that the Demos will react angrily and stone Euripides (κοὐκ ἐβάλλετο, 778), just as the angry chorus of Acharnians intends to do to Dicaeopolis when they hear of his treason (*Ach.* 236), and as Tyndareus plans to inspire the Assembly to do in Euripides' *Orestes* (612–14). Instead of venting their notorious anger, however, the Demos calls for a referendum on the matter (779–80):

μὰ Δί', ἀλλ' ὁ δῆμος ἀνεβόα κρίσιν ποιεῖν
ὁπότερος εἴη τὴν τέχνην σοφώτερος.

Not at all. Instead the Demos called out for a judgment
about which one was the wiser in their profession.

Aristophanes thus acknowledges but subverts the harsh appraisal of the Demos' judgment dramatized in *Orestes* (and which he dramatized himself two decades earlier). The surface appeal of Euripides is once again not to be denied, but conflict arises when it comes to the content, the wisdom, of what he says. The contest will play on this disjunction repeatedly, but there is more to be explicated from this passage. While there is always ambivalence about Euripides, the harshness of the scenario here is unique. In *Acharnians* and *Thesmophoriazusae*, Euripides is a distinctive and bizarre artist, but ultimately innocuous. In *Frogs* he is a villain, an antagonist to the rightful ruler, Aeschylus, and additionally opposed by Sophocles, who serves as a sort of second to Aeschylus. At the concept of Euripides taking the throne, the Demos is expected to vent its rage as it would toward a traitor. Why? I argued earlier in this chapter that the harsh view of Euripides results from a perception that Euripides turned traitor against the democracy subsequent to the season of 409, when tragedy was so important to the Demos' renewal following the coup of 411. In the past, Euripides had been overtly patriotic about Athens (e.g., in *Heracleidae* and *Suppliants* of the 420s). The *Thesmophoriazusae* indicates that, following the poor reception of his tetralogy in 415, Euripides rose to popularity again by 412. It is this rehabilitation that Dionysus happily remembers early in the play, when he is reading *Andromeda*. Since then, whether it was *Orestes*, *Archelaus* or more likely some combination of these plays, statements and actions (some of which are not recoverable now), Euripides betrayed the Demos in the sense that he was supposed to celebrate the restored democracy as a favored son but offered satirical critique instead and even praise of a non-Greek monarchy. Accordingly, Aristophanes refers to the expected response from the Demos: anger. His faith and support of the Demos, however, mean that he dramatizes instead debate and deliberation about Euripides and about what tragedy means to the Demos under these circumstances. The lengthy *agon* tackles many technical and superficial qualities of tragedy, and undermining Euripides' appeal in these regards is key to insuring his loss in the contest, but overall the contest reads effectively as a referendum before the Demos, exploring the issues set before the Athenian democracy, about what tragedy will mean, and what composer of tragedy will represent them. That author will prove to be Aeschylus, but Aristophanes also knows that this is a problematic proposal. Much of what Aristophanes says about Aeschylus and Euripides makes sense, if the Athenian Demos is in 405 wrestling with how best to promote a tragedian and tragedy as the face of its civic identity. Broadly, Euripides has superficial appeal, but ultimately the content of his plays lets the Demos down. Aeschylus is imperious at a superficial level, but ultimately the proper choice because he pulls the Demos in the direction of Athens' greatness.

Aristophanes had incorporated the nucleus of this contrast between the two authors already in *Clouds*. When Strepsiades asks his son to recite a passage from Aeschylus, Pheidippides describes Aeschylus as a premiere poet, but bombastic and incoherent (1364–67). Pheidippides follows up by reciting Euripides instead, a speech reportedly about incest (1371–72). That Aeschylus is difficult to comprehend and that Euripides can be shocking and subversive seems to be uncontroversial, and it is hardly a problematic statement even among modern admirers. Aristophanes' project in *Frogs* is more problematic, however. Aeschylus will need to be politically appealing, and the undeniable appeal of Euripides' technique must be put in its place.

Making Aeschylus politically palatable is a not unproblematic process that Aristophanes makes unfold over the course of the *agon*. He seems to recognize that Aeschylus is perceived as inaccessible, so he begins with this problem and steadily brings Aeschylus to the fore as the *agon* goes along. So, when the contest is first being set up, Aeschylus rejects the Athenian Demos as judges (οὔτε γὰρ Ἀθηναίοισι συνέβαιν' Αἰσχύλος, 807), but later passages will bring him ever closer to the contemporary world of the

Demos. Still, back when the contest begins, Aeschylus refuses to speak at all, and, once he does, after being provoked by Euripides, Dionysus has to talk him down off of his anger (856–59):

σὺ δὲ μὴ πρὸς ὀργὴν, Αἰσχύλ᾽, ἀλλὰ πραόνως
ἔλεγχ᾽, ἐλέγχου: λοιδορεῖσθαι δ᾽ οὐ πρέπει
ἄνδρας ποιητὰς ὥσπερ ἀρτοπώλιδας·
σὺ δ᾽ εὐθὺς ὥσπερ πρῖνος ἐμπρησθεὶς βοᾷς.

Aeschylus, not so angry. Just gently
question and cross-examine. It's not appropriate for poets to wrangle
like some bread sellers.
You shout right away like an oak tree on fire.

Shouting (βοᾷς) and wrangling (λοιδορεῖσθαι) are typical of political debate that does not constitute meaningful deliberation (see the Appendix), and suggest the demagoguery of a leader like Cleon. In calming Aeschylus down, then, Dionysus is treating him the way Aristophanes treats the Demos, acknowledging the anger but pushing him toward calmer discussion. As it is, the Demos in the play is already calling for rational debate and judgment, so Dionysus is encouraging Aeschylus to participate on the Demos' terms, which in turn makes Aeschylus more palatable and acceptable to the real-life Demos, present in the form of the spectators in the theater. By the end of the *agon,* this appeal is successful, and Aeschylus is the better adviser and deliberator. By contrast, at the start of the *agon* Euripides identifies himself as the "stronger" of the two (κρείττων, 831) and Aeschylus calls him a "collector of mouthings" (στωμυλιοσυλλεκτάδη, 841), but to no particular effect.[65] As the *agon* unfolds, Aristophanes makes Aeschylus more and more a figure suitable to represent the democratic Demos and edges Euripides outside the realm of acceptability.

The change begins in the initial exchanges between the two contestants. Euripides begins by characterizing Aeschylus' dramaturgy as deceptive and hollow (908–13). When Dionysus interjects that he enjoys Aeschylean silence over modern chatter (τῇ σιωπῇ . . . νῦν οἱ λαλοῦντες, 916–17), Euripides calls him stupid (ἠλίθιος, 918), but the implicit defense of chatter foreshadows the weakening of Euripides' position. Aeschylus in the mean-

---

65. Cf. Chapter 3 on κρείττων and the more positive "mouth," rather than a tongue, at the root of this word.

time again stews in silence and barks out occasionally, replicating his earlier anger. By contrast, Euripides is still able to lay claim to the rational refutation the Demos and Dionysus called for (922).

As the focus shifts to Euripides' own dramaturgy, however, the momentum shifts, as do the politics. Euripides makes an unrefuted claim about how he slims down bloated tragedy, but then there is trouble. He trumpets the characters who speak for him (949–50):

ἀλλ᾽ ἔλεγεν ἡ γυνή τέ μοι χὠ δοῦλος οὐδὲν ἧττον,
τοῦ δεσπότου χἠ παρθένος χἠ γραῦς ἄν.

And more the woman spoke for me, and the slave no less
than the master, and the girl and the old woman.

Such inclusiveness, in and of itself, is a virtue in Aristophanes. His plays have all these characters speaking out prominently and often with benefit for the *polis*, but Euripides' following claim, that he acted democratically (δημοκρατικὸν γὰρ αὔτ᾽ ἔδρων, 952) gets him in trouble, and Dionysus rebukes him (953–54):

τοῦτο μὲν ἔασον, ὦ τᾶν.
οὐ σοὶ γάρ ἐστι περίπατος κάλλιστα περί γε τούτου.

Now sir, let that one go.
In your case, it's not the best idea to pursue that.

If Aristophanes had any desire to, he could easily have incorporated quotes from Euripides from various stages of his career that trumpet the virtues of democracy. As I have argued, however, at this particular time Euripides was suffering the reputation of having betrayed the democracy, and Aristophanes was not inclined to dispute the point. With this crucial barrier quickly but solidly established, Euripides' credentials continue to erode. He immediately claims another problematic achievement, teaching people to babble (λαλεῖν ἐδίδαξα, 954), which he had implicitly defended a little earlier. Aristophanes has Aeschylus readily assent to his claim, of course, because this is the sort of unhelpful talk that consumes public discourse without helping the Demos render its better judgment. Euripides digs himself deeper as he takes credit for having people question and pursue trivialities in a passage that culminates in taking credit for the politicians Cleitophon and Theramenes (967). Dionysus spins out a joke about Theramenes' uncanny knack for coming up like a rose no matter the smelliness of his surroundings (968–70). Theramenes' history with the Four Hundred could hardly make him seem democratic, even if he managed to avoid serious trouble up to this point.[66] Likewise, Cleitophon's efforts to further the coup of the Four Hundred (Arist. *Ath. Pol.* 29.3) could not give him a reputation as a useful advocate for the Demos, even if he managed to avoid outright condemnation. No ancient reference to Cleitophon suggests any democratic sympathies.[67] And yet the sort of duplicity that enables men like Theramenes and Cleitophon to be oligarchic supporters and yet survive under the restored democracy is what Aristophanes links to Euripides, for, after Dionysus' interjection, Euripides immediately takes credit for teaching them this type of reasoning (971–74).

With Euripides' democratic credentials shredded, the next exchange focuses on poets' ability to make better citizens (1009–10). This round (1010–98) goes easily to Aeschylus, who cites plays that fostered the warriors of the days of Athens' greatness in empire. Euripides is reduced to offering feeds that allow Aeschylus to expound on the superiority of his position. Aeschylus comes off as the one who inspires greatness in citizens, while Euripides' characters lead to immoral behavior and difficulties for the democratic government, such as the wealthy finding ways to dodge liturgies (1065–66). Again among the charges is λαλιά, the empty babble that takes up time and distracts even the rowers in the fleet from their duties (1069–73; cf. the Appendix).

The choral interlude that follows offers a reminder that the stakes in this choice are high (1099–1100) and reiterates the faith in the spectators (τοῖς θεωμένοισιν, 1110) to make wise decisions. In setting up the contest, there was the expectation that the Demos would proceed with a vengeance, but they called for judgment about the wisdom of the two playwrights. Aeschylus was skeptical about the Athenians' capacity to judge the poets, but now the chorus assures Aeschylus that the spectators are themselves wise (θεατῶν γ' οὕνεχ', ὡς ὄντων σοφῶν, 1118). Thucydides once made his Cleon chastise the Demos in the Assembly for being mere "spectators of speeches" (see the Introduction), but now Aristophanes appropriates the image, as he does for the *ochlos* (mob). They *are* spectators of speeches, but they have the wisdom to handle sophistication and will make the right judgment.

---

66. See Harding (1974) for the vicissitudes of Theramenes' reputation in the fourth century.

67. Cleitophon later belonged to the oligarchic faction that supported the Thirty (*Ath. Pol.* 34.3), and Plato (*Rep.* 340a–b) has him attempt to support Thrasymachus' contention that justice consists of the weak obeying the will of the stronger. Cf. [Plato,] *Clit.* 410e.

With the basic political point made, the next three stages of the debate maintain suspense by turning to technical aspects of dramaturgy: prologues (1119–1250), lyrics (1261–1364) and the "weight" of their verses (1371–1410). Although Aristophanes normally acknowledges the superficial and stylistic appeal of Euripides, in these contests Euripides at best comes off at a draw (prologues and lyrics) or at a loss (the weighing), thereby negating his greatest asset. When Dionysus returns to the matter of making judgment, he is divided, because he reckons one playwright wise and enjoys the other (τὸν μὲν γὰρ ἡγοῦμαι σοφόν, τῷ δ' ἥδομαι, 1413). Since wisdom was the original criterion for judgment (766, 776, 780), the contest should be over, but Aristophanes wants to explicate on the nature of this wisdom at issue, so Dionysus recapitulates the situation (1418–21):

> ἐγὼ κατῆλθον ἐπὶ ποιητήν. τοῦ χάριν;
> ἵν' ἡ πόλις σωθεῖσα τοὺς χοροὺς ἄγῃ.
> ὁπότερος οὖν ἂν τῇ πόλει παραινέσειν
> μέλλει τι χρηστόν, τοῦτον ἄξειν μοι δοκῶ.

> I came down for a poet. What for?
> So the city can be saved and put on its choruses.
> So, whichever one will provide the city
> some useful advice, I think I'll take.

The merging of the purpose of saving the *polis* and putting on its festivals makes all the more topical sense, since the democracy invested heavily in its identity through the production of tragedy. Aristophanes returns explicitly to the substantive political advice to be gleaned from each tragedian. Dionysus first asks about Alcibiades. After each contestant gives answers, Dionysus finds himself in the familiar quandary of one speaking wisely and one clearly (ὁ μὲν σοφῶς γὰρ εἶπεν, ὁ δ' ἕτερος σαφῶς, 1434), although wisdom is still supposed to be the criterion.[68] The second round of questioning finds Dionysus sarcastically referring to Euripides as a wise Palamedes, which would relegate him back to his unpopularity in 415. Despite extended interrogation, Aeschylus actually does not give out his exact wisdom for saving the city, but it is not necessary. Aeschylus has long been the winner.

---

68. Lines 1431–32 are a notorious crux, in that either Aeschylus' lines appear in doublet form (probably reflecting different versions in the original performance and in the encore) or the lines represent the marginal intrusion of a quotation from a similar line from Eupolis' *Demes*. Neither solution affects my reading, but see note 70 below on the indirect association with Pericles. See Dover (1993, 372) for the best overview of the issue.

It has just been Aristophanes' suspense that has dragged it out. To cap off the choice, Euripides protests, and Dionysus rebukes him with his notorious line, "My tongue swore" (ἡ γλῶττ' ὀμώμοκ', 1471), once again, and for the final time, invoking the tongue as the sophistic vehicle of unhelpful speech. Euripides has effectively been no more than a demagogue who fills up time with, at best, innocuous verbiage and, at worst, socially subversive ideas.

The chorus now celebrates the victory of substance over style. Blessings come to the man who benefits his citizens, family and friends (1482–90). There is in fact no graceful appeal (χαρίεν, 1491) in composing tragedy using the babble (λαλεῖν) of Socrates, a reference to Euripides' style.[69] Preferring such drivel to art is insane (παραφρονοῦντος, 1498). Ultimately, Aeschylus wins on both style and content. Aeschylus is to rise to modern Athens to save it with the content of his ideas (γνώμαις, 1502), while Euripides remains in the underworld, a moral nitwit, liar and clown (ὁ πανοῦργος ἀνὴρ / καὶ ψευδολόγος καὶ βωμολόχος, 1520–21), forever blocked from the throne of tragedy by Sophocles. The chorus echoes the blessings, including peace, that Aeschylus will bring to the city.

With this resurrection, Aristophanes completes the emotional journey he initiated early in the play, when Dionysus was reading *Andromeda* and yearning for Euripides, longing for the time, years earlier, before the oligarchic revolution, when Athens and its drama seemed more confident and enjoyable. In the dark days that followed, comprising revolution, bloody restoration of the democracy, the vicissitudes of the Peloponnesian War, the losses of Agathon, Euripides and Sophocles, the Demos reacted, often rashly, to the difficulties as the Athenians struggled militarily, politically, and with the future of its treasured cultural creation, tragedy. Aristophanes gives the Demos its due in recognizing the tumult and pain of these years, naturally looking back at better days, but he uses his decades of political clout to advise the Demos to settle down, render sensible judgments as spectators and find better models than Euripides to aspire to. While the *agon* of *Frogs* shares many formal characteristics with that of *Clouds,* the resurrection of Aeschylus here has its closest parallel in the rejuvenation of Demos in *Knights,* and they share the return of Athens' golden, pre-Periclean age of successful imperialism, peace and wisdom.[70] This is the cultural ideal in

---

69. Cf. Aristophanes fr. 392 and Callias fr. 15, as well as Teleclides frr. 41–42, which link Socrates and Euripides.

70. Sidwell (2009, 44, 293–95) tries to maintain a chain of associations from Aeschylus to Pericles to Eupolis, all ironically satirized as antidemocratic. Even though there has been, ever since antiquity (notably at Valerius Maximus 7.2), a tradition associating Aeschylus with Pericles, Aristophanes

all of Aristophanes' plays, and, although there is a foreboding awareness in *Frogs* of the looming catastrophe, there is nothing ironic or less than idealistic in restoring Aeschylus. Aeschylus himself was some fifty years dead, but the revival of productions of his plays provided cultural continuity, and, for Aristophanes, a sustained link to the best of democratic Athens.

---

never praises Pericles or the Periclean age. For Aristophanes, Athens' greatness lay in its pre-Periclean empire. Aeschylus is victorious, but the metaphor of the lion cub alone is sufficient to invoke Aeschylus (*Ag.* 717–36), and Dionysus' response (1434) that Aeschylus spoke wisely (σοφῶς) and Euripides clearly (σαφῶς) indicates that there is little or nothing to be gained from trying to generate specific policy from Aeschylus' enigmatic profundity, to say nothing of aligning him with Periclean war policy from twenty-five years earlier, which Aristophanes was quite willing to mock in other plays (see Chapters 2 and 3).

Epilogue

ἔστιν δ' ὁ μὲν περὶ τῶν μελλόντων κρίνων οἷον ἐκκλησιαστής.

A man at the Assembly is a judge of what will happen in the future.
—Aristotle, *Rhet.* 1.3.2.1358b4–5

More than a decade intervenes between *Frogs* and the next extant comedy. That these were the years of the tyranny of the Thirty and the more expansive reincarnation of the Athenian democracy makes it all the more regrettable that there is so little to reconstruct of comedy's characterization of this difficult but fascinating period. Legal speeches of the time testify to continuing debate about how to deal with the legacy of the Thirty, both in terms of appropriate punishment and how to properly understand the development of the regime (Lys. 13 and 30), but also how to vet the future participants in the democracy (Lys. 25).

The most intriguing topical comic fragments from the period belong to Archippus, and these all shade into issues of politics and rhetoric. The title of Archippus' *Donkey's Shadow* was proverbial for a dispute over something trivial, and all references to the saying appear in the context of Athenian courts, so perhaps the play also had a forensic context, but the fragments (35–36) are unhelpful.[1] Another of Archippus' comedies, *Fish,* seems to have

---

1. See *Wasps* 191 and Σ for an aetiology of the phrase, a story also found in [Plut.] *Mor.* 848ab

satirized the political machinery of Athens. One fragment complains about the double jeopardy officeholders face with their audits (fr. 14); another has an orator addressing the (chorus of?) fish, not with the customary address of a jury as ἄνδρες Ἀθηναῖοι, "gentlemen of Athens," but with the more context-appropriate ἄνδρες Ἰχθύες, "Gentlemen Fish" (fr. 30). Yet another writes up a mock peace treaty between the Athenians and the fish (fr. 27).[2] It would be fascinating to know, then, how Archippus handled one of the key figures in the aftermath of the tyranny of Thirty in 403, when he staged *Rhinon,* but the remains (frr. 42–44) are unhelpful.

When Aristophanes surfaces again with extant plays, his approach to the political environment and the role of rhetorical speech within it displays some continuity, but the differences are more marked. The chain to the glorious past of Athens that Aristophanes fervently clung to in *Frogs* now seems broken. Given the broader context, this is not surprising. Ober has demonstrated that the period 403–322 B.C.E. for the Athenian democracy marks a new, ideologically coherent era deserving its own synchronic study.[3] Thus, the plays of this period merit a separate study to analyze fully how Aristophanes' last two extant plays fit into the intellectual milieu of the fourth century, as he pursues new ways to envision the political and cultural landscape. I offer only a few comments outlining this approach. In many ways, it is remarkable how radically and energetically Aristophanes works to articulate a new, progressive vision of Athens, given that he seems to have forsaken the optimistic idealization of Athens that propelled nearly all his plays of the fifth century.[4]

Assemblywomen, of the late 390s, already benefits from progressive scholarship about its vision of democratic culture in its early renewal, along with the role of rhetorical speech in the public arena.[5] Rothwell finds the protagonist Praxagora the very embodiment of a new articulation of persuasion (*peitho*).[6] She is a successful *rhetor* who leads the contingent of women in the Assembly on a new venture for Athens' civic community and opens up a new space for effective rhetorical speech to benefit the Athenian Demos. On the other hand, the range and domain of her reforms bespeak a cynicism or lack of faith in current institutions not found in the fifth-century plays.[7]

(Lives of Ten Orators), where Demosthenes employs it.
    2. Cf. Rothwell (2007, 126–28).
    3. Ober (1989, 36–38).
    4. See Zumbrunnen (2012, 99–122) for a fresh look at these issues.
    5. Ober and Strauss (1990, 264–69).
    6. Rothwell (1990).
    7. For Aristophanes' vision in *Assemblywomen* compared to Plato's political vision in *Republic* 5,

Aristophanes' vision is, if anything, more radically inclusive, egalitarian and democratic, perhaps the most hopeful scenario the comedian can offer in Athens' depressed situation.

In *Wealth,* of 388, Aristophanes offers another total re-creation of the Athenian *polis* by redistributing wealth based on merit, and the time-honored institutions of the democracy have barely any relevance this time. A range of "political" readings of the play have been proposed over the years, from the "ironic" reading to the dark readings that expose the ideological irrationality of Athens to deeply cynical charades.[8] Subsequent readings have found more positive elements in its literary technique and sociological foregrounding of desire.[9] Sommerstein's earlier reading of the play as a somewhat hard-edged defense of the poorest of the democracy's supporters comes closest to continuity with the Aristophanes I propose in this book.

Interestingly, somewhere in this period, Aristophanes himself served in the institution he had so long championed, the Council (*IG* II^2 1740.24 = T9 PCG = *Ath. Agora* XV.12.26). It is tempting to speculate that this service and the radical politics of his last plays are related. Serving on the Council could have been discouraging and led him to believe deeper structural change was needed, perhaps explaining why in the late plays the Council no longer factors in social reform or provides stability. Conversely, Aristophanes' increasingly committed politics focusing on social reform might have contributed to his pursuing and being selected by his tribe to serve. While such scenarios remain entirely speculative, his service at this time, as Sommerstein points out, means that Aristophanes passed his *dokimasia,* and the audits of other litigants at the time demonstrate that his past behavior, especially his loyalty to oligarchy or democracy, would have been an issue.[10] Perhaps it was problematic, but those insisting that Aristophanes espoused an antidemocratic line for decades must reckon how and why Aristophanes then served in one of the bastions of the democracy at a time when the democracy was vigilant about who participated, and anyone linked to oligarchy was vulnerable politically and in court.

Another consequence of the coherent ideological landscape Ober charts for 403–322 is the development of the focused use of formal rhetoric. As Ober argues, formal rhetoric developed in this period as the established

---

see now Tordoff (2007). Cf. Reinders (2001, 243–79).

8. Sommerstein (1984) surveys the ironic readings, such as Konstan and Dillon (1981). For an even more cynical reading, see Olson (1990).

9. Sfyroeras (1995); McGlew (2002, 174–91).

10. Sommerstein (2009, 5 n. 15; revised from 1993).

medium of communication between the democratic body and the elite subpopulation of Athens, the means by which each party continually renegotiated their relationship, but with the Demos holding the ultimate authority of interpretation.[11] In a sense, Aristophanes was on the wrong side of history yet again. He had repeatedly characterized and dramatized the development of technical speech as a drag on the democratic deliberative process, but it in fact became the efficient means of maintaining stability. There is perhaps some hint that Aristophanes is aware of this growing reality in *Assemblywomen,* with its speech by Praxagora before the Assembly, and in *Wealth,* in the debate between Poverty and Chremylus, each allowing considerable development of organized speech and developed argumentation in ways that actually forward the positive goals of the protagonists to benefit Athens.

Even so, it is a long way from the formal rhetorical devices systematized by Aristotle and others later in the century. Later comedy would respond to these developments. Specific philosophical schools, and sometimes the speech habits of their students, are recognized.[12] Eventually a passage full of technical rigmarole will hit the comic stage (Cratinus Jr. fr. 7, of the Pythagoreans):

ἔθος ἐστὶν αὐτοῖς, ἄν τιν' ἰδιώτην ποθὲν
λάβωσιν εἰσελθόντα, διαπειρωμένοις
τῆς τῶν λόγων ῥώμης ταράττειν καὶ κυκᾶν
τοῖς ἀντιθέτοις, τοῖς πέρασι, τοῖς παρισώμασιν,
τοῖς ἀποπλάνοις, τοῖς μεγέθεσιν νουβυστικῶς.

This is their character: if they catch some ordinary person coming along, they test his strength in argumentation, assault and batter him with antitheses, conclusions, balanced clauses, digressions, quantities enough to stuff your brain!

Comedy gradually proceeds from reacting to and reflecting formal rhetoric until plays incorporate speeches that later students will recognize as models to be emulated. In the Roman world, Quintilian recommends a half dozen plays of Menander that contain speeches that are both prime specimens of rhetoric and whose content benefits the orator in training (10.1.69). Much to the exasperation of the staunch Atticist Phrynichus a century later, a

---

11. Ober (1989).
12. See Olson (2007, 227–55) for a survey.

certain Balbus of Tralles was known to prefer Menander over Demosthenes (*Epit.* 394 Fischer = Menander T119 PCG).

While Aristophanes would be crucial for Atticists as a source of unimpeachable Attic vocabulary, and he would win points for style, it has only been in modern scholarship that he has been credited with formal construction of speeches following precepts neither he nor his contemporaries knew. While the basis for such work is understandable, we can now securely say that Aristophanes in fact opposed and attacked the early developments that would blossom in the generations after his lifetime into formal instruction in rhetoric. In the fifth century he supported, even as he criticized, the democracy of Athens, which in the fourth century, in a way that would likely have surprised and perhaps disturbed him, thrived by appropriating the very type of speech he despised.

In any case, Aristophanes' legacy and determination to dramatize the importance of public free speech certainly continued. Some sources in antiquity said that the fourth-century comic playwright Nicostratus was a son of Aristophanes. As it happens, in one brief passage surviving from his comedies (fr. 29), a character quotes a line from Euripides (οὐκ ἔστιν ὅστις πάντ' ἀνὴρ εὐδαιμονεῖ, "No man is completely happy," fr. 661.1 *Stheneboea*), the same line that Aristophanes' own version of Euripides used in desperation when trying to avoid Aeschylus' little bottle of oil (*Frogs* 1217–19). It is ironic in one way that Aristophanes in *Frogs* disparages a playwright when, six years earlier, one of his characters, Inlaw, invoked freedom of speech under the democracy (παρρησία, *Th.* 541) to defend Euripides. But freedom of speech has been the more enduring legacy of Aristophanes. Another stray line of Nicostratus champions the idea as if to pick up where Aristophanes' career leaves off (fr. 30, first line unmetrical):

ἆρ' οἶσθ' ὅτι τῆς πενίας ὅπλον ἐστιν ἡ
παρρησία; ταύτην ἐάν τις ἀπολέσῃ,
τὴν ἀσπίδ' ἀποβέβληκεν οὗτος τοῦ βίου.

Don't you know that the weapon against poverty
is freedom of speech? If you lose that,
then you've lost the shield of your life.

Perhaps then, in the end, as caustically as he sometimes used language, at his core Aristophanes believed in freedom of speech as a shield rather than as a weapon, and so he perennially objected to the use of language to harm the Demos while he himself sought to shield the Athenian democracy, to protect it, so that better, wiser natures would render sound judgment, and its citizens would enjoy a success and prosperity approaching the fantastic worlds he was able to create on stage before the Demos. Such sound judgment, of course, had to include the spectators in the theater voting Aristophanes' comedies, which dramatized these worlds, first prize.

Appendix

Catalog of Terminology, Practitioners, and Institutions Related to Rhetoric in the Remains of Fifth-Century Comedy

This appendix collects and catalogues references to "rhetorical" language, its practitioners and its contexts in fifth-century Greek comedy. In the main text, many of the subjects of these entries are discussed in the context of a chronological progression. Here, entries group all the relevant citations by subject for ease of consultation and reference.

This catalog comprises three categories. (1) The first section catalogues terminology in comedy that designates or characterizes "proto-rhetorical" language in the fifth century, i.e., the language that later came to be reckoned as the beginnings of formal rhetoric. By "proto-rhetorical," I mean language that comedy singles out for its unorthodoxy (and usually its ethical dimension as well), but which was not yet focalized in the discipline later known as "rhetoric" (cf. the Introduction). (2) The next section catalogues references to speakers and theoretical explorers of language, including those who later come to be reckoned the pioneers of rhetoric. These practitioners include individuals and groups, sometimes named and sometimes not, from politicians who had to deliver public speeches as part of their activity to philosophers who contributed to the debate and development of rhetorical theory. (3) The last section lists and summarizes passages that describe or dramatize institutions associated with the theory and practice of rhetoric in the political arena (the Assembly, Council, and courts), as well as training or philosophical mechanisms for transmitting and advancing the intellectual exploration that would become formalized as rhetoric. References to political and philosophical institutions focus on how comedy depicts their relationship to rhetoric, but other references to them in comedy are cited as necessary to provide context for the depictions of these institutions more generally.

The few relevant references to comedy and rhetoric from Sicily in the fifth century and its reception in Athens in the fifth and fourth centuries are presented in their entirety and discussed in Chapter 1, and so are not repeated here.

CHRONOLOGICAL LIMITS FOR OLD COMEDY AND RHETORIC

Since antiquity, scholars have divided the history of Greek comedy into Old, Middle and New. These are not hard, fixed categories, and some fragments cannot be comfortably placed under just one of these rubrics, but the distinction remains helpful, and the historical periods underpinning these categories are meaningful for the debate about the development of rhetoric, so the nomenclature is used here. For the purposes of this book and this appendix, Old Comedy covers Athenian comedy belonging to the fifth century down to 403 B.C.E. Ancient testimony says comic productions at Athens were institutionalized in the 480s, and any history of comic performance prior to that is opaque to us now. Scarcely any fragments point to events prior to the 440s, so all the material presented here, although some of it cannot be dated, is overwhelmingly likely to belong to the second half of the century. It was during this same time frame that traditionally the first precepts of formal rhetoric were developed by the intellectuals now known as the Sophists, and the phenomenon spread through the cultural and political life of Athens.

Terminology

Consistent with recent research into the development of early rhetorical theory, the remains of Old Comedy do not include the word ῥητορική or any of the formal terms canonized in the curriculum of rhetoric from the late fourth century onward, such as names for parts of speech.

Listed in (Greek) alphabetical order below are entries for the terms (and clusters of related terms) attested in Old Comedy for designating or characterizing "proto-rhetorical" language in the later part of century, terms which, for purposes of comedy, took place mostly in public, political settings.

ᾄδειν: A snatch of dialogue from Aristophanes' *Farmers* (fr. 101) says that "singing" can mean a poor defense in court.

> A. καὶ τὰς δίκας οὖν ἔλεγον ᾄδοντες τότε;
> B. νὴ Δία· φράσω δ' ἐγώ μέγα σοι τεκμήριον.
> ἔτι γὰρ λέγουσ' οἱ πρεσβύτεροι καθήμενοι,
> ὅταν κακῶς τις ἀπολογῆται τὴν δίκην·
> ᾄδεις.

> A. So did they speak their cases by singing them that time?
> B. By Zeus, yes! I'll give you real proof:
> The old men sitting (on a jury) still say,
> when a defendant presents his case poorly,
> "You're singing!"

No other extant passage uses the phrase this way, but the term does appear in some brief jokes with forensic contexts (*Wasps* 100–101, 268–70, 815–17; *Birds* 39–41).

ἀδολεσχεῖν: This is a strong term for verbal blather. Eupolis has a line addressing a σοφιστής (see the entry for this term below), probably sarcastically or ironically, to teach ἀδολεσχεῖν (fr. 388). Eupolis also applies ἀδολεσχεῖν to Socrates (fr. 386; cf. below under "Practitioners"). A fragment of Aristophanes references Prodicus (fr. 506; cf. below under "Practitioners") with respect to the corrupting influence of someone engaged in ἀδολεσχεῖν.[1] Strepsiades uses it twice when deliberating with "Hermes" to determine his revenge on the residents of Socrates' *Phrontisterion* (*Clouds* 1480, 1485). Hermippus fr. 21 has λεπτολογία, "refined talk," glossed as the equivalent of ἀδολεσχεῖν.[2]

ἀντίθετον: This word, attested only once (Aristophanes fr. 341), comes the closest of any term to matching its meaning, if not its exact form (later ἀντίθεσις), in later technical vocabulary. Only the reference to Agathon confirms that its meaning seems the same as later (καὶ κατ' Ἀγάθων' ἀντίθετον ἐξυρημένον, "and a shaven antithesis in the manner of Agathon"), since antitheses were a hallmark of his style (cf. under "Practitioners").[3]

βοᾶν: This is a regular word for shouting, but it frequently occurs in the context of political deliberation and thus in contexts where proto-rhetorical language also appears. Shouting can be a legitimately aggressive tactic, e.g., at *Ach.* 38, where Dicaeopolis will shout down anyone at the Assembly who refuses to deliberate about peace, and *Ach.* 711, where Thucydides son of Milesias could once have outshouted his prosecutors (cf. under "Practitioners"). More often shouting is unproductive, e.g., at *Ach.* 185–86 and 353 (of the hostile chorus of Acharnians), *Kn.* 286 (Paphlagonian will shout down the Sausage-Seller), 311 (the chorus of Knights refers to Cleon's shouting), 728 (Demos responds to the noise of the Paphlagonian and Sausage-Seller), *Wasps* 471 and 750 (Bdelycleon responds to Philocleon's cries of anguish), 921 (Philocleon says the case cries out clearly for conviction), 1228 (Bdelycleon says Philocleon will be shouted down by Cleon at a banquet), and 859 (Dionysus tries to convince Aeschylus to respond to debate, ἐλέγχου, calmly instead of shouting).[4] Other nonverbal body noises can be associated with this sort of unproductive dialogue, such as farts and snores (πέρδεται and ῥέγκεται, *Kn.* 115) or clearing the throat (χρέμπτεται, *Th.* 381).[5] Whereas the standard term for responding in a debate is ἀντιλέγειν and engaging in

---

1. See Chapter 4, 117 for this fragment.
2. Cratinus fr. 342 similarly applies ὑπολεπτολόγος to Aristophanes for resembling Euripides.
3. The fragment is problematic and the subject of some debate. Karachalios (2006) argues that it is not a fragment of the lost *Thesmophoriazusae* at all, but a gloss reference to the extant one. If he is right, this unique instance of ἀντίθετον in the fifth century would disappear.
4. *Frogs* 779, where the Demos calls for a contest between Aeschylus and Euripides, plays against the stereotype of the angry Demos by having the group call for judgment (see Chapter 6).
5. Major (2002) has fourth-century parallels for farting as oratory.

conversation διαλέγεσθαι, a participant should also "listen back" (ἀντακούειν),[6] but the counterpart to shouting is open-mouthed gaping, which Aristophanes repeatedly criticizes among the citizen Demos (*Ach.* 105, 635; *Kn.* 651, 755, 1119, 1263; *Wasps* 695, 1007; and cf. Chapter 3).

βροντᾶν: Thundering is a metaphor found in comedy to describe some speakers (most notably Pericles). O'Sullivan attempts to make a case that it is a technical term (1992, 107–10), but Willi (2003) has refuted this conclusion (cf. the Introduction).

γλῶττα: The tongue, as the organ of speech and synecdoche for language, generates its own group of metaphors.[7] The comic playwright Plato offers praise of the tongue (fr. 52):

> γλώττης ἀγαθῆς οὐκ ἔστ' ἄμεινον οὐδὲ ἕν
> ...
> ἡ γλῶττα δύναμιν τοὺς λόγους ἐκτήσατο,
> ἐκ τῶν λόγων δ' ἅττ' αὐτὸς ἐπιθυμεῖς ἔχεις.

> There's not a thing better than a tongue when it's good.
> ...
> The tongue provides power for words,
> And from the words you have what you desire.

Cratinus offers a similar evaluation of the tongue (fr. 128):

> ἀλλὰ μὰ Δί' οὐκ οἶδ' ἔγωγε γράμματ' οὐδ' ἐπίσταμαι,
> ἀλλ' ἀπὸ γλώττης φράσω σοι· μνημονεύω γὰρ καλῶς.

> Well, by Zeus I don't know my letters and I can't think,
> But I'll just speak to you from the tongue, because I remember just fine.

Context is not available for either of these fragments, but in the extant plays, or where the context or tone is evident for a fragment, the tongue regularly implies negative or less-than-candid speech.[8] Another passage from the comic playwright Plato (fr. 176) is typical, where a speaker says one thing in his mind while he does another with his tongue (νοεῖ μὲν ἕτερ', ἕτερα δὲ τῇ γλώττῃ λέγει). Cratinus sarcastically

---

6. As the speaker in Crates fr. 45 commands someone to do; cf. similar commands in Euripides at *Supp.* 569 and *Hec.* 321 and adesp. 572, where λεσχαίνειν is equated with διαλέγεσθαι.

7. See Rosenbloom (2009, 200–209) for a rich discussion of orators' tongues in fifth-century literature, although he does not specifically recognize that γλῶττα tilts toward the negative in drama. Fr. 233 (*Banqueters*) seems to use γλῶττα in its later technical meaning of "gloss," but this mostly likely reflects the usage of Galen (our source for the fragment), rather than an early attestation of this meaning.

8. The only positive compound of the tongue occurs at *Knights* 782, where Demos was able to provide greatness for striking up with the tongue (μεγάλως ἐγγλωττοτυπεῖν) after Marathon. More than a century later, Philemon offers this positive statement (fr. 24): πρόχειρον ἐπὶ τὴν γλῶτταν εὐλόγῳ τρέχειν, "running to the tongue is handy for the sensible."

refers to Pericles as "the greatest tongue of the Greeks" (μεγίστη ... γλῶττα τῶν Ἑλληνίδων, fr. 324). Another fragment of Cratinus might elaborate on what Pericles can do with his tongue (from *Dionysalexandros,* possibly Athena's offer in the parody of the judgment of Paris):

γλῶττάν τε σοι
δίδωσιν ἐν δήμῳ φορεῖν
καλῶν λόγων ἀείνων,
ᾗ πάντα κινήσεις.

... gives you a tongue of beautiful eternally flowing words to bring to the Demos with which you will move them all. (fr. 327 = Olson B16; cf. Pericles under "Practitioners" below)

Another fragment (adesp. fr. 213) offers the compound neologism γλωσσοκηλο-κόμπης, "charming with a noisy tongue." Dicaeopolis refers to a tongue-lashing from Cleon (*Ach.* 380). The Sausage-Seller's unsavory credentials include an effective tongue (*Kn.* 637). He also invokes the image of the city gagged speechless by Cleon's tongue (351–52). The Cloud chorus predicts Strepsiades will be able to fight with his tongue (*Clouds* 419), a talent Strepsiades himself admits he needs (792) and later relishes (1160). Kreitton Logos promises Pheidippides a small tongue (1013) but threatens that Hetton Logos would make him have a big one (1018). Hetton Logos himself endorses the tongue (1058). The Wasp chorus urges Philocleon to use his whole tongue in defense of jury service (*Wasps* 547). The Bird chorus sings a song of "tongue-bellies" (*Birds* 1694–1705), which hinges on the Athenian obsession with court drama and cites specifically Gorgias and Philippus (see the entries under "Practitioners"). Agathon's song makes InLaw think of tongue-gagging (*Th.* 131).

Of course the most notorious tongue is that of Euripides' *Hippolytus* (612, ἡ γλῶσσ' ὀμώμοχ', ἡ δὲ φρὴν ἀνώμοτος, "My tongue swore, but my heart is unsworn"), which Aristotle reports was even used against Euripides in a court case (*Rhet.* 3.15.8.1416a28–34). Aristophanes turns this line on Euripides himself, in passing at *Th.* 176 (cf. *Frogs* 102), and crucially at *Frogs* 1471 (cf. Euripides' invocation of the tongue at 892, the chorus's response about wild tongues at 898 and earlier of Euripides at 828; Socrates invokes the tongue at *Clouds* 424). Elsewhere Aristophanes speaks of measuring the tongue Euripides used to "wipe out speeches" (ῥήματ' <ἐξεσ>μήχετο, fr. 656).[9]

In a potentially related metaphor, licking sometimes appears, providing a variant and twist on the negative activities of the tongue. At *Kn.* 103 and 1094 and *Wasps* 904, licking is equivalent to embezzlement. Two phrases without context could belong to this cluster of metaphors. At adesp. fr. 328, ἐλλείχοντα τῶν Ἀθηνῶν, "licking on the Athenians," is glossed as referring to what incorporated citizens (πρόσγραφοι) do, on the analogy of licking honey, in order to appear as citizens. Also, adesp. fr. 438 glosses φοινικελίκτην καὶ λόγων ἀλαζόνα as a deceitful speaker.[10]

---

9. See Chapter 6 n14 for more on this fragment.
10. I wonder if φοινικελίκτης ("red-licker"?) does not carry an obscene sense. Cf. Henderson (1991, 186) on cunnilingus, with Eupolis fr. 60, Storey (2003, 88–89), *Kn.* 1285 and Σ *Peace* 883.

By comparison, στόμα, "mouth," is benign.[11] Consequently, Aristophanes uses στόμα to refer to the positive things he takes from Euripides (fr. 488), and he has sweet honey bedew the mouth of Sophocles (fr. 598).[12] Phrynichus has the braggart Aeschines (not the famous orator) admire the mouth of Dionysus (fr. 10).

Diminutives and compounds of στόμα, however, always have negative connotations, and Euripides is usually involved. Euripides accuses Aeschylus of an ungated mouth (*Frogs* 838). Aeschylus calls Euripides a mouthing-collector (*Frogs* 841). In *Frogs*, the chorus says Euripides has a "mouth-working tongue" (*Frogs* 826–27) and that both have powerful mouths (880). For the consistently pejorative uses of στωμύλλω and related words, see *Ach.* 429 (Dicaeopolis of Euripides), 579 (Dicaeopolis to Lamachus, a parody of Euripides?); *Kn.* 1376 (followers of Phaeax); *Clouds* 1003 (Kreitton of Hetton Logos); *Peace* 995 (Greeks mouthing each other in war); *Th.* 461 (chorus on the Garland-Seller), 1073 (Inlaw and Echo); *Frogs* 92 ("worse than Euripides"), 841, 1069, 1160 (Aeschylus of Euripides), 1071 (Aeschylus of punks), 1310 (Aechylus parodying Euripides), 943 (Euripides of his own writing); and adesp. fr. 115 dub. (στωμυλήθραι δαιταλεῖς, "mouthy banqueters").

On the other hand, φωνή, "voice," is neutral and unmarked. See, e.g., *Kn.* 637–38, where the Sausage-Seller need only refer to his "effective tongue" (γλῶτταν εὔπορον) for it to be awful, but he has to specify "shameless" to indicate his voice has a negative quality (φωνήν τ' ἀναιδῆ; cf. 218 for another example).

εἰκός: This key term is associated with the "Sophistic" movement at the end of the fifth century for arguments using probability, which were a hallmark of fifth-century thinkers and speakers engaging in the new, rational means for constructing arguments.[13] Consistent with Old Comedy's antagonistic stance toward the new intellectuals and their distinctive language, comic idiom uses εἰκός in its value-laden, more traditional senses of "normal" or "proper." Thus Pherecrates deploys the term in a fragment probably spoken by a young man to an elder, perhaps his father, that "it is proper [εἰκός] for me to be in love, but past your season" (fr. 77). Cratinus says the tragedian Acestor will get a beating unless he tidies up his business, where εἰκός could yield either sense, but certainly there is some hint of propriety ("he deserves it"). In the context of natural phenomena, it means activity that is natural or normal, as in the action of plants (Aristophanes fr. 572) and thunder (*Clouds* 393). Otherwise, propriety, not probability, is always the key. A chorus asks whether it is proper that Thucydides son of Milesias (cf. under "Practitioners") should be hounded by prosecutors (*Ach.* 703), for example. Even Pheidippides after his training with Hetton Logos uses an argument of propriety, not probability (*Clouds* 1418), and Strepsiades concedes it in these terms as well (1439). There is no evidence of a probability argument in comedy, even in parody.

---

11. Plato, *Theaetetus* 142d illustrates the more positive στόμα: Eucleides, to express that he could not recite something from memory, says: οὔκουν οὕτω γε ἀπὸ στόματος· ἀλλ' ἐγραψάμην ... ὑπομνήματα ... ἀναμιμνῃσκόμενος ἔγραφον, "No, definitely not from memory [lit., "from the mouth"], but I wrote down what I remembered ... and drawing on my memory wrote it out."

12. The mouth on occasion can be a potential source of trouble. The mouth does need to be restrained in situations calling for holy silence (*Kn.* 670, 1316; *Th.* 40). The mouth of the sycophant Nicarchus should be arrested (*Ach.* 926).

13. See Schiappa (1999, 36) on this term in early rhetoric and some scholars' speculative use of it. Cf. Tindale (2010, 69–82).

ἐλέγχειν: In *Clouds*, Hetton Logos announces he will "cross-examine" Kreitton Logos (1043) and later, after defending the tongue (see above), invites Kreitton Logos to "refute" him in turn (μ' ἐξέλεγξον εἰπών, 1062). The Paphlagonian engages in questioning of Sausage-Seller (*Kn.* 1232), and the men's chorus urges the Proboulos to pursue thorough cross-examination of Lysistrata (*Lys.* 484). The contest between Aeschylus and Euripides in *Frogs* is first described as a ἔλεγκον τῆς τέχνης (786). Dionysus tells Aeschylus to ἐλέγχειν instead of being angry (857). Euripides several times engages in it (894, 908 and 922) and offers that spectators of his plays could examine what he said, so he had to be honest (960–61). Despite the negative association of *elenchus* in the fourth century and later, in *Frogs* it thus seems like a more civilized process of cross-examination.[14]

ἔπος: This is the most precise term for an individual word, although colloquially it can refer to a saying or remark (cf. the entry for ῥῆμα below). Dionysus describes the analysis of Euripides' prologues as προλόγων τῆς ὀρθότητος ἐπῶν, "the correctness of your prologue words" (*Frogs* 1181). The comic poet Phrynichus mentions τῇ διαθέσει τῶν ἐπῶν ("the arrangement of words," fr. 58), but there is no context to help define the phrase precisely. Eupolis (fr. 326) sets διάθεσιν ᾠδῆς, "arrangement of song," in opposition to the traditional form (ἀρχαῖον). Given that there was decidedly a move toward "new music" by the end of the fifth century, perhaps Phrynichus' fragment refers to an analogous phenomenon in prose.[15]

καιρός: This word for "the right time" is attested to have been of great interest to Gorgias (82 B13 DK), but little detail survives. Aristophanes uses the word, but never in the context of anything philosphical, argumentative or oratorical.

κράζειν: Much like βοᾶν (above), κράζω and related words mean "to shout or scream." This cluster of words can refer to oratory or wrangling in political debate. Cleon's screaming is pervasive in *Knights* (256, 284, 487, 863, 1018), and he will continue screaming even after being cast out of the city (1403). Aristophanes invokes Cleon's screaming two years later in the *parabasis* of *Wasps* (1287), where the chorus of Cleon's wasp supporters also screams, but this is just as likely because they are aggressive (226) or threatened (415) as because they are associated with courts. Similarly, the chorus of Acharnians initially screams (*Ach.* 182), and later Thucydides son of Milesias could have outscreamed his prosecutors (711; cf. under "Practitioners"). Finally, in *Peace* (637), generic orators rouse the people with their screaming.

λαλεῖν: In succeeding centuries, this word becomes an ordinary one for talking, but in the fifth century it retains its sense of empty chatter or small talk. Eupolis succinctly summarizes λαλεῖν ἄριστος, ἀδυνώτατος λέγειν, "superb at chatter, incapable of speaking" (fr. 116). This is the idea behind Paphlagonian Cleon's dismissal of an amateur speaker who chatters (*Kn.* 348; cf. 295). Aristophanes does not distinguish

---

14. Aristophanes fr. 257 uses the term, but it lacks context.
15. See Csapo (2004) on the political dimension of the "New Music," although he does not discuss this fragment in particular.

types of chatter, so the idea gets applied to many speakers and situations.[16] Among them, a scholiast reports Aristophanes describing Gorgias and Philippus as λάλοι (fr. 118, but there is no certainty that the scholiast uses Aristophanes' exact wording). Aristophanes links Socrates to such chatter (*Frogs* 1492). Since Euripides receives as much criticism for being a sophist (in the modern sense) as anyone in Greek comedy (see "Practitioners" below), it is unsurprising that his tragedies are not just λάλοι but "chatter around" (περιλαλούσας, Aristophanes fr. 392) and elsewhere need more salt and less chatter (Aristophanes fr. 595; cf. fr. 158 for the salt metaphor). Euripides in *Frogs* asserts that he promoted chatter (*Frogs* 954), and Aeschylus is happy to agree (955, 1069, where also note the pairing of λαλία and στωμυλία). Dionysus finds Aeschylean silence preferable to other playwrights' chatter (917). In *Clouds*, Kreitton Logos complains about young men chattering (931, 1053), and later the chorus characterizes Pheidippides' upcoming speech as chatter (1394). In *Acharnians*, people are chattering in the Agora instead of at the Assembly (21). Aristophanes' use of the related words καταλαλεῖν (fr. 151) and λάλησις (fr. 949) is also recorded.[17]

λέγω/λόγος: These and related terms are broad, multivalent words and concepts that the ancient Greeks themselves discussed, debated and redefined constantly for centuries, and have consequently had full-length modern studies devoted to them.[18] As such they go well beyond the limits of stable, controlled technical vocabulary and beyond the reach of the catalog here.[19]

ληρεῖν: This word refers more strongly to verbal nonsense than λαλεῖν. While Euripides admits to λαλία, he denies ληρεῖν (945), although both he and Aeschylus accuse each other of it (923, 1136, 1197). The choruses of both *Clouds* (359) and *Frogs* (1497) link Socrates to this nonsense.

λοιδορεῖν: This word covers a range of harsh exchanges, from mean-spirited arguing, to arrogant disdain to harsh (yet righteous) advice (cf. the ironic definition at *Kn.* 1274). It characterizes the bickering Logoi in *Clouds* (934), the argument between Strepsiades and Pheidippides (*Clouds* 1353) and the start of trouble between Aeschylus and Euripides (*Frogs* 757, along with θόρυβος and βοᾶν), although Dionysus will say such bickering is not appropriate for them (857). Like βοᾶν, it can be a legitimately aggressive tactic, as at *Ach.* 38, where Dicaeopolis will shout down anyone at the Assembly who refuses to deliberate about peace. It is, of course, an activity of Cleon (*Peace* 656), even when he is exiled at the end of *Knights* (1400).

---

16. See Willi (2003, 168–69) for the gender associations Aristophanes links to this cluster of words.

17. Aristophanes otherwise uses λαλεῖν in contexts not connected with proto-rhetoric or its usual contexts. For other instances of λαλεῖν in comic fragments, where the context is unclear, or at least there is no indication of political or philosophical content, see Pherecrates frr. 2, 70, 138; Strattis fr. 54; adesp. 1005.

18. For studies with particular relevance to Old Comedy, see O'Regan (1992), Schiappa (2003, esp. 87–116, 157–89) and Freydberg (2008).

19. Chapter 3 discusses the *logoi* of *Clouds* and notes the unique use of *legontes* as "orators" in *Peace* (635).

θόρυβος is a more general word for chaos and hubbub, but no surviving comic passage uses it specifically of an angry group at assembly or deliberations.

προοίμια: Proemium, as a designation for the initial section of a formally organized speech, does not appear until the fourth century. In the fifth century, the word refers to greetings. Its single attestation in surviving fifth-century comedy (*Knights* 1353) conforms to standard fifth-century usage (cf. the Introduction and Chapter 3 on *Knights*).

ῥῆμα; This noun refers to an utterance or unit of speech, generally more than individual words. Thus Aeschylus in *Frogs* refers to analyzing each of Euripides' ῥήματα "by the word" (κατ' ἔπος, 1198; cf. entry on ἔπος above), and in the contest of scales, a ῥῆμα equals a single line of verse to be weighed (*Frogs* 1379). It is the more common term used when the character of a speaker's language is to be described, whether it is Ionic pronunciation (*Peace* 521), the bloated style of Aeschylus (*Frogs* 940) or "prettied up" (ῥήματα κομψά, Aristophanes fr. 719).[20] A ῥῆσις refers to a passage or speech and does not carry any particular evaluative connotation.[21] By contrast, diminutive ῥημάτια are linked in a pejorative way with creative speakers (e.g., Euripides at *Ach*. 447 and *Peace* 534; Hetton Logos at *Clouds* 942; fear-mongering threats at *Wasps* 668). Cf. the entry under "Practitioners" for ῥήτωρ.

τεκμήριον: Hubbard cites ὑποτεκμαίρῃ (Aristophanes fr. 205) as an example of technical vocabulary with regard to rhetoric, but no evidence (no pun intended) supports his assertion.[22] Neither the noun nor the verb is restricted technical vocabulary, and neither is limited to forensic or rhetorical contexts (e.g. at *Wasps* 76, the verb τεκμαίρεται is used of a medical diagnosis).

Miscellaneous Terminology from Fragments

Even with the helpful editions of Rusten and Storey, the fragments of Old Comedy are less accessible than the complete plays of Aristophanes.[23] For convenience and reference, then, I collect here the remaining notable references to speech and language in the fragments of fifth-century comedy.

A passage in Eupolis' *Marikas* gave an ancient commentator reason to reference Cleon sputtering in *Knights* (παφλάζειν, fr. 192.135–36; cf. *Knights* 919 and *Peace* 314 for the same metaphor). In Pherecrates fr. 56, an unidentified speaker is silent, until the verbal torrent has poured out. Another voice breaks out sharply and loudly (Pherecrates fr. 153). In Phrynichus fr. 3 (= Olson J14), an old man fears younger men who scratch up

---

20. Cf. adesp. fr. 442 ψυχροκομψεύματα, "cold and prettied up," perhaps of speech; for "cold" speaking, see *Th*. 170 (of the tragedian Theognis), 848 (of Euripides' *Palamedes*), and Theophilus fr. 4 (of *rhetores*).
21. If the gloss cited at Crates fr. 59 does belong to Old Comedy, it is the earliest use of ῥῆσις in comedy, apparently meaning a decree of some sort.
22. Hubbard (2007); cf. the Introduction.
23. Rusten (2011) and Storey (2011).

their elders with words, although they speak sweetly (τούτοις οἷς ἡδυλογοῦσι μεγάλας ἀμυχὰς καταμύξαντες). Syracosius yaps like a puppy when he speaks at the *bema* (Eupolis fr. 220; cf. the barking at *Wasps* 904).The longest fragment from Aristophanes' first play, *Banqueters* (205), hinges on the issue of orthodox language.[24]

Another fragment (fr. 233) features part of the same debate, but about words in older authors such as Homer and Solon, still a type of discussion associated with the new intellectualism in the idea of analyzing language.

Because many fragments derive from lexicographers hunting for rare words, a happy number of creative neologisms referring to language survive. Euripides' skill is στρεψιμάλλος, "wool-tangled" (Aristophanes fr. 682).[25] Cratinus coins λυπησιλόγος as someone who causes pain with their words (fr. 381), and describes running down someone with words like running over them with a horse (fr. 389 ἐφιππάσασθαι λόγοις). Such might be the goal of a politician engaged in knock-down politics (πολιτικοκοπεῖν in Sannyrio fr. 7 and glossed at Plato fr. 113 as λοιδορεῖν and κωμῳδεῖν). Suetonius (adesp. frr. 930–31) collects several heavy compound creations used to characterize busybodies in the Agora, some attested from Aristophanes' extant plays but some not known from other comic remains, including πολυκαλινδήτους, "lots of rolling." It is important to keep in mind that these more isolated items could apply equally well to speakers or situations quite apart from those using formal rhetoric (e.g., to a lyric poet).

Practitioners

Comedy devotes at least as much time and effort to characterizing the speakers and theorizers of language as to the language itself. This section on people has two parts. The first has entries for terms that label a class of speakers, including those who might not be *defined* by being such speakers, but who form groups typically employing such language. The second part proceeds alphabetically through the individuals cited in comedy in this connection. In comedy, proto-rhetorical language was to be found primarily in public, political environments, so this section overlaps with discussions of political leadership or creatures of the political environment.[26]

ἀλαζών: This is a strictly pejorative term, "faker," which in the fifth century is applied to a range of characters employing pretentious quackery, but all of whom use decidedly verbal trickery, whereas in later periods it is used of a wider range of braggarts and fools.[27] The residents of Socrates' Phrontisterion are such fakers (102, naming Chaerephon, and see individual entry below on Socrates, and 1492; cf. 449). Eupolis uses it of Protagoras (fr. 157; see below). Other practitioners include Cleon (*Kn.* 269, 290, 902, the last with him on the receiving end from the Sausage-Seller). Dicaeopolis calls out several of them (63, 87, 109, all of an unnamed ambassador, 135 of Theorus),

---

24. See Introduction and Chapter 2 for more discussion.
25. See Chapter 6 n11 for more on this metaphor.
26. See Connor (1971, 108–19) for the history of ῥήτωρ and δημαγωγεῖν in the politics of Athens in the last third of the fifth century. See the discussion in Chapter 3 for the third term Connor discusses, προστάτης τοῦ δήμου, "protector of the people." For a similar account of συνήγορος, see L. B. Carter (1985, 120–25).
27. MacDowell (1990).

including a generic one who speaks δίκαια κἄδικα to swindle rural folk (371–73). Adesp. fr. 438 mentions a λόγων ἀλαζόνα ("faker in his words"), and Cratinus might, appropriately enough, pair it with κόμπος, "noise" (fr. 375). Euripides applies the label to Aeschylus, somewhat ironically, of his silences (*Frogs* 919).[28]

ῥήτωρ: This term is etymologically related to ῥῆσις (see the entry under "Terminology" above), and this origin may explain its usage, insofar as it refers to someone publicly engaged in policy debate.[29] The word has a different range from English "orator" (as a professional speaker or someone especially skilled in delivering speeches), often corresponding more to "politician" in the sense of someone whose occupation involves regular debate in public, political institutions. Aristophanes places them in the courts (*Ach.* 680) and in the Assembly (*Ach.* 38; *Kn.* 1360). A passage from *Banqueters* (fr. 205) links them directly with strange, new phrasing. Otherwise, they come in for general abuse as politicians (*Kn.* 358, 423–26; *Th.* 530; *Frogs* 367). Similarly, references to ῥήτορες in fragments of Old Comedy do not mention them in the act but refer to them more as a species.[30]

Although the word ῥητορική derives directly from this term, there is no reference to it or to any technical skill or training for *rhetores*.[31]

σοφιστής: Studies have established that, by the fifth century, this word refers broadly to performers and to those who have some prestige for their wisdom. In Old Comedy it never refers to the intellectuals now known as the Sophists.[32] For example, Cratinus calls a group of poets a swarm of σοφισταί (fr. 2). Eupolis applies it to a rhapsode (fr. 483). Plato the comic poet wrote a play titled Σοφισταί, in which he identifies Bacchylides (a flute-player, not the choral poet) as a σοφιστής (fr. 149). A σοφιστής is addressed in Eupolis, but given parallel usage, this is most likely someone who in modern terms would be identified as a poet or performer (fr. 388). In the complete comedies, the word appears only in *Clouds*. According to Socrates, the Clouds nourish "sophists" (331), probably meant in the most general way. Hetton Logos promises to make Pheidippides a sophist (1111), i.e., to make him smart and accomplished. Later, the chorus uses the term ironically of Strepsiades (1309). Athenaeus records that the term was also a widespread one for comic performers (14.621d–e), but it is not clear to what time period he refers.

συνήγορος: A few passages use the term συνήγορος, a legal advocate in the courts. In comedy, there seems to be little difference between a ῥήτωρ and a συνήγορος, except that συνήγοροι are more specifically aggressive prosecutors. Indeed, one fragment mentions both ῥήτορες and συνήγοροι, without any indication that they are meaningfully different groups (Aristophanes fr. 205.6–9). The συνήγορος at this time was associated with young, aggressive prosecutors, a group likely, as comedy

---

28. In a nonrhetorical, but still verbal, sense, it is used of deceit through oracles (*Peace* 1045, 1069 and 1121 of Hierocles; *Birds* 983) and of Meton (*Birds* 1016).
29. Connor (1971, 116 esp. n. 51); and cf. Crates fr. 59.
30. See Chapter 2 for more references and dicussion.
31. For the public, political ramification of the training in *Clouds*, see Chapter 3.
32. Kerferd (1950).

depicts them, to use the new dubious style of speaking to achieve their ends. The chorus at *Acharnians* 703–18 describes a chattering (cf. λαλεῖν under terminology) prosecutor of this sort, and one more fragment (Aristophanes fr. 424) assumes the idea.³³ In *Knights*, Agoracritus asks the rejuvenated Demos how he will handle a *bomolochic* prosecutor, and Demos responds that he would hurl one to his death (1358–63).³⁴

Below is an alphabetical list of historical individuals either (1) linked to the history and development of rhetoric and mentioned in fifth-century comedy³⁵ or (2) mentioned in comedy in connection with the new intellectualism or because their speech characterized them in some fashion. In general, the entries focus on references germane to these areas, so that passages without any discernible connection to language are omitted.³⁶ This list also does not include poets mentioned in connection with their poetry unless they also are linked to progressive, proto-rhetorical language.³⁷

- Aeschines (PA 337, PAA 114830; not the famous orator): Aeschines is linked to hyperbolic speech at Phrynichus fr. 10; *Wasps* 459 and 1243 (cf. *Wasps* 325, 1220; and *Birds* 823).

- Agathon (PA 83, PAA 105185): Like Euripides, this tragic poet was mocked for his novel and experimental work on the tragic stage. A long scene in Aristophanes' extant *Thesmophoriazusae* satirizes his effeminacy and creative process (1–294).³⁸ A fragment from Aristophanes' other *Thesmophoriazusae* (fr. 341) mentions κατ' Ἀγάθων' ἀντίθετον ἐξυρημένον, "a shaven antithesis in the manner of Agathon," referring both to the tragedian's effeminacy and his verbal style influenced by Gorgias.³⁹

---

33. See Chapter 3, 97–98 for details.

34. The chorus of *Wasps* makes a passing mention of a συνήγορος as an aggressive prosecutor (482). The position of συνήγορος changed in the coming years, but a fragment from the third century suggests their reputation only worsened:

μόνῳ δ' ἰατρῷ τοῦτο καὶ συνηγόρῳ
ἔξεστιν, ἀποκτείνειν μέν, ἀποθνῄσκειν δὲ μή.

It's possible only for a doctor and a *synegoros*
to commit murder and not die for it. (Philemon Jr. fr. 3)

35. Where applicable, for each name I include PAA numbers, cross-references to Diels-Kranz (DK) and to Radermacher's *Artium scriptores* (AS). Of those who could have overlapped with the period being surveyed, the following have left no trace in comedy: Antisthenes (AS 19), Cephalus (AS 18), Critias (DK 88, AS 17), Corax and Tisias (AS 2), Empedocles (AS 1), Erginus (AS 5), Evenus (AS 20), Hippias (DK 86, AS 11), Licymnius (AS 16), Nicias of Syracuse (AS 4), Polus (AS 14) and Theodorus (AS 12). The remains of Greek Old Comedy are far too sparse to make any substantive claims from the silence about these individuals, a number of whom are shadowy figures even in broader contexts.

36. For more comprehensive references, see Sommerstein (1996) and Storey (2011, 3: 453–58). On the other hand, I have endeavored to be as thorough as possible about references in fragments, since these are more difficult to research.

37. For discussion and debate about broader issues with respect to the way Aristophanes makes comedy of historical individuals, see Ercolani (2002) and Saetta Cottone (2005).

38. See Given (2007) for a careful analysis of this scene and its role in the play as a whole.

39. This fragment is problematic and part of recent debate about the date of the lost *Thesmophoriazusae* and how it fits into the career of Agathon. See Butrica (2001, 2004), Austin and Olson

- Alcibiades (PA 600, PAA 121630): The notorious and charismatic Alcibiades represented much of what was upsetting to comic poets (and others) about the young generation of intelligent but unusual speakers. He was known for, apparently in a positive way, a distinct lisp when he spoke (mocked at *Wasps* 42–45). One fragment mocks Alcibiades' son (also named Alcibiades) for emulating his father, including his lisp (Archippus fr. 48). Much earlier, in 427 B.C.E., Aristophanes (fr. 205, cf. pp. 40–41) includes Alcibiades among the notorious speakers emulated by a young delinquent. Plutarch states generally that Alcibiades was an able speaker and that comic poets testified to his being a very powerful one among the *rhetores* (adesp. fr. 695, δυνατὸς ἦν εἰπεῖν ... τῶν ῥητόρων ὁ δυνατώτατος). The reference to him as an aggressive *synegoros* in *Acharnians* (716) fits this generalization, but most extant references to him in comedy focus on other aspects of his reputation.[40] One fragment (Eupolis fr. 385) blends Alcibiades' excesses with the boldness of his speech and assertions:

(Αλκ.) ... ὃς δὲ πρῶτος ἐξηῦρον τὸ πρῴ 'πιπίνειν.
(Α.) πολλήν γε λακκοπρωκτίαν ἡμῖν ἐπίστασ' εὑρών.
(Αλκ.) εἶεν· τίς εἶπεν "ἀμίδα, παῖ" πρῶτος μεταξὺ πίνων;
(Β.) Παλαμηδικόν γε τοῦτο τοὐξεύρημα καὶ σοφόν σου.

Alcibiades: ... and who was the first to invent drinking in the morning?
B: You sure set up a lot of ass-hollowing for us when you invented that.
Alcibiades: OK. Who was the first to say "Boy! Pisspot!" right in the middle of drinking?
B: That invention is just like Palamedes, so clever of you.

Whereas in Aristophanes fr. 205 an unusual word is linked to Alcibiades, here a drunken Alcibiades on stage himself lays claim to innovation, both in action and in a new saying. The respondent's citation of Palamedes provides an indirect link to the new intellectualism.[41]

(2003–4) and Karachalios (2006). Athenaeus comments that Plato also mocked Agathon's balanced clauses and antitheses: χλευάζει τε τὰ ἰσόκωλα τὰ Ἀγάθωνος καὶ τὰ ἀντίθετα (187c). See Dover (1980, 123–24) for analysis of the way Plato represents these traits, with parallels from Gorgias' funeral oration (B6 DK), in Agathon's speech at *Symp.* 194e–97e. An unattributed fragment of Aristophanes, but possibly also belonging to the other *Thesmophoriazusae*, attributes the phrase "light-bringing fir torches" to Agathon (πεύκας ... φωσφόρους, fr. 592.35 = TrGF 39 15).

40. See Gribble (1999, 74–79) for a survey of the depiction of Alcibiades in comedy. Some scholars have hunted for a number of further allusions to Alcibiades in comedy, but see the cautionary notes of Storey (2003, 194), Dover (2004) and Olson (2007, 218).

41. Palamedes has some associations with the new thinkers through Gorgias' speech on Palamedes, and Euripides' play about him seems to have portrayed him as a condemned intellectual (frr. 578–89, esp. 578 on his inventions) and was staged in 415 (cf. Chapter 6). If Eupolis fr. 385 belongs to *Baptai*, it could belong to near or after the time Euripides' play was staged; cf. Storey (2003, 108–10, 355). In the next century, the trope of "inventor" appears often in comic fragments, on which, see Hunter (1983, 162).

- Antiphon (PA 1304, PAA 138625; R 10; cf. DK 87): Antiphon the Rhamnusian, the first orator whose works survive, and leader of the oligarchic Four Hundred who briefly ruled Athens in 411, was mentioned by the comic playwright Plato in his *Pisander* for his greed (φιλαργυρία, fr. 110). Philostratus (*Lives of the Sophists* 1.15.2) adds that comedy attacked Antiphon as a devious legal expert who provided, at great cost, speeches composed contrary to justice, especially for those with risky cases (τοῦ Ἀντιφῶντος ὡς δεινοῦ τὰ δικανικὰ καὶ λόγους κατὰ τοῦ δικαίου ξυγκειμένους ἀποδιδομένου πολλῶν χρημάτων αὐτοῖς μάλιστα τοῖς κινδυνεύουσιν).[42]

- Callias (PA 7826, PAA 554500): Callias, son of Hipponicus, in comedy was notorious for wasting the resources of his very wealthy family. This image played some role in Aristophanes' *Horai* (fr. 583) but probably not a central one. Eupolis' *Kolakes* was set at Callias' house and dramatized the decadence at length. Later sources testify also to Callias' reputation for supporting and housing the famous intellectuals of his day. The fragments of Eupolis' *Kolakes* (421 B.C.E.) are consistent with these accounts, naming Protagoras, Alcibiades, Chaerephon and possibly Socrates among the guests.[43]

- Cleon (PA 8674, PAA 579130): Cleon dominated politics in Athens from the death of Pericles (the earliest reference to him, Hermippus fr. 47, cites Cleon's opposition to Pericles during the first two seasons of the Peloponnesian War) until his own death in 422 B.C.E. (Eupolis fr. 211 and *Peace* 269–70 note his death; adesp. 846 notes this and the subsequent rise of Hyperbolus to prominence). Aristophanes pursued him relentlessly on stage, devoting virtually all of *Knights* and much of *Wasps* to him. Jokes about him turn on everything from his appearance (Cratinus fr. 228 on his face, eyebrows and μανία, "madness") to his profession of tanner (adesp. fr. 297). His harsh manner of speaking was another regular target. Aristophanes literally makes him a barking dog in *Wasps,* and this idea probably lies behind the comic playwright Plato calling him Cerberus (fr. 236). One fragment ridicules him for publicly hailing χαῖρε, "Hello! Rejoice!" while he was actually hurting the city (Eupolis fr. 331 = Olson E17). Another criticizes the lack of free speech (ἰσογορία) under him (Eupolis fr. 316 = Olson E18).[44]

- Cleophon (PA 8638, PAA 578250): A difficult passage in *Frogs* (676–85) satirizes Cleophon as a foreigner, perhaps including a characterization of his speaking style (see Chapter 6 for discussion).

- Demostratus (PA 3611, PAA 319245): Aristophanes in *Lysistrata* (391–97) depicts him as a raving speaker, possibly reckoned as "Bouzyges," who helped

---

42. Scholars remain divided about whether this Antiphon is Antiphon "the Sophist" (DK 87). Gagarin (2002) and Pendrick (2002) each summarize the position of the two camps. Cratinus mentions an Antiphon son of Lyconides (fr. 212), certainly different from the Rhamnusian, but who cannot be securely identified with any other "Antiphon."

43. Storey (1985 and 2003, 179–97).

44. The fragmentary commentary on Eupolis' *Marikas* mentions Cleon παφλάζειν, "sputtering" (fr. 192.135–36, probably citing the parallel at *Knights* 919). For a reconstruction of the feud between Aristophanes and Cleon, along with helpful surveys of relevant bibliography, see Storey (1995) and Olson (2007, 210–13).

lead Athens into the disastrous Sicilian expedition. Two fragments of Eupolis' *Demes* mention a speaker as "Bouzyges," one (fr. 103) of someone sarcastically identified as the best speaker after Pericles, and another (fr. 113) as shouting like Bouzyges. These two fragments may refer to Demostratus, but the identification is uncertain.[45]

- Diopeithes (PA 4309, PAA 363105): This man, known from a reference in Plutarch's biography of Pericles as a prosecutor of atheists and intellectuals, is cited by a scholiast to *Birds* 988 as a ὑπομανιώδης ῥήτωρ, "slightly mad *rhetor*," in Teleclides (fr. 7) and likewise παραμαινομένῳ, "raving," in Amipsias (fr. 10), with a couplet from Phrynichus (fr. 9) describing him as a frantic runner with a tambourine. Most references also link him to oracles, but *Wasps* 380 urges the jury-addicted Philocleon to inhale the spirit of Diopeithes, suggesting that he was a vigorous prosecutor, so perhaps his frantic activity was notable in court.[46]

- Euathlos (PA 5238, PAA 425665; R 6): A scholiast says that this aggressive prosecutor, known from Aristophanes' *Acharnians* (703–12), *Wasps* (590–93) and *Holkades* (fr. 424), was also cited in Cratinus' *Thrattai* (fr. 82) and Plato's *Peisander* (fr. 109), but gives no further information. His nickname of "archer" would seem to place him with those using aggressive new language (with words as his arrows), but the available references do not elaborate.

- Euripides: Chapter 6 discusses Euripides, but included here are a few comic references of a more technical nature. Cratinus charges Aristophanes himself with writing like Euripides, using the charged vocabulary associated with the new intellectual speech (fr. 342 = Olson B41):[47]

> τίς δὲ σύ; κομψός τις ἔροιτο θεατής.
> ὑπολεπτολόγος, γνωμιδιώκτης, εὐριπιδαριστοφανίζειν.

> "And who are you?" some shrewd spectator may ask.
> A rather pretty-worded, platitude-pursuing Euripidaristophanizer.

Aristophanes himself responds to the comparison (fr. 488):

> χρῶμαι γὰρ αὐτοῦ τοῦ στόματος τῷ στρογγύλῳ,
> τοὺς νοῦς δ' ἀγοραίους ἧττον ἢ 'κεῖνος ποιῶ.

> I employ the smooth roundness of his style,
> But I have less crude ideas than he does.

---

45. Storey (2003, 135–36).
46. On Diopeithes' political career, see Connor (1963, 115–18); and on the hyperbehavior of a prosecutor at court, cf. Syracosius running around the bema like a puppy in Eupolis fr. 220.
47. Bakola (2010, 24–29) discusses how Cratinus distances himself from, and aligns Aristophanes with, sophistic doctrine here.

Note that Aristophanes uses στόμα, "mouth," here for what he appropriates, rather than the more abusive "tongue" (see the entry above in "Terminology"). The στόματος ... στρογγύλῳ may also pick up on a running joke about Euripides' fondness for sigma sounds. The comic Plato parodies a very sigmatic line from Euripides' *Medea* (ἔσωσά σ,' ὡς ἴσασιν Ἑλλήνων ὅσοι, "I saved you, as all the Greeks know," 476) by saying, ἔσωσας ἐκ τῶν σίγμα τῶν Εὐριπίδου, "You saved us from the sigmas of Euripides" (fr. 29).[48] Elsewhere Aristophanes economizes the connection between Euripides' tragedies and the new intellectualism by having Socrates ghostwrite them (fr. 392), again using vocabulary associated with the new slippery style (for περιλαλούσας, see on λαλεῖν above in "Terminology"):[49]

Εὐριπίδῃ δ' ὁ τὰς τραγῳδίας ποιῶν
τὰς περιλαλούσας οὗτός ἐστι, τὰς σοφάς.

Composing tragedies for Euripides
that are clever and chatter around.

- Gorgias (DK 82; R 7): The famous speaker is linked with Philippus at *Wasps* 421 and *Birds* 1701, where a scholiast says Aristophanes also mentioned Gorgias as a babbling *rhetor* (λαλὸς ῥήτωρ) in *Farmers* (fr. 118), but offers no details.[50]
- Hyperbolus (PA 13910, PAA 902050): Apparently entering politics at a relatively young age (Cratinus fr. 283 and Eupolis fr. 252), Hyperbolus was perceived as the immediate successor to Cleon (adesp. 846) in 422 B.C.E. until his ostracism in 415. Hyperbolus was a popular target in comedy, being the principal target of at least three plays, Eupolis' *Marikas*, Hermippus' *Artopolides* and Plato's *Hyperbolus*.[51] Unlike slippery, sophisticated speakers, Hyperbolus was mocked for not sounding like an Athenian and thus immediately as a non-Greek (e.g., a Phrygian in Polyzelus fr. 5). Rather than unusual phrasing or vocabulary (such as is cited in Aristophanes fr. 205), attacks focus on specific quirks of pronunciation: a stuttering δοκικῶ for δοκῶ (Hermippus fr. 12), loss of "i" in δῃτώμην for διῃτώμην and loss of "g" in ὀλίον for ὀλίγον (Plato fr. 183 = Olson E24).[52]

---

48. Eubulus fr. 26 (= Olson D11) from the next century has a similar joke; Clayman (1987) demonstrates that the perception is based on some famous lines, not a widespread trend in Euripides' style.

49. Teleclides frr. 41 (= Olson F5) and 42 and Callias fr. 15 (= Olson F3) are cited together by Diogenes Laertius (2.18) as passages asserting that Socrates contributed to Euripides' writing, although he does not explain the connection of Callias fr. 15 with Euripides (which mentions only Socrates by name); cf. Olson (2007, 178).

50. See the Introduction and Schiappa (1999, 85–152) for Gorgias' role in pre-Aristotelian rhetorical theory.

51. See Olson (2007, 214–15) for a survey.

52. Cf. Pherecrates fr. 11 on Lycurgus (grandfather of the canonical orator) perceived as Egyptian in a corrupt passage that might comment on his diction (λέξεις).

- Lysistratus (PA 9630, PAA 618290): Lysistratus is cited among the speakers linked to unorthodox language in Aristophanes fr. 205. There may be multiple men named Lysistratus referred to by Aristophanes in various plays and by Antiphon and Andocides in speeches, but there is no definitive way to separate them or establish them under a single identity.[53] None of the other references play on his manner of oratory or speaking.
- Pandeletus (PAA 763615): Named at *Clouds* 924, where Kreitton Logos characterizes Hetton Logos as "munching Pandeletian platitudes from a little bag" (ἐκ πηριδίου γνώμας τρώγων Πανδελετείους), Pandeletus, according to the Suda, was in Cratinus' *Cheirones* (fr. 260), but there are no details. He is also characterized in the Suda entry as an active prosecutor, perhaps a hint at Cratinus' characterization.
- Pericles: See the section on Pericles in Chapter 2 for comic references to Pericles during his lifetime, and Chapter 4 on Eupolis' *Demes* for the famous lines praising him (fr. 102).
- Phaeax (PA 13921, PAA 911410; R 13): At *Knights* 1377–80, the followers of Phaeax are characterized by a half-dozen newly coined adjectives in -ικός:[54]

    σοφός γ' ὁ Φαίαξ δεξιῶς τ' οὐκ ἀπέθανεν.
    συνερτικὸς γάρ ἐστι καὶ περαντικός,
    καὶ γνωμοτυπικὸς καὶ σαφὴς καὶ κρουστικός,
    καταληπτικός τ' ἄριστα τοῦ θορυβητικοῦ.

    That really wise Phaeax avoids death so cleverly.
    because he's cooperative, conclusive,
    idea-impressitive, clear, strikitive,
    and most repressative of the provocative.

    Whether this characterization was meant to reflect the speaking style of Phaeax himself is uncertain. Plutarch says that Phaeax was inferior to Alcibiades as a speaker and explains: ἐντευκτικὸς γὰρ ἰδίᾳ καὶ πιθανὸς ἐδόκει μᾶλλον ἢ φέρειν ἀγῶνας ἐνδήμῳ δυνατός, "for he seemed affable and persuasive in private more than capable in public debate" (Alc. 13.1–2). He then quotes a succinct line from Eupolis (fr. 116, quoted above with regard to λαλεῖν) that implies Phaeax was better at small talk than speech making.
- Philippus: A scholiast says Aristophanes mentioned this babbling *rhetor* (λαλὸς ῥήτωρ) in *Georgoi* (fr. 118; linked with Gorgias at *Wasps* 421 and *Birds* 1701), but offers no details, and this may not be the exact wording used by Aristophanes.
- Prodicus (DK 84, R 8): In Aristophanes fr. 506 (quoted above), either a book or Prodicus or someone of the ἀδολεσχῶν has ruined someone. Storey sug-

---

53. MacDowell (1971, 238).
54. See discussion Chapter 3, 81.

gests the teacher of grammar and music (fr. 17) in Eupolis' *Aiges*, Prodamus, could be meant to evoke Prodicus.[55] The chorus of *Clouds* refers to Prodicus' intelligence, but not in terms of his verbal ability (360–61). Papageorgiou (2004b) argues that the moral dimension of the two *Logoi* in *Clouds* is derived from Prodicus' parable of Virtue and Vice.[56]

- Protagoras (DK 80, R 3): Like Plato's dialogue about him, the one comedy in which we know Protagoras had some importance, Eupolis' *Kolakes*, has him at the house of Callias (see above). Two fragments mention him (frr. 157–58):

ἔνδον μέν ἐστι Πρωταγόρας ὁ Τήϊος,
ὃς ἀλαζονεύεται μὲν ἀλιτῆρος
περὶ τῶν μετεώρων, τὰ δὲ χαμᾶθεν ἐσθίει.

Inside is Protagoras of Teos,
who is an accursed faker
about cosmic matters but eats earthly things.

πίνειν γὰρ αὐτὸν Πρωταγόρας ἐκέλευ', ἵνα
πρὸ τοῦ κυνὸς τὸν πλεύμον' ἔκπλυτον φορῇ.

For Protagoras ordered him to drink, so that
he would have his lungs washed out before the Dog [i.e., before
the star Sirius rose].

Other than referring to his being an ἀλαζών, these two fragments do not address Protagoras' importance for the development of rhetoric. An indirect link between Protagoras and comedy is found in Plato, who has his caricature of Protagoras cite Pherecrates' *Savages* in arguing about the teachability of ἀρετή, "excellence" (*Prot.* 327c = T2 in PCG). This Protagoras says that even the most unjust person, raised among laws and fellow humans (νόμοις καὶ ἄνθρωποις), is more civilized than those lacking in education, courts and laws (μήτε παιδεία μήτε δικηστήρια μήτε νόμοι), such as the savage chorus of Pherecrates' play. It is possible that Plato makes this link because the play made some association with Protagoras' anthropological theories, but there is no specific evidence. See Chapter 3 for a discussion of the importance of Kreitton and Hetton Logos for understanding Aristophanes' reaction to Protagoras.

- Socrates: Athens' most famous and notorious intellectual seems to have been a relatively popular target on the comic stage.[57] As far as his language or proto-rhetoric, the most blunt criticism of him in comedy comes from Eupolis (fr. 386 = Olson F1), but the context is unknown:

---

55. Storey (2003, 70–74).
56. Papageorgiou (2004b).
57. For broader and more detailed analyses of Socrates in Greek comedy, see Patzer (1994), Noël (2000), Mitscherling (2003) and Cavallero (2007).

μισῶ δὲ καὶ <τὸν> Σωκράτην
τὸν πτωχὸν ἀδολέσχην,
ὃς τἄλλα μὲν πεφρόντικεν,
ὁπόθεν δὲ καταφαγεῖν ἔχοι,
τούτου κατημέληκεν.

And I hate Socrates,
the blathering beggar,
who's thought about various things,
but to where to get something to eat,
he's paid no attention.

The criticism here targets the disjunction between Socrates' intellectual interests, expressed verbally through ἀδολεσχία (see "Terminology" above), and basic nutritional needs, much as do Eupolis' references to Protagoras (frr. 157–58; see the entry above).[58] As with Pericles, the posthumous tradition seems different, in this case with a reference to one of his accusers (adesp. 940, probably Meletus, cited in the fifth century by Sannyrio fr. 2 for being as emaciated as a corpse):

κεῖται δ' ὁ τλήμων τὸ στόμα παρεστραμμένος,
ὃ τὸν διάμορφον Σωκράτην ἀπώλεσεν.

He lies still now, the wretch, perverted in the mouth
which destroyed the polymorphous Socrates.

Thus Socrates, after all his talk (or blather) is ruined by a mouth, however, rather than a type of tongue.

- Syracosius (PA 13041, PAA 853435): Scholars most often discuss Syracosius for his reputed role in censoring comic speech, but the scholiasts' information about his supposed legislation could well derive from comedy, although even if so, it tells us little new about how comedy portrayed him.[59]
- Teleas (PA 13500, PAA 878910): Cited for his shiftiness in *Birds* (168–70), in the comic playwright Plato (fr. 176), Teleas says one thing in his mind while he does another with his tongue (νοεῖ μὲν ἕτερ', ἕτερα δὲ τῇ γλώττῃ λέγει; cf. above in "Terminology").
- Theogenes (Theagenes? See Storey [2003, 147–49] on the multiple candidates with whom this individual might be identified): In Eupolis (fr. 135), a Theogenes is noted to have the nickname καπνός, "smoke," because he promised much but did not deliver. At Aristophanes fr. 582 and Eupolis fr. 99.5–10, he

---

58. See the entry on Euripides for his collaboration with Socrates (Aristophanes fr. 392; Callias fr. 15; Teleclides frr. 41–42).
59. See Ercolani (2002) for debate and further references. See Chapter 4, 116–17 for Syracosius as orator in Eupolis fr. 220.

is satirized for excessive farting, which for other speakers can designate fatuous oratory.[60]

- Theramenes (PA 7234, PAA 513930): Theramenes is targeted in *Frogs* (533–41, 967–70) for his slippery political activities, where Euripides claims him as a student. In later antiquity (e.g., Cicero, *De or.* 2.93), rhetorical works were attributed to Theramenes, but these are of doubtful authenticity.[61]
- Thrasymachus (R 9): Thrasymachus is cited for an unusual phrase (Aristophanes fr. 205), but Storey (1988) argues that this is not the famous Sophist.
- Thucydides son of Milesias (PAA 515450): Aristophanes twice cites Thucydides on the occasion of his failed defense in court late in life (*Ach.* 703–12; *Wasps* 946–48). The passage in *Acharnians* makes explicit that he had been a powerful speaker in court (cf. the entries for shouting and screaming above), but there is no more information about his style. Since Aristophanes is using him as an example of the good old days, it is unlikely he would have been linked to the progressive "proto-rhetorical" language.[62]

Institutions

Aristophanes dramatizes directly or reports explicitly on the three main institutions of the Athenian democracy—the Assembly, the Council and the courts—and projects an anxiety about the role of the new style of speech in each of them. This final section outlines the dramatizations of activity in these areas and collects comic fragments that provide hints that other comedies dramatized the proceedings in these institutions as well.

Assembly

- *Acharnians:* The play opens with a failed meeting of the Assembly (1–173), including examples of public language (not so much proto-rhetorical as political humbug). The policy speech that Dicaeopolis could not deliver at the meeting, he delivers to the hostile chorus of *Acharnians* (496–555).
- *Knights:* As the play begins, Cleon (as Paphlagonian) dominates the Assembly (305). Later, Demos presides over an Assembly debate between Cleon and the Sausage-Seller (752–972).[63]
- *Wasps:* In the prologue, the slave Sosias has a satirical dream about the Assembly, which he and Xanthias interpret (31–51). It includes references to the speaking styles of Cleon and Alcibiades.

---

60. Major (2002).
61. Dover (1993, 261).
62. See Olson (2002, 252) for a survey of what is known of Thucydides' life.
63. Rhodes (2010) analyzes how these scenes match up to historical information about the proceedings of the Assembly.

- Eupolis' *Demes:* One section of the lengthy papyrus fragment (99.23–34) refers to action in the Assembly, but interpretation is difficult.[64]
- *Birds:* The birds hold something of an assembly to hear Peisetaerus' proposal (431–637), which is the most ambitious and successful bit of persuasive deliberation in extant comedy.
- *Lysistrata:* The Proboulos briefly recalls an incident in the Assembly from a few years earlier, when Demostratus supported the Sicilian expedition, while women shrieked inauspiciously during a celebration of the Adonia (388–97). Lysistrata later refers to failed activity in the Assembly as motivation for the women's activism (507–25).
- *Thesmophoriazusae:* This play features an extensive and detailed dramatization of the Assembly.[65] The women hold an assembly, complete with the longest continuous speeches in extant comedy (295–573).
- *Frogs:* The Demos in the underworld calls for judgment on Aeschylus and Euripides, perhaps in a manner suggesting Assembly trials (779–80).

Council

- *Knights:* In this play, control of the Athenian democracy by demagogues involves dominating both the Assembly and the Council (166–67, 363, 395–96, 475–79, 774–76). The Sausage-Seller reports the dysfunctional debate before the Council between himself and the Paphlagonian (624–82), which features much of the shouting typical of comedy's characterization of the language and deliberations of public debate.
- *Peace:* Since the play celebrates the return of success and prosperity, it does not dramatize a dysfunctional Council but indicates its future in a peaceful Athens (894–908). Trygeaus is to return the divine *Theoria* to the Council (713–18), which he does in extraordinary fashion by presenting her to the *Bouletikon* in the theater, where the real-life Prytaneis were seated (887, 905).
- *Lysistrata:* The central antagonist in the play is the Proboulos, whose very office represented a restriction on the Council's authority. He is routed by Lysistrata and the women (387–610), and later in the play a representative of the Council is to be chosen for the peace negotiations (1011–12).
- *Thesmophoriazusae:* The Council is closed (79), but the women's assembly receives its proposal from the Council (372–75). Later, a Prytanis arrives to arrest Inlaw for invading the assembly, acting on the authority of the Council (943).

---

64. Storey (2003, 149–60).
65. Haldane (1965) analyzes how these scenes match up to historical information about the proceedings of the Assembly.

Courts

- *Acharnians:* In the *parabasis*, the chorus laments the situation in the courts where aggressive young prosecutors pummel venerable citizens (676–718). The metaphors of the youths' language as weaponry indicate a link of the new, proto-rhetorical language with this sort of prosecution.
- *Knights:* Control of the Athenian democracy by demagogues involves dominating the courts (307, 973–84), but Demos will liberate the courts when he is rejuvenated (1316–18).
- *Wasps:* The bulk of this play turns on jurors and courts (1–1002) and includes a satirical domestic trial of a dog (764–997), whose mock proceedings include fragmented speeches by the prosecution and defense. Scholars' attempts to make these speeches conform to structural principles of the fourth century do not hold up (see Chapter 3), but the proceedings do give a sense of comedy's ridicule of forensic practice.
- *Peace:* Euripides is briefly linked with courts (532–34).
- *Birds:* The chorus sings a song that hinges on the Athenian obsession with court drama (1694–1705). The song's "tongue-bellies" indicate language and speech are central to this obsession (cf. the entry on the tongue under "Terminology").

References to the Courts in Comic Fragments

As it happens, virtually all the references among comic fragments that pertain to proto-rhetorical speech making, and for which some context is evident, pertain to the courts. Chapter 2 surveys these brief references.

Bibliography

Andò, V. 2004. "Saperi femminili in un mondo alla rovescia: Le donne in *Lisistrata* e *Ecclesiazuse*." *Dioniso* 3: 90–107.
Arai, Naoshi. 2004. "Do Spectators See the Frogs in the *Frogs?*" *JCS* 52: 32–44.
Arnott, W. Geoffrey. 2010. "Middle Comedy." In Gregory W. Dobrov, ed., *Brill's Companion to the Study of Greek Comedy*, 279–331. Leiden.
Austin, C., and S. D. Olson. 2003-4. "On the Date and Plot of Aristophanes' Lost *Thesmophoriazusae*." *LICS* 3: 1–11.
———. 2004. *Aristophanes: Thesmophoriazusae*. Oxford.
Bakola, E. 2010. *Cratinus and the Art of Comedy*. Oxford.
Barker, Elton T. E. 2011. "'Possessing an Unbridled Tongue': Frank Speech and Speaking Back in Euripides' *Orestes*." In D. M. Carter, ed., *Why Athens? A Reappraisal of Tragic Politics*, 145–62. Oxford.
Berlin, James A. 1992. "Aristotle's *Rhetoric* in Context: Interpreting Historically." In Stephen P. Witte, Neil Nakadate, and Roger D. Cherry, eds., *A Rhetoric of Doing: Essays on Written Discourse in Honor of James L. Kinneavy*, 55–65. Carbondale, IL.
Bers, Victor. 1997. *Speech in Speech: Studies in Incorporated "Oratio Recta" in Attic Drama and Oratory*. Lanham, MD.
Biles, Zachary. 2011. *Aristophanes and the Poetics of Competition*. Cambridge.
Bonanno, Maria Grazia. 1983. "Aristoph. fr. 198 K. (ὀνόματα καινά)." *MCr* 18: 61–70.
———. 2005. "Un novo frammento di Aristofane? (Com. Adesp. fr. *480 K.-A.)." *Eikasmos* 16: 105–9.
Bons, Jeroen A. E. 2007. "Gorgias the Sophist and Early Rhetoric." In Ian Worthington, ed., *A Companion to Greek Rhetoric*, 37–46. Oxford.

Borthwick, E. K. 1994. "New Interpretations of Aristophanes *Frogs* 1249–1328." *Phoenix* 48: 21–41.

Braun, Thomas. 2000. "The Choice of Dead Politicians in Eupolis' *Demoi:* Themistocles' Exile, Hero-Cult and Delayed Rehabilitation; Pericles and the Origins of the Peloponnesian War." In F. D. Harvey and J. Wilkins, eds. *The Rivals of Aristophanes: Studies in Athenian Old Comedy,* 191–231. London.

Brock, Roger. 2009. "Did the Athenian Empire Promote Democracy?" In John Ma, Nikolaus Papazarkadas, and Robert Parker, eds., *Interpreting the Athenian Empire,* 149–66. London.

Brockmann, Christian. 2003. *Aristophanes und die Freiheit der Komödie: Untersuchungen zu den frühen Stücken unter besonderer Berücksichtigung der "Acharner."* Munich.

Buis, Emiliano Jerónimo. 2005. "Cómo plagiar la litigiosidad del enemigom y no perder en el intento: La estrategia desvergonzada de la mímesis jurídica como clave de lectura en *Caballeros.*" *Eirene* 41: 140–60.

———. 2008. "Diplomáticos y farsantes (Ar. *Ach.* 61–174): Estrategias para una desarticulación cómica de la política exterior ateniense." *CFC (G)* 18: 249–66.

Burian, Peter. 2011. "Athenian Tragedy as Democratic Discourse." In D. M. Carter, ed., *Why Athens? A Reappraisal of Tragic Politics,* 95–117. Oxford.

Butrica, J. 2001. "The Lost *Thesmophoriazusae* of Aristophanes." *Phoenix* 55: 44–76.

———. 2004. "The Date of Aristophanes' Lost *Thesmophoriazusae:* A Response to Austin and Olson." *LICS* 3: 1–5.

Byl, S. 1991. "Le stéréotype de la femme athénienne dans *Lysistrata.*" *RBPh* 69: 33–43.

Carawan, E. 2010. "The Case against Nikomachos." *TAPA* 140: 71–95.

Carey, Christopher. 2000. "Old Comedy and the Sophists." In F. D. Harvey and J. Wilkins, eds., *The Rivals of Aristophanes: Studies in Athenian Old Comedy,* 419–36. London.

Carlevale, John. 2000. "Education, 'Phusis,' and Freedom in Sophocles' *Philoctetes.*" *Arion,* 3rd series, 8: 26–60.

Carrière, Jean-Claude. 2003. "Les banquets de Démos dans les comédies d'Aristophane: Stratégies poétiques et message politique." *Pallas* 61: 175–202.

———. 2004. "Politique, éducation et pulsions 'naturelles' dan les *Guêpes:* De la comédie sociale 'réaliste' à la subversion comique 'carnivalesque' et au triomphe de Dionysos." *Dionisio* n.s. 3: 66–89.

Carter, David M. 2004. "Was Attic Tragedy Democratic?" *Polis* 21: 1–25.

———. 2007. *The Politics of Greek Tragedy.* Exeter.

———. 2011. "Plato, Drama, and Rhetoric." In D. M. Carter, ed., *Why Athens? A Reappraisal of Tragic Politics,* 45–67. Oxford.

Carter, L. B. 1985. *The Quiet Athenian.* Oxford.

Cassio, Albio Cesare. 1985. *Commedia e partecipazione: La "Pace" di Aristofane.* Naples.

Cavallero, Pablo A. 2007. "La historicidad del Sócrates de Aristófanes y la coincidencia de las fuentes." *REA* 109: 449–64.

Ceccarelli, Paola. 2000. "Life among the Savages and Escape from the City in Old Comedy." In F. D. Harvey and J. Wilkins, eds., *The Rivals of Aristophanes: Studies in Athenian Old Comedy,* 453–71. London.

Christ, Matthew R. 1998. *The Litigious Athenian.* Baltimore.

———. 2006. *The Bad Citizen in Classical Athens.* Cambridge.

Clay, Jenny Strauss. 2007. "Hesiod's Rhetorical Art." In Ian Worthington, ed., *A Companion to Greek Rhetoric,* 447–57. Oxford.

Clayman, D. 1987. "Sigmatism in Greek Poetry." *TAPA* 117: 69–84.
Cole, Thomas. 1991a. *The Origins of Rhetoric in Ancient Greece.* Baltimore.
———. 1991b. "Who Was Corax?" *ICS* 16: 65–84.
Compton-Engle, Gwendolyn. 2001. "Mock-Tragic Priamels in Aristophanes' *Acharnians* and Euripides' *Cyclops.*" *Hermes* 129: 558–61.
———. 2013. "The Blind Leading: Aristophanes' *Wealth* and *Oedipus at Colonus.*" *CW* 106: 155–70.
Conacher, Desmond. 1998. *Euripides and the Sophists.* London.
Connor, W. R. 1963. "Two Notes on Diopeithes the Seer." *CPh* 58: 115–18.
———. 1971. *The New Politicians of Fifth-Century Athens.* Princeton, NJ.
Consigny, Scott. 2001. *Gorgias: Sophist and Artist.* Columbia, SC.
Crick, Nathan. 2010. "The Sophistical Attitude and the Invention of Rhetoric." *Quarterly Journal of Speech* 96: 25–45.
Croally, N. T. 1994. *Euripidean Polemic: The "Trojan Women" and the Function of Tragedy.* Cambridge.
Cropp, Martin, and Gordon Fick. 1985. *Resolution and Chronology in Euripides: The Fragmentary Tragedies.* BICS Supp. 43. London.
Csapo, Eric. 2004. "The Politics of the New Music." In Penelope Murray and Peter Wilson, eds., *Music and the Muses: The Culture of "Mousikē" in the Classical Athenian City,* 207–48. Oxford.
Davidson, J. 1997. *Courtesans and Fishcakes: The Consuming Passions of Classical Athens.* New York.
de Brauw, Michael. 2007. "The Parts of the Speech." In Ian Worthington, ed., *A Companion to Greek Rhetoric,* 187–202. Oxford.
Denniston, J. D. 1927. "Technical Terms in Aristophanes." *CQ* 21: 113–21.
Dillon, John. 2004. "Euripides and the Philosophy of His Time." *Classics Ireland* 11: 47–73.
Dover, Kenneth J. 1968. *Aristophanes: Clouds.* Oxford.
———. 1974. *Greek Popular Morality in the Time of Plato and Aristotle.* London and Berkeley.
———. 1980. *Plato: Symposium.* Cambridge.
———. 1993. *Aristophanes: Frogs.* Oxford.
———. 2004. "The Limits of Allegory and Allusion in Aristophanes." In D. L. Cairns and R. A. Knox, eds., *Law, Rhetoric, and Comedy in Classical Athens: Essays in Honour of Douglas M. MacDowell,* 239–49. Swansea.
Dunbar, Nan. 1995. *Aristophanes: Birds.* Oxford.
———. 1997. "Editing *Birds*: Problems and Perspectives." In A. Tsakmakis and M. Khristopoulos, eds., Ὄρνιθες: Ὄψεις καὶ Ἀναγνώσεις μίας Ἀριστοφανικῆς Κωμωδίας, 69–85. Athens.
Duncan, Anne. 2011. "Nothing to Do with Athens? Tragedians at the Courts of Tyrants." In D. M. Carter, ed., *Why Athens? A Reappraisal of Tragic Politics,* 69–84. Oxford.
Edmunds, Lowell. 1980. "Aristophanes' *Acharnians.*" In Jeffrey Henderson, ed., *Aristophanes: Essays in Interpretation,* 1–41. Yale Classical Studies 26. New Haven, CT.
———. 1987a. "The Aristophanic Cleon's 'Disturbance of Athens.'" *AJP* 108: 233–63.
———. 1987b. *Cleon, "Knights," and Aristophanes' Politics.* Lanham, MD.
Egli, Franziska. 2003. *Euripides im Kontext zeitgenössischer intellektueller Strömungen: Analyse der Funktion philosophischer Themen in den Tragödien und Fragmenten.* Beiträge zur Altertumskunde 189. Munich.

Elster, Jon. 1998. *Deliberative Democracy.* Cambridge.
English, Mary C. 2007. "Reconstructing Aristophanic Performance: Stage Properties in *Acharnians.*" *CW* 100: 199–227.
Ercolani, Andrea, ed. 2002. *Spoudaiogeloion: Form und Funktion der Verspottung in der aristophanischen Komödie.* Stuttgart.
Erp Taalman Kip, A. M. van. 1987. "Euripides and Melos." *Mnemosyne* 40: 414–19.
Faraone, C. A. 2006. "Priestess and Courtesan: The Ambivalence of Female Leadership in Aristophanes' *Lysistrata.*" In Christopher A. Faraone and Laura K. McClure, eds., *Prostitutes and Courtesans in the Ancient World,* 207–23. Madison, WI.
Farenga, Vincent. 2006. *Citizen and Self in Ancient Greece: Individuals Performing Justice and the Law.* Cambridge.
Foley, Helene. 1988. "Tragedy and Politics in Aristophanes' *Acharnians.*" *JHS* 108: 32–47.
———. 2008. "Generic Boundaries in Late Fifth-Century Athens." In Martin Revermann and Peter Wilson, eds., *Performance, Iconography, Reception: Studies in Honour of Oliver Taplin,* 15–36. Oxford.
Ford, Andrew. 2002. *The Origins of Criticism: Literary Culture and Poetic Theory in Classical Greece.* Princeton, NJ.
Foster, Edith. 2010. *Thucydides, Pericles, and Periclean Imperialism.* Cambridge.
Fox, Matthew, and Niall Livingstone. 2007. "Rhetoric and Historiography." In Ian Worthington, ed., *A Companion to Greek Rhetoric,* 542–61. Oxford.
Freydberg, Bernard. 2008. *Philosophy and Comedy: Aristophanes, Logos, and Eros.* Bloomington, IN.
Gagarin, Michael. 1994. "Probability and Persuasion: Plato and Early Greek Rhetoric." In I. Worthington, ed., *Persuasion: Greek Rhetoric in Action,* 46–68. London.
———. 1997. *Antiphon: The Speeches.* Cambridge.
———. 2002. *Antiphon the Athenian: Oratory, Law, and Justice in the Age of the Sophists.* Austin, TX.
———. 2007. "Background and Origins: Oratory and Rhetoric before the Sophists." In Ian Worthington, ed., *A Companion to Greek Rhetoric,* 27–36. Oxford.
Gallagher, Robert L. 2003. "Making the Stronger Argument the Weaker: Euripides, *Electra* 518–44." *CQ* 53: 401–15.
Gallego, Julián. 2005–6. "Los *dissoi logoi* en las *Nubes* de Aristófanes: Esquema formal y punto de detención de la proliferación discursiva." *Circe* 10: 177–93.
Garver, Eugene. 1996. "The Political Irrelevance of Aristotle's *Rhetoric.*" *Philosophy and Rhetoric* 29: 179–99.
Gigante, M. 1957. "Un nuovo frammento politico (P. Heid. 182)." *Maia* 9: 68–74.
Given, John. 2007. "The Agathon Scene in Aristophanes' *Thesmophoriazusae.*" *Symbolae Osloenses* 82: 35–51.
Goldhill, Simon. 1990. "The Great Dionysia and Civic Ideology." In John J. Winkler and Froma I. Zeitlin, eds., *Nothing to Do with Dionysos?: Athenian Drama in Its Social Context,* 97–129. Princeton, NJ.
———. 1991. *The Poet's Voice: Essays on Poetics and Greek Literature.* Cambridge.
———. 2009. "The Audience on Stage: Rhetoric, Emotion, and Judgment in Sophoclean Theatre." In Simon Goldhill and Edith Hall, eds., *Sophocles and the Greek Tragic Tradition,* 27–47. Cambridge.
Gomme, A. W. 1938. "Aristophanes and Politics." *CR* 52: 97–119.
Gordziejew, V. 1938. "De prologo *Acharnensium.*" *Eos* 39: 321–50, 449–76.

Gregory, Justina. 1999/2000. "Comic Elements in Euripides." In M. Cropp, K. Lee, and D. Sansone, eds., *Euripides and Tragic Theater in the Late Fifth Century,* 59–74. *ICS* 24/25. Champaign, IL.
———. 2002. "Euripides as Social Critic." *G&R* 49: 145–62.
Gribble, D. 1999. *Alcibiades and Athens.* Oxford.
Griffin, Jasper. 1998. "The Social Function of Attic Tragedy." *CQ* 48: 39–61.
Gross, Alan G., and Marcelo Dascal. 2001. "The Conceptual Unity of Aristotle's *Rhetoric.*" *Philosophy and Rhetoric* 34: 275–91.
Gutmann, Amy, and Dennis Thompson. 2004. *Why Deliberative Democracy?* Princeton, NJ.
Habash, Martha. 2002. "Dionysos' Roles in Aristophanes' *Frogs.*" *Mnemosyne* 55: 1–17.
Haldane, J. A. 1965. "A Scene in the *Thesmophoriazusae* (295–371)." *Philologus* 109: 39–46.
Hall, Edith. 2006. *The Theatrical Cast of Athens: Interactions between Ancient Greek Drama and Society.* Oxford.
———. 2009. "Deianeira Deliberates: Precipitate Decision-Making and *Trachiniae.*" In Simon Goldhill and Edith Hall, eds., *Sophocles and the Greek Tragic Tradition,* 69–96. Cambridge.
Hanink, Johanna. 2011. "Aristotle and the Tragic Theater in the Fourth Century B.C.: A Response to Jennifer Wise." *Arethusa* 44: 311–28.
Hansen, Moses. 1978. "*Demos, Ecclesia,* and *Dicasterion* in Classical Athens." *GRBS* 19: 127–46.
Harding, Phillip. 1974. "The Theramenes Myth." *Phoenix* 28: 101–11.
———. 1994. "Comedy and Rhetoric." In Ian Worthington, ed., *Persuasion: Greek Rhetoric in Action,* 196–221. London.
Harriott, Rosemary M. 1986. *Aristophanes: Poet and Dramatist.* Baltimore.
Haskins, Ekaterina V. 2004. *Logos and Power in Isocrates and Aristotle.* Columbia, SC.
Heath, Malcolm. 1998. "Aristophanes and the Discourse of Politics." In Gregory W. Dobrov, ed., *The City as Comedy: Society and Representation in Athenian Drama,* 230–49. Chapel Hill, NC.
———. 2011. "Response to Burian, Hesk and Barker." In D. M. Carter, ed., *Why Athens? A Reappraisal of Tragic Politics,* 163–71. Oxford.
Henderson, Jeffrey J. 1980. "*Lysistrate:* The Play and Its Themes." In Jeffrey Henderson, ed., *Aristophanes: Essays in Interpretation,* 153–218. Yale Classical Studies 26. New Haven, CT.
———. 1990. "The *Dêmos* and Comic Competition." In John J. Winkler and Froma I. Zeitlin, eds., *Nothing to Do with Dionysos?: Athenian Drama in Its Social Context,* 271–313. Princeton, NJ.
———. 1991. *The Maculate Muse: Obscene Language in Attic Comedy.* Rev. ed. Oxford.
———. 1993. "Problems in Greek Literary History: The Case of Aristophanes' *Clouds.*" In R. Rosen and J. Farrell, eds., *Nomodeiktes: Greek Studies in Honor of Martin Ostwald,* 591–601. Ann Arbor, MI.
———. 1998a. "Mass versus Elite and the Comic Heroism of Peisetairos." In G. W. Dobrov, ed., *The City as Comedy: Society and Representation in Athenian Drama,* 135–48. Chapel Hill, NC.
———. 1998b. "Attic Old Comedy, Frank Speech, and Democracy." In Deborah Boedeker and Kurt Raaflaub, eds., *Democracy, Empire, and the Arts in 5th-Century Athens,* 255–73. Cambridge.

———. 2003. "Demos, Demagogue, Tyrant in Attic Old Comedy." In Kathryn A. Morgan, ed., *Popular Tyranny: Sovereignty and Its Discontents in Ancient Greece,* 155–79. Austin, TX.
Henry, M. H. 1995. *Aspasia, Prisoner of History: Aspasia of Miletus and Her Biographical Tradition.* Oxford.
Hesk, Jon. 2011. "Euripidean *euboulia* and the Problem of 'Tragic Politics.'" In D. M. Carter, ed., *Why Athens?: A Reappraisal of Tragic Politics,* 119–43. Oxford.
Holzhausen, Jens. 2003. *Euripides Politikos: Recht und Rache in "Orestes" und "Bakchen."* BzA 185. Munich.
Hubbard, Thomas K. 1991. *The Mask of Comedy: Aristophanes and the Intertextual Parabasis.* Ithaca, NY.
———. 1998. "Utopianism and the Sophistic City in Aristophanes." In G. W. Dobrov, ed., *The City as Comedy: Society and Representation in Athenian Drama,* 23–50. Chapel Hill, NC.
———. 2007. "Attic Comedy and the Development of Theoretical Rhetoric." In Ian Worthington, ed., *A Companion to Greek Rhetoric,* 490–508. Oxford.
Hughes, Alan. 2012. *Performing Greek Comedy.* Cambridge.
Hunter, Richard L. 1983. *Eubulus: The Fragments.* Cambridge.
———. 2009. *Critical Moments in Classical Literature: Studies in the Ancient View of Literature and Its Uses.* Cambridge.
Hunzinger, Christine. 2000. "Aristophane, lecteur d'Euripide." In Jean LeClant and Jacques Jouanna, eds., *Le théâtre grec antique: La comédie; Actes du 10ème colloque de la villa Kérylos à Beaulieu-sur-Mer, les 1er et 2 octobre 1999,* 99–110. Cahiers de la Villa Kérylos 8. Paris.
Jacob, Bernard. 1996. "What If Aristotle Took Sophists Seriously? New Readings in Aristotle's *Rhetoric.*" *Rhetoric Review* 14: 237–52.
Kaimio, Maarit, and Nicola Nykopp. 1997. "Bad Poets' Society: Censure of the Style of Minor Tragedians in Old Comedy." In Jyri Vaahtera and Raija Vainio, eds., *Utriusque linguae peritus: Studia in honorem Toivo Viljanaa,* 23–37. Turku.
Kallet, Lisa. 2003. "*Dēmos Tyrannos:* Wealth, Power, and Economic Patronage." In Kathryn A. Morgan, ed., *Popular Tyranny: Sovereignty and Its Discontents in Ancient Greece,* 117–53. Austin, TX.
Karachalios, Foivos-Spyridon. 2006. "Aristophanes' Lost *Thesmophoriazusae* Revisited: On the Date and Plot." *LICS* 5: 1–23.
Kassel, Rudolph, and Colin Austin. 1983–2001. *Poetae comici graeci.* 8 vols. Berlin.
Kerferd, G. B. 1950. "The First Greek Sophists." *CR* 64: 8–10.
———. 1981. *The Sophistic Movement.* Cambridge.
Kerkhof, R. 2001. *Dorische Posse, Epicharm und attische Komödie.* Munich.
Kloss, Gerrit. 2001. *Erscheinungsformen komischen Sprechens bei Aristophanes.* Untersuchungen zur antiken Literatur und Geschichte 59. Berlin.
Konstan, David. 1998. "The Greek Polis and Its Negations: Versions of Utopia in Aristophanes' *Birds.*" In G. W. Dobrov, ed., *The City as Comedy: Society and Representation in Athenian Drama,* 3–22. Chapel Hill, NC.
———. 2010. "Ridiculing a Popular War: Old Comedy and Militarism in Classical Athens." In David Pritchard, ed., *War, Democracy, and Culture in Classical Athens,* 184–99. Cambridge.
Konstan, David, and Matthew Dillon. 1981. "The Ideology of Aristophanes' *Wealth.*" *AJP* 102: 371–64.

Kopff, E. C. 1990. "The Date of Aristophanes, *Nubes II.*" *AJP* 111: 318–29.
Lada-Richards, Ismene. 1999. *Initiating Dionysus: Ritual and Theatre in Aristophanes' "Frogs."* Oxford.
Lefkowitz, Mary R. 2012. *The Lives of the Greek Poets.* 2nd ed. Baltimore.
Leo, Friedrich. 1960. *Ausgewählte kleine Schriften.* 2 vols. Rome and Oxford.
Lloyd, Michael. 1992. *The Agon in Euripides.* Oxford.
MacDowell, D. M. 1971. *Aristophanes: Wasps.* Oxford.
———. 1990. "The Meaning of ἀλαζών." In E. M. Craik, ed., *"Owls to Athens": Essays on Classical Subjects Presented to Sir Kenneth Dover,* 287–92. Oxford.
———. 1995. *Aristophanes and Athens.* Oxford.
Major, Wilfred E. 2002. "Farting for Dollars: Agyrrhios in Aristophanes' *Wealth* 176." *AJP* 123: 549–57.
———. 2006. "Aristophanes and *Alazoneia:* Laughing at the Parabasis of the *Clouds.*" *CW* 99: 131–44.
Markantonatos, Andreas. 2007. *Oedipus at Colonus: Sophocles, Athens, and the World.* Berlin.
Marshall, C. W. 2009. "Sophocles' *Chryses* and the Date of *Iphigenia in Tauris.*" In J. R. C. Cousland, James Rutherford Hume, and Martin Cropp, eds., *The Play of Texts and Fragments: Essays in Honour of Martin Cropp,* 141–56. Mnemosyne Supp. 314. Leiden.
Marzullo, B. 1953. "Strepsiade." *Maia* 6: 99–124.
Mastromarco, G. 1997. "La *Lisistrata* di Aristofane: Emanzipazione femminile, società fallocratica e utopia comica." In Antonio López Eire, ed., *Sociedad, política y literatura: Comedia griega antigua; Actas del I Congreso Internacional: Salamanca, noviembre 1996,* 103–16. Salamanca.
Mastronarde, Donald J. 1995. *Euripides: Phoenissae.* Cambridge.
———. 2010. *The Art of Euripides: Dramatic Technique and Social Context.* Cambridge.
McCabe, Mary Margaret. 1994. "Arguments in Context: Aristotle's Defense of Rhetoric." In David Furley and Alexander Nehamas, eds., *Aristotle's "Rhetoric": Philosophical Essays,* 129–65. Princeton, NJ.
McClain, T. Davina. 1998. "When Families Fight: Aeschylus' *Seven against Thebes* and Aristophanes' *Lysistrata.*" Unpublished paper read at the meeting of the Classical Association of the Middle West and South. Charlottesville, VA.
McComiskey, B. 2002. *Gorgias and the New Sophistic Rhetoric.* Carbondale, IL.
McCoy, Marina. 2007. *Plato on the Rhetoric of Philosophers and Sophists.* Cambridge.
McDonald, Marianne. 2007. "Rhetoric and Tragedy: Weapons of Mass Persuasion." In Ian Worthington, ed., *A Companion to Greek Rhetoric,* 473–89. Oxford.
McGlew, J. F. 2002. *Citizens on Stage: Comedy and Political Culture in the Athenian Democracy.* Ann Arbor, MI.
———. 2004. "'Speak on My Behalf': Persuasion and Purification in Aristophanes' *Wasps.*" *Arethusa* 37: 11–36.
Mendelsohn, Daniel. 2002. *Gender and the City in Euripides' Political Plays.* Oxford.
Mendelson, Michael. 2002. *Many Sides: A Protagorean Approach to the Theory, Practice, and Pedagogy of Argument.* Dordrecht.
Michelakis, Pantelis. 2006. *Euripides: Iphigenia at Aulis.* Duckworth Companions to Greek and Roman Tragedy. London.
Michelini, Ann N. 1987. *Euripides and the Tragic Tradition.* Madison, WI.
Mirhady, David. 2009. "Is the Wasps' Anger Democratic?" In J. R. C. Cousland, James

Rutherford Hume, and Martin Cropp, eds., *The Play of Texts and Fragments: Essays in Honour of Martin Cropp*, 371–88. *Mnemosyne* Supp. 314. Leiden.

Mitscherling, Jeff. 2003. "Socrates and the Comic Poets." *Apeiron: A Journal for Ancient Philosophy and Science* 36: 67–72.

Morgan, Teresa. 2007. "Rhetoric and Education." In Ian Worthington, ed., *A Companion to Greek Rhetoric*, 303–19. Oxford.

Most, Glenn W. 1994. "The Use of Endoxa: Philosophy and Rhetoric in the *Rhetoric*." In David Furley and Alexander Nehamas, eds., *Aristotle's "Rhetoric": Philosophical Essays*, 167–99. Princeton, NJ.

Muir, J. V. 2001. *Alcidamas: The Works and Fragments*. London.

Müller, D. 1974. "Die Verspottung der metaphorischen Ausdruckweise durch Aristophanes." In U. Reinhardt and K. Sallman, eds., *Musa jocosa: Arbeiten über Humor und Witz, Komik and Komödie der Antike (Festschrift für Andreas Theirfelder zum 70. Geburtstag)*. Hildesheim.

Müller-Strübing, Hermann. 1873. *Aristophanes und die historische Kritik: Polemische studien zur Geschichte von Athen im fünften Jahrhundert vor Ch.* Leipzig.

Murphy, Charles T. 1938. "Aristophanes and the Art of Rhetoric." *HSCP* 49: 69–113.

Naiden, Fred. 2010. "The Legal (and Other) Trials of Orestes." In Edward M. Harris, Delfim F. Leão, and P. J. Rhodes, eds., *Law and Drama in Ancient Greece*, 61–77. London.

Neil, Robert A. 1901. *The Knights of Aristophanes*. Cambridge.

Newiger, Hans-Joachim. 1957. *Metapher und Allegorie: Studien zu Aristophanes*. Zetemata 16. Munich.

Nightingale, Andrea W. 1995. *Genres in Dialogue: Plato and the Construct of Philosophy*. Cambridge.

Noël, Marie-Pierre. 2000. "Aristophanes et les intellectuels: Le portrait de Socrate et des sophistes dan les *Nubes*." In Jean LeClant and Jacques Jouanna, eds., *Le théâtre grec antique: La comédie; Actes du 10ème colloque de la villa Kérylos à Beaulieu-sur-Mer, les 1er et 2 octobre 1999*, 111–28. Cahiers de la Villa Kérylos 8. Paris.

Nussbaum, Martha. 1980. "Aristophanes and Socrates on Learning Practical Wisdom." In Jeffrey Henderson, ed., *Aristophanes: Essays in Interpretation*, 43–97. Yale Classical Studies 26. New Haven, CT.

Ober, Josiah. 1989. *Mass and Elite in Democratic Athens: Rhetoric, Ideology, and the Power of the People*. Princeton, NJ.

———. 1998. *Political Dissent in Democratic Athens: Intellectual Critics of Popular Rule*. Princeton, NJ.

———. 2008. *Democracy and Knowledge: Innovation and Learning in Classical Athens*. Princeton, NJ.

Ober, Josiah, and Barry Strauss. 1990. "Drama, Political Rhetoric, and the Discourse of the Athenian Democracy." In John J. Winkler and Froma I. Zeitlin, eds., *Nothing to Do with Dionysos?: Athenian Drama in Its Social Context*, 237–70. Princeton, NJ.

O'Higgins, Laurie. 2003. *Women and Humor in Classical Greece*. Cambridge.

Olson, S. D. 1990. "Economics and Ideology in Aristophanes' *Wealth*." *HSCP* 93: 223–42.

———. 2002. *Aristophanes: Acharnians*. Oxford.

———. 2007. *Broken Laughter: Select Fragments of Greek Comedy*. Oxford.

———. 2010a. "Comedy, Politics, and Society." In Gregory W. Dobrov, ed., *Brill's Companion to the Study of Greek Comedy*, 35–69. Leiden.

———. 2010b. "The Comic Poet Pherecrates, a War-Casualty of the Late 410s B.C." *JHS* 130: 49–50.
O'Regan, Daphne Elizabeth. 1992. *Rhetoric, Comedy, and the Violence of Language in Aristophanes' "Clouds."* Oxford.
O'Sullivan, Neil. 1992. *Alcidamas, Aristophanes, and the Beginnings of Greek Stylistic Theory.* Hermes Einzelschriften 60. Stuttgart.
———. 1993. "Plato and ἡ καλουμένη ῥητορική." *Mnemosyne* 46: 87–89.
Papageorgiou, Nikolaos. 2004a. "Ambiguities in *Kreitton Logos?*" *Mnemosyne* 57: 284–94.
———. 2004b. "Prodicus and the Agon of the *Logoi* in Aristophanes' *Clouds.*" *QUCC* n.s. 78: 61–69.
———. 2004c. "Rhetoric and Arithmetic in Aristophanes' *Wasps.*" *Maia* 56: 525–35.
Parker, L. P. E. 1997. *The Songs of Aristophanes.* Oxford.
Patzer, Andrea. 1994. "Sokrates in den Fragmenten der attischen Komödie." In A. Bierl and P. von Möllendorf, eds., *Orchestra: Drama-Mythos-Bühne*, 50–81. Leipzig.
Pendrick, Gerard J. 1998. "Plato and RHETORIKH." *RhM* 141: 10–23.
———. 2002. *Antiphon the Sophist: The Fragments.* Cambridge.
Peppler, Charles W. 1910. "The Termination –ικός, as Used by Aristophanes for Comic Effect." *AJP* 31: 428–44.
Pernot, L. 2005. *Rhetoric in Antiquity.* Trans. W. E. Higgins. Washington, DC.
Piltz, W. 1934. *Der Rhetor im attischen Staat.* Leipzig.
Platter, Charles. 2007. *Aristophanes and the Carnival of Genres.* Baltimore.
Podlecki, A. J. 1998. *Perikles and His Circle.* London.
Pontani, Filippomaria. 2009. "Demosthenes, Parody, and the *Frogs.*" *Mnemosyne* 62: 401–16.
Pope, Maurice. 1988. "Thucydides and Democracy." *Historia* 37: 276–96.
Poulakos, John. 1995. *Sophistical Rhetoric in Classical Greece.* Columbia, SC.
Poulakos, Takis, and David J. Depew, eds. 2004. *Isocrates and Civic Education.* Austin, TX.
Poster, Carol. 1997. "Aristotle's *Rhetoric* against Rhetoric: Unitarian Reading and Esoteric Hermeneutics." *AJP* 118: 219–49.
Pritchard, D. M. 2012. "Aristophanes and De Ste. Croix: The Value of Old Comedy as Evidence for Athenian Popular Culture." *Antichthon* 44: 14–51.
Raaflaub, Kurt A. 1980. "Des freien Burgers Recht der freien Rede: Ein Beitrag zur Begriffs- und Sozialgeschichte der athenischen Demokratie." In Werner Eck, Hartmut Galsterer, and Hartmut Wolff, eds., *Studien zur antiken Sozialgeschichte: Festschrift Friedrich Vittinghoff*, 7–57. Cologne and Vienna.
———. 2003. "Stick and Glue: The Function of Tyranny in Fifth-Century Athenian Democracy." In Kathryn A. Morgan, ed., *Popular Tyranny: Sovereignty and Its Discontents in Ancient Greece*, 59–93. Austin, TX.
Race, William H. 1982. *The Classical Priamel from Homer to Boethius. Mnemosyne* Supp. 74. Leiden.
Radermacher, Ludwig. 1951. *Artium scriptores: Reste der voraristotelischen Rhetorik.* SAWW 227.3. Vienna.
Reckford, Kenneth J. 1987. *Aristophanes' Old-and-New Comedy: Six Essays in Perspective.* Chapel Hill, NC.
Reinders, P. 2001. *Demos Pyknites: Untersuchungen zur Darstellung des Demos in der Alten Komödie.* Stuttgart.

Reitzammer, L. 2008. "Aristophanes' *Adôniazousai*." *CA* 27: 282–333.
Revermann, Martin. 2006. *Comic Business: Theatricality, Dramatic Technique, and Performance Contexts of Aristophanic Comedy*. Oxford.
Rhodes, P. J. 1972. *The Athenian Boule*. Oxford.
———. 1986. "Political Activity in Classical Athens." *JHS* 106: 132–44.
———. 2003. "Nothing to Do with Democracy: Athenian Drama and the *Polis*." *JHS* 123: 106–7.
———. 2010. "The 'Assembly' at the End of Aristophanes' *Knights*." In Edward M. Harris, Delfim F. Leäo, and P. J. Rhodes, eds., *Law and Drama in Ancient Greece*, 158–68. London.
———. 2011a. "Appeals to the Past in Classical Athens." In Gabriel Herman, ed., *Stability and Crisis in the Athenian Democracy*, 13–30. Stuttgart.
———. 2011b. "The Dionysia and Democracy Again." *CQ* 61: 71–74.
Roberts, W. R. 1904. "The New Rhetorical Fragment (Oxyrhynchus Papyri, Part III., Pp. 27–30) in Relation to the Sicilian Rhetoric of Corax and Tisias." *CR* 18: 18–21.
Robson, James. 2009. *Aristophanes: An Introduction*. London.
Roisman, Hanna M. 2007. "Right Rhetoric in Homer." In Ian Worthington, ed., *A Companion to Greek Rhetoric*, 429–48. Oxford.
Romer, F. E. 1998. "Good Intentions and the ὁδὸς ἡ κόρακας." In G. W. Dobrov, ed., *The City as Comedy: Society and Representation in Athenian Drama*, 51–74. Chapel Hill, NC.
Romilly, Jacqueline de. 1992. *The Great Sophists in Periclean Athens*. Trans. J. Lloyd. Oxford. 1992.
Rose, Peter. 1976. "Sophocles' *Philoctetes* and the Teaching of the Sophists." *HSCP* 80: 49–105.
Roselli, David Kawalko. 2011. *Theater of the People: Spectators and Society in Ancient Athens*. Austin, TX.
Rosen, Ralph M. 2004. "Aristophanes' *Frogs* and the Contest of Homer and Hesiod." *TAPA* 134: 295–322.
Rosenbloom, D. 2002. "From *poneros* to *pharmakos:* Theater, Social Drama, and Revolution in Athens, 428–404 B.C.E." *CA* 21: 283–346.
———. 2009. "Staging Rhetoric in Athens." In Erik Gunderson, ed., *The Cambridge Companion to Ancient Rhetoric*, 194–211. Cambridge.
Rothfield, Tom. 1999. *Classical Comedy: Armoury of Laughter, Democracy's Bastion of Defence; Introducing a Law of Opposites*. Lanham, MD.
Rothwell, Kenneth S. 1990. *Politics and Persuasion in Aristophanes' "Ecclesiazusae."* Mnemosyne Supp. 101. Leiden.
———. 2007. *Nature, Culture, and the Origins of Greek Comedy: A Study of Animal Choruses*. Cambridge.
Rowe, C. J. 1986. "The Argument and Structure of Plato's *Phaedrus*." *PCPS* 32: 106–25.
Rusten, Jeffrey, ed. 2011. *The Birth of Comedy: Texts, Documents, and Art from Athenian Comic Competitions, 486–280*. Baltimore.
Saetta Cottone, Rossella. 2005. *Aristofane e la poetica dell' ingiuria: Per una introduzione alla "loidoria" comica*. Rome.
Scharffenberger, Elizabeth W. 1995. "A Tragic *Lysistrata?* Jocasta in the 'Reconciliation Scene' of the *Phoenician Women*." *RhM* 138: 312–36.
———. 1998. "Parody, Satire, Irony, and Politics: From Euripides' *Orestes* to Aristophanes' *Frogs*." *T&P* 19: 111–22.

———. 2007. "*Deinon Eribremetas:* The Sound and Sense of Aeschylus in Aristophanes' *Frogs.*" *CW* 100: 229–49.
———. 2008. "Aristophanic Imaginings: Reflections on Martin Revermann's *Comic Business.*" *International Journal of the Classical Tradition* 15: 428–39.
Schiappa, Edward. 1990a. "Did Plato Coin *Rhêtorikê?*" *AJP* 111: 460–73.
———. 1990b. "Neo-Sophistic Rhetorical Criticism or the Historical Reconstruction of Sophistic Doctrine?" *Philosophy and Rhetoric* 23: 192–217.
———. 1991. "Sophistic Rhetoric: Oasis or Mirage." *Rhetoric Review* 10: 5–18.
———. 1994. "Plato and ἡ καλουμένη ῥητορική: A Response to O'Sullivan." *Mnemosyne* 47: 512–14.
———. 1999. *The Beginnings of Rhetorical Theory in Classical Greece.* New Haven, CT.
———. 2003. *Protagoras and Logos: A Study in Greek Philosophy and Rhetoric.* 2nd ed. Columbia, SC.
Schiappa, Edward, and Jim Hamm. 2007. "Rhetorical Questions." In Ian Worthington, ed., *A Companion to Greek Rhetoric,* 3–15. Oxford.
Schwinge, Ernst-Richard. 1997. *Griechische Tragödie und zeitgenössische Rezeption: Aristophanes und Gorgias; Zur Frage einer angemessenen Tragödiendeutung.* Berichte aus den Sitzungen der Joachim Jungius-Gesellschaft der Wissenschaften, Hamburg, 15.2. Hamburg.
———. 2002. "Aristophanes und Euripides." In Andrea Ercolani, ed., *Spoudaiogeloion: Form und Funktion der Verspottung in der aristophanischen Komödie,* 3–43. Stuttgart.
Scodel, Ruth. 1980. *The Trojan Trilogy of Euripides.* Hypomnemata 60. Göttingen.
Scullion, S. 2003. "Euripides and Macedon, or the Silence of the *Frogs.*" *CQ* n.s. 53: 389–400.
———. 2006. "The Opening of Euripides' *Archelaus.*" In Douglas Cairns and Vayos Liapis, eds., *Dionysalexandros: Essays on Aeschylus and His Fellow Tragedians in Honour of Alexander F. Garvie,* 185–200. Swansea.
Seaford, Richard. 2000. "The Social Function of Attic Tragedy: A Response to Jasper Griffin." *CQ* 50: 30–44.
———. 2003. "Tragic Tyranny." In Kathryn A. Morgan, ed., *Popular Tyranny: Sovereignty and Its Discontents in Ancient Greece,* 95–115. Austin, TX.
Segal, Charles P. 1961. "The Character and Cults of Dionysus and the Unity of the *Frogs.*" *HSCP* 65: 207–42.
Seidensticker, Bernd. 1982. *Palintonos Harmonia: Studien zu komischen Elementen in der griechischen Tragödie.* Hypomnemata 72. Göttingen.
Sfyroeras, Pavlos. 1995. "What Wealth Has to Do with Dionysus: From Economy to Poetics in Aristophanes' *Plutus.*" *GRBS* 36: 231–61.
———. 2008. "Πόθος Εὐριπίδου: Reading *Andromeda* in Aristophanes' *Frogs.*" *AJP* 129: 299–317.
Shear, Julia L. 2011. *Polis and Revolution: Responding to Oligarchy in Classical Athens.* Cambridge.
Sidwell, Keith. 2009. *Aristophanes the Democrat.* Cambridge.
Silva, Maria de Fátima. 2007. "Um Deus em busca de identidade: Dioniso em *Rãs.*" *Minerva* 20: 53–64.
———. 2010. "Euripides' *Orestes:* The Chronicle of a Trial." In Edward M. Harris, Delfim F. Leão, and P. J. Rhodes, eds., *Law and Drama in Ancient Greece,* 77–93. London.
Simmons, Robert Holschuh. 2012. "Cleon's Pederasty of the *Demos?* The Case of Aristo-

phanes' *Knights*." Unpublished paper read at the meeting of the Classical Association of the Middle West and South. Baton Rouge, LA.

Slater, Niall W. 1998. "Performing the City in *Birds*." In G. W. Dobrov, ed., *The City as Comedy: Society and Representation in Athenian Drama*, 75–94. Chapel Hill, NC.

———. 2002. *Spectator Politics: Metatheatre and Performance in Aristophanes*. Philadelphia.

Sluiter, I., and R. M. Rosen, eds. 2004. *Free Speech in Classical Antiquity*. Mnemosyne Supp. 254. Leiden.

Sommerstein, A. H. 1980. "Notes on Aristophanes' *Knights*." *CQ* 30: 46–56.

———. 1984. "Aristophanes and the Demon Poverty." *CQ* 34: 314–33.

———. 1993. "Cleophon and the Restaging of *Frogs*." In A. H. Sommerstein, S. Halliwell, J. J. Henderson, and B. Zimmermann, eds., *Tragedy, Comedy, and the Polis*, 461–76. Bari. Reprinted in *Talking about Laughter and Other Studies in Greek Comedy*, 254–71. Oxford, 2009.

———. 1996. "How to Avoid Being a *Komodoumenos*." *CQ* 46: 327–56.

———. 2000. "Platon, Eupolis, and the 'Demagogue-Comedy.'" In F. D. Harvey and J. Wilkins, eds., *The Rivals of Aristophanes: Studies in Athenian Old Comedy*, 437–51. London.

———. 2005. "An Alternative Democracy and an Alternative to Democracy in Aristophanic Comedy." In U. Bultrighini, ed., *Democrazia e antidemocrazia nel mondo greco: Atti del convegno internazionale di studi, Chieti, 9–11 aprile 2003*, 195–207 (discussion, 229–33). Alexandria. Reprinted with corrections and additions in *Talking about Laughter and Other Studies in Greek Comedy*, 204–22. Oxford, 2009.

Sousa e Silva, Maria de Fátima. 1987–88. "Crítica à retórica na comédia de Aristófanes." *Humanitas* 39–40: 34–104.

Spielvogel, Jörg. 2003. "Die politische Position des athenischen Komödiendichters Aristophanes." *Historia* 52: 3–22.

Sprute, Jürgen. 1994. "Aristotle and the Legitimacy of Rhetoric." In David Furley and Alexander Nehamas, eds., *Aristotle's "Rhetoric": Philosophical Essays*, 117–28. Princeton, NJ.

Ste Croix, G. E. M. de. 1972. "The Political Outlook of Aristophanes." Appendix 29 in *The Origins of the Peloponnesian War*, 355–76. Ithaca, NY.

Storey, Ian C. 1985. "Eupolis 352 K." *Phoenix* 39: 154–57.

———. 1988. "Thrasymachus at Athens: Aristophanes fr. 205 (*Daitales*)." *Phoenix* 42: 212–18.

———. 1993. "The Dates of Aristophanes' *Clouds II* and Eupolis' *Baptai*: A Reply to E. C. Kopff." *AJP* 114: 71–84.

———. 1995. "*Wasps* 1284–91 and the Portrait of Cleon in *Wasps*." *Scholia* 4: 3–23.

———. 2003. *Eupolis: Poet of Old Comedy*. Oxford.

———. 2011. *Fragments of Old Comedy*. 3 vols. Loeb Classical Library. Cambridge, MA.

Strauss, Barry. 1997. "The Problem of Periodization: The Case of the Peloponnesian War." In Mark Golden and Peter Toohey, eds., *Inventing Ancient Culture: Historicism, Periodization, and the Ancient World*, 165–75. London.

Stadter, Philip A. 1989. *A Commentary on Plutarch's Pericles*. Chapel Hill, NC.

Suter, Ann C. 1997–98. "Back from the Dead: Euripides' *Orestes* and Aristophanes' *Frogs*." *NECN* 25: 3–7.

Sutton, D. F. 1987. *Two Lost Plays of Euripides*. New York.

Taaffe, Lauren K. 1994. *Aristophanes and Women*. London.

Tell, Håkan. 2009. "Wisdom for Sale? The Sophists and Money." *CP* 104: 13–33.
———. 2011. *Plato's Counterfeit Sophists*. Cambridge, MA.
Telò, Mario. 2007. *Eupolidis Demi*. Testi con commento filologico 14. Florence.
Timmerman, David M., and Edward Schiappa. 2010. *Classical Greek Rhetorical Theory and the Disciplining of Discourse*. Cambridge.
Tindale, Christopher W. 2010. *Reason's Dark Champions: Constructive Strategies of Sophistic Argument*. Columbia, SC.
Tordoff, Robert. 2007. "Aristophanes' *Assembly Women* and Plato, *Republic* Book 5." In Robin Osborne, ed., *Debating the Athenian Cultural Revolution: Art, Literature, Philosophy, and Politics, 430–380 B.C.*, 242–63. Cambridge.
Usher, S. 1999. *Greek Oratory: Tradition and Originality*. Oxford.
Versnel, Henk S. 1995. "Religion and Democracy." In Walter Eder, ed., *Die athenische Demokratie im vierten vorchristlichen Jahrhundert*, 367–87. Stuttgart.
Voelke, Pierre. 2004. "Euripide, héros et poète aristophanien (à propos des *Acharniens* et des *Thesmophories*)." In Claude Calame, ed., *Poétique d'Aristophane et langue d'Euripide en dialogue*, 117–38. Lausanne.
Walsh, Philip. 2009. "A Study in Reception: The British Debates over Aristophanes' Politics and Influence." *Classical Receptions Journal* 1: 55–72.
Wardy, Robert. 1996. *The Birth of Rhetoric: Gorgias, Plato, and Their Successors*. London.
———. 2009. "The Philosophy of Rhetoric and the Rhetoric of Philosophy." In Erik Gunderson, ed., *The Cambridge Companion to Ancient Rhetoric*, 43–58. Cambridge.
Westlake, H. D. 1980. "The *Lysistrata* and the War." *Phoenix* 34: 38–54.
Whitehead, David. 1977. *The Ideology of the Athenian Metic*. PCPS Supp. 4. Cambridge.
Whitehorne, John. 2002. "Aristophanes' Representations of 'Intellectuals.'" *Hermes* 130: 28–35.
Wilkins, J. 2000. *The Boastful Chef: The Discourse of Food in Ancient Greek Comedy*. Oxford.
Willi, Andreas. 2003. *The Languages of Aristophanes: Aspects of Linguistic Variation in Classical Attic Greek*. Oxford.
Willink, C. W. 1986. *Euripides: Orestes*. Oxford.
Wilson, N. G. 2007a. *Aristophanea: Studies in the Text of Aristophanes*. Oxford.
———. 2007b. *Aristophanis: Fabulae*. 2 vols. Oxford.
Wilson, Peter. 2007. "*Nikē*'s Cosmetics: Dramatic Victory, the End of Comedy, and Beyond." In Chris Kraus, Simon Goldhill, Helene P. Foley, and Jas Elsner, eds., *Visualizing the Tragic: Drama, Myth, and Ritual in Greek Art and Literature; Essays in Honour of Froma Zeitlin*, 257–87. Oxford.
———. 2009. "Tragic Honours and Democracy: Neglected Evidence for the Politics of the Athenian Dionysia." *CQ* 59: 8–29.
Wise, Jennifer. 2008. "Tragedy as 'An Augury of a Happy Life.'" *Arethusa* 41: 381–410.
Wohl, Victoria. 2009. "Rhetoric of the Athenian Citizen." In Erik Gunderson, ed., *The Cambridge Companion to Ancient Rhetoric*, 162–77. Cambridge.
Worthington, Ian, ed. 2007. *A Companion to Greek Rhetoric*. Oxford.
Yunis, Harvey. 1991. "How Do the People Decide? Thucydides on Periclean Rhetoric and Civic Instruction." *AJP* 112: 179–200.
Zimmerman, Christiane. 1993. *Der Antigone-Mythos in der antiken Literatur und Kunst*. Mainz.
Zimmermann, Bernhard. 2005. "*Spoudaiogeloion:* Poetik und Politik in den Komödien des Aristophanes." *Gymnasium* 112: 531–46.

Zumbrunnen, John G. 2008. *Silence and Democracy: Athenian Politics in Thucydides' History.* University Park, PA.
———. 2012. *Aristophanic Comedy and the Challenge of Democratic Citizenship.* Rochester, NY.
Zuntz, Günther. 1949. "Once Again the Antiphontean Tetralogies." *MH* 6: 100–103.

Index locorum

Aristophanes
  Acharnians
    37–39, 54
    496–556, **52, 56–60**
    504–8, **58**
    513–14, **58–59**
    555–56, **59**
    627–28, **60**
    630–42, **61–62**
    656–58, **62**
    680–88, **63–64**
  Banqueters
    fr. 205, 5, **40–41**, 42, 64, 97
    fr. 233, 5, 41
  Birds
    371–82, **127–28**
    460–66, **128**
    1074–75, **124**
    1280–84, **129**
    1553–64, **124**
    1570–71, **130**
    1583–85, **130**
    1694–1705, **124–25**
  Clouds
    97–99, **84**
    101–4, **85**
    112–18, **85**
    551–59, **116**
    882–85, **90**
    934–38, **92**
    941–60, **92–94**
    1421–24, **94–95**
    1437–51, **95–96**
    1478–85, **96**
  Frogs
    676–85, **164**
    686–87, **168**
    779–80, **171**
    856–59, **173**
    949–50, **174**
    953–54, **174**
    1418–21, **176**
  Knights
    41–43, **65**
    90–94, **65**
    99–100, **66**

137, **66**
164–67, **66**
191–93, **67**
217–19, **67**
274–83, **69**
294–95, **69–70**
303–12, **70**
324–27, **70–71**
344–52, **72–73**
395–96, **74**
475–79, **74**
703–4, **75**
752–55, **76**
973–84, **98–99**
1111–30, **77–78**
1209–10, **79**
1261–63, **80**
1316–18, **99**
1340–44, **13, 80–81**
1375–80, **81**
1381–83, **81–82**
Lysistrata
    527–28, **137–38**
Peace
    532–34, **149–50**
    632–37, **110–11**
Thesmophoriazusae
    78–79, **140–41**
    301–11, **141**
    335–39, **141**
    352–67, **142–43**
    381–82, **143**
    528–30, **143–44**
    1143–44, **140**
Wasps
    409–14, **100–101**
    471–72, **101**
    488–90, **101–2**
    559–96, **103**
    666–71, **103–4**
    679–86, **97**
    885–90, **104–5**
    907–30, **106–8**
    1003–7, **108–9**
Fragments
    fr. 32, **123**
    fr. 328, **123**
    fr. 392, **117**

fr. 424, **98**
fr. 488, **150**
fr. 506, **117**
fr. 581, **123**
fr. 595, **117**
fr. 706, **39n**
Archippus
    Rhinon
        frr. 42–44, **180**
    Fragments
        fr. 14, **180**
        fr. 27, **180**
        fr. 30, **180**
Aristotle
    Nichomachean Ethics
        9.7.1167b17, **29**
    Rhetoric
        1.1.5.1354a, **9**
        1.2.7.1356a27–28, **51**
        1.3.2.1358b2–3, **1**
        1.3.2.1358b4–5, **179**
        1.4.9.1360a3–6, **115**
        1.4.12.1360a25–27, **133**
        1.11.8.1370b1, **162**
        2.6.20.1384b9–11, **44**
        3.9.10.1410b3–5, **23, 26**
Callias
    fr. 21, **49**
Cephisodorus
    fr. 13, **44**
Cicero
    De inventione
        2.2.6, **8n**
Comica Fragmenta Adespota
    fr. 115, **41**
    fr. 438, **43**
    fr. 587, **490**
    fr. 591, **44**
    fr. 649, **44**
    fr. 701, **45–46**
    fr. 930–31, **41**
    fr. 1095, **39**
Crates
    fr. 30, **42**
    fr. 45, **39**
    fr. 59, **42**
Cratinus
    Dionysalexandros

Index locorum

Hypothesis 44–48, **47**
Fragments
    fr. 52, **39**
    fr. 324, **48**
    fr. 327, **48**
    fr. 353, **44**
    fr. 375, **43**
    fr. 381, **41**
    fr. 476, **40**
Cratinus Junior
    fr. 7, **182**
Diodorus Siculus
  Library
    12.53.3–5, **3**
Diogenes Laertius
  Lives of the Eminent Philosophers
    3.11, **32–33**
Epicharmus
    fr. 76, **26**
    fr. 77, **26**
    fr. 78, **26**
    fr. 113, **28**
    fr. 136, **28, 29, 32–33**
    fr. 140, **31**
    fr. 142, **29**
    fr. 144, **27**
    fr. 145, **23, 26**
    fr. 146, **29–30, 32–33**
    fr. 161, **27**
    fr. 163, **27**
    fr. 175, **27**
    fr. 184, **27**
    fr. 219, **27**
[Epicharmus]
    fr. 276, **32–33**
Eupolis
  Aiges
    fr. 17, **118**
  Cities
    fr. 220, **116–17**
  Demes
    fr. 99.23–34, **119**
    fr. 99.31, **122**
    fr. 102, **20, 122**
    fr. 103, **122**
    fr. 108, **39n, 122**
    fr. 115, **120**
    fr. 116, **117, 122**
    fr. 118, **117**
    fr. 126, **121**
  Marikas
    fr. 192 13–15, **118**
    fr. 192.135–36, **116**
  Fragments
    fr. 76, **123**
    fr. 98, **123**
    fr. 331, **116**
    fr. 386, **117, 118**
Euripides
  Andromeda
    fr. 133, **162**
  Antigone
    fr. 172, **154**
  Auge
    fr. 275, **156–57**
  Orestes
    696–701, **159**
  Stheneboea
    fr. 661.1, **183**
Hermippus
    fr. 47, **48**
Lysias
  Orations
    21.1, **147**
    30.13, **167**
Nicostratus
    fr. 29, **183**
    fr. 30, **183**
Pherecrates
    fr. 56, **40**
    fr. 153, **40**
Phrynichus
    fr. 3, **40**
    fr. 19, **39**
Plato
  Protagoras
    311e–12e, **38n**
  Theaetetus
    152e, **28**
Plato Comicus
    fr. 202, **42–43n**
Plutarch
  De Sera numinis vindicta
    15.559a–b, **29**
  Life of Pericles
    3.7, **120**

8.2–3, **45–46**
13.15–16.160e, **45**
15.2–3, **46**
32, **49**
Protagoras
    fr. 80B1, **89**
    fr. 80B6a, **88**
    fr. 80B6b, **89**
Teleclides
    fr. 2, **43–44**

Thucydides
    History of the Peloponnesian War
        2.65, **46**
        3.36.6, **3**
        3.38.4–7, **3–4, 54, 56**
        8.1.1, **134**
Thugenides
    fr. 1, **43**

adolcschein, 117
Aeschylus: in *Clouds*, 172; in *Frogs*, 151, 153, 162–64, 166, 170–78; language of, 41–42; persuasive speech in, 16; as savior of Athens, 173, 177; in Sicily, 41–42
agon: of *Clouds*, 87–89; of *Frogs*, 164, 170, 172–77; of *Knights*, 69–74; of *Lysistrata*, 135–37, 139; of *Wasps*, 102–4
Agoracritus, 80–82, 99
alazōn, 43
Alcibiades, 5, 123; as speaker, 20; comic views of, 116
Alcimus, 31–32, 34
allegory, in A., 126
Amphitheos, 55, 60, 87
antilegein, 39
Antiphon, 38
antitheton, 14
Arai, N., 164n
Archedemus, 164
Archelas, meaning of, 66–67, 68

Archeptolemus, 72
Archippus, 179–80
Aristophanes: *Acharnians*, 19–20, 51–52, 53–64, 87, 97, 99, 109, 113, 129, 149, 171; *Assemblywomen*, 180–81, 182; *Babylonians*, 53; *Banqueters*, 5, 6, 14, 40–41, 42, 50, 64, 83; *Birds*, 20, 123–32; civic crown awarded to, 148, 169–70; *Clouds*, 31, 82–97, 113, 177; early career of, 5–6; *Frogs*, 21, 146–78, 183; ideology of, 16–19, 22, 43, 52, 60–61, 63, 71, 93, 100, 113, 131–32, 168; *Knights*, 13–14, 20, 64–82, 83, 99, 109, 113, 119, 121, 131, 138, 177; *Lysistrata*, 21, 133–34, 135–39, 155; *Peace*, 52, 110–12; political career of, 181; as source for the history of rhetoric, 5–7, 11–12; style of, 183; *Thesmophoriazusae*, 139–45, 150–51, 157–58, 171; *Wasps*, 20, 31, 35, 97–109, 113, 123; *Wealth*, 123, 181–82
Aristotle: on comedy, 11–12, 44; on the

development of rhetoric, 7–10, 16, 24–26, 182; on rhetoric and politics, 1–2, 9, 51
Aspasia, 48–49, 50
Assembly: in *Acharnians,* 52, 53–56; attendance at, 54; in *Congresswomen,* 140–41; dysfunctional, 20, 52, 54–56, 61–63, 66, 100, 113; in *Knights,* 20; procedures in, 140–41; as spectators, 1, 3–4, 56, 57; in *Thesmophoriazusae,* 140–41, 143; trials in, 159; of women, 140; *see also* Council; deliberation; success, of the Demos

Bakola, E., 47
Bdelycleon, 100–104, 108
Borthwick, E. K., 153
Braun, T., 120–21
Brauw, M. de, 11
Brock, R., 102n
Brockmann, C., 53n
Bruce, Lenny, 146
Burian, P., 16n, 156n
Burnett, Carol, 146n

Callias, 83, 118
Carter, D., 156n
Christ, M., 16n
City Dionysia, 147–48
class: and the Demos, 109; in *Wasps,* 102, 109
Cleigenes, 169n
Cleitophon, 174–75
Cleon, 6, 7, 113, 175; in *Acharnians,* 53, 62; career of, 5; compared to Pericles, 68, 75; courts corrupted by, 98–99, 100, 103, 105; death of, 110; in Eupolis, 116; as flatterer, 64, 67; in *Knights,* 66–77, 79–82; language of, 41–42; as monster, 70, 99; oratory of, 66; privileges of, 75–76; as protector, 104; as shouter, 69, 75, 101, 111, 173; in Thucydides, 3–4, 54, 56, 62–63; in *Wasps,* 100

Cleophon, 164–68, 169; and oligarchy, 166; reputation of, 167
Cloudcuckooland, as reconfigured Athens, 126, 129–30
Cole, T., 10, 11, 12, 13n, 25, 26, 34, 88
comedy: Aristotle on, 11–12; ideology of, 17; in Sicily, 19, 25–35; as source for rhetoric, 7–8
Compton-Engle, G., 55n, 148n
Connor, W. R., 70
Corax, 9, 19, 24–25; historicity of, 24
Council: A.'s faith in, 139, 168; A.'s service in, 181; A.'s staging of, 18; Cleon's abuse of, 67; deliberations of, 52, 64, 112, 113; in the *Knights,* 73–74, 113; oligarchic, 166; and the Proboulos, 135–36; trials before, 165; *see also* Assembly; deliberation; success, of the Demos
courts: in *Acharnians,* 63–64; A.'s mistrust of, 99, 100–101; A.'s staging of, 18; Cleon's corruption of, 98–99, 100, 103, 105; dysfunction of, 20, 97–99, 105, 113, 150; in Old Comedy, 44; translocation of, 104–5; as unnecessary, 99, 109, 104–5, 113; in *Wasps,* 97–109; *see also* deliberation
Crates, 37, 42
Cratinus, 37, 38, 41, 44; language of, 41–42; on Pericles, 47–48

debate: as central to comedy, 26; in Old Comedy, 39; *see also* agon; deliberation
deliberation, 4, 17, 21, 51–52, 54, 60–61, 72, 127–28, 145, 170, 182; A.'s faith in, 100, 113; barriers to, 65; in *Birds,* 126; broadened inclusion in, 72–73, 79n, 127–28, 137–39, 145, 174, 181; Cleon's effects on, 64, 67–68; contrasted with spectating, 1, 53–54, 60, 72, 75–76, 80, 175; displayed to foreigners, 62; and drinking, 65–66; dysfunctional, 55–56, 63–64, 69, 76, 80, 101, 111, 113, 158–60; and education, 94; in

Eupolis, 119; about Euripides, 172; in Euripides, 154–55; and flattery, 61–63, 65, 75–76, 79–81; and justice, 95; in *Knights,* 75, 109; and language, 82; in *Lysistrata,* 134–35; and the Sicilian expedition, 134–35; successful, 64, 66, 77, 79–80, 82, 96–97, 99, 103, 139, 141, 156; and zero-sum debate, 93; *see also* agon; Assembly; translocation
dēmagōgia, 100, 120, 122, 164; meaning of, 67–68
demēgorein, 119
democracy: A.'s criticism of, 52; A.'s dramatization of, 16; A.'s faith in, 113, 131; and free speech, 16; and language, 6; protection of, 130–31; restoration of, 153, 171–72; restricted participation in, 136–37; successful functioning of, 60–61; *see also* Assembly; Council; courts; deliberation; oligarchy; success, of the Demos; tyranny
Demos: anger of, 65, 171–73; A.'s faith in, 63, 93; authority of, 71; civic benefactors of, 148; deception of, 64; definition of, 3n; enslavement of, 102; Euripides rejected by, 163; identified with the theater audience, 94; judgment by, 21, 79, 100, 131–32, 158–60, 169, 171, 183–84; success of, 65–66, 77, 79, 82, 100, 109, 112–13, 129, 138, 139, 144, 145, 156, 159–60, 184; tyranny of, 101–2, 131; *see also* deliberation
Demos (*Knights*), 64–65, 76–82, 109, 113; rejuvenation of, 80–81
Demosthenes (*Knights*), 65
Demostratus, 135
dialegesthai, 39
diathesis, 38
Dicaeopolis, 20, 53–56, 82, 87, 109, 113, 149; as speaker, 52, 56–64
didaskaloi, 83
diēgēsis, 59, 106–7
Diodorus Siculus, 2, 5, 7
Dionysus (*Frogs*), 162, 176, 177

Dover, K. J., 86, 91n
drunkenness, as virtue, 65–66
Dunbar, N., 130n

Edmunds, L., 54n
education: aristocratic, 83; comedy on, 118; in *Clouds,* 82–97; and deliberation, 94; and language, 82–83, 92; and moral decadence, 90; and rhetoric, 2, 6, 7; and the Sophists, 91
eikos, 38–39
empire, Athenian, 2, 5–6, 20, 64, 69, 77, 102, 126, 131, 175, 177; economics of, 103–4, 109; nostalgia for, 109
Epicharmus, 19, 25–30; in Aristotle and Plato, 34; argumentation in, 28–29; date of, 33; debate scenes in, 26; formal rhetoric absent from, 30–31; forgeries of, 27n, 31–34; as influence on Athenian comedy, 35; and Pythagoreanism, 28; sources for, 28–29, 34; symposium scenes in, 29–30
epilogos, 57, 59–60, 106, 108, 128
epitropos, 111; see also *prostatēs*
ethics: in comedy, 91; and rhetoric, 91–92
Eupolis, 37–38, 116–18; *Baptai,* 123; compared to A., 119; *Demes,* 20, 118–19, 121–22; ideology of, 118–20; *Kolakes,* 83; on Pericles, 49; on Protagoras, 89
Euripides: in *Acharnians,* 149; *Andromeda,* 144, 152, 158, 162, 171, 177; *Antigone,* 154; *Archelaus,* 160–61; as anti-democratic, 131, 155, 157, 159–60, 171–72, 174–75; in *Clouds,* 149, 172; contrasted with Sophocles, 163; as corrupting influence, 91; as demagogue, 177; as democrat, 174; Demos' judgment of, 159–60, 163; in *Frogs,* 151, 162–78, 183; *Helen,* 144, 152, 158; *Hippolytus,* 157; *Hypsipyle,* 152, 153, 158, 162; *Iphigenia at Aulis,* 160; language and style of, 150, 153, 171, 172, 174, 176, 177; late career of, 151–52,

157; and Macedon, 160–61; misogyny of, 151, 158; *Oedipus,* 153; as opposed to peace, 150; *Orestes,* 152, 153, 158–59, 161, 171–72; *Palamedes,* 144, 151, 157; parodied by A., 57–58, 140, 144; in *Peace,* 149–50; *Phoenician Women,* 152, 153, 154–56, 158, 160, 161, 162; popularity of, 164, 171; restored reputation of, 158; as sophist, 117; superficial appeal of, 171, 172, 176; in *Thesmophoriazusae,* 140, 141, 143–45, 150–51, 157–58, 171; *Telephus,* 144; *Trojan Women,* 157–58; tongue of, 150; unpopularity of, 176; as villain, 151, 171

flattery: by Cleon, 62, 63, 64–65, 67, 75, of the Demos, 63, 64–65, 67, 69, 75, 76, 78–81; dangers of, 61–62, 65; of the Prytaneis, 75
Foley, H., 56
foreigners, included in deliberation, 73, 79n, 139n; *see also* inclusion
free speech; see *isēgoria; parrhēsia*

Gagarin, M., 25, 33
Gallagher, R. L., 58n
Gallego, J., 89n
gaping, as reaction to speech, 75, 76, 78, 80, 103–4
glōtta; see tongue
Gomme, A. W., 16
Gorgias: on persuasion, 9; on Palamedes, 157; rhetoric and style of, 3, 5, 6–7, 19, 51; and the Sophists, 8–9; visit to Athens by, 2–3, 5, 24, 35

Haldane, J. A., 140
Hansen, M., 100n
Haskins, E., 11
Heath, M., 16–17
Henderson, J., 16, 131, 132n

Hermes: in *Clouds,* 96; in *Peace,* 110–12
Hermippus, 48–49, 50, 116, 121
heroes, Athenian, 123–24; *see also* nostalgia
Hetton Logos and *Kreitton Logos,* 85–91, 92–94; moral components of, 90; in Protagoras, 89–91
Hubbard, T. K., 12, 13–14, 15, 106–7, 108, 130n, 168n
Hughes, A., 18
Hyperbolus, 111, 116

inclusion, of non-citizens in deliberation, 72–73, 127–28, 137–38, 139, 174, 181
Inlaw, 143–44
institutions, Athenian, in Old Comedy, 43–44, 49
isēgoria, 73

judgment; *see* deliberation
jurors, status of, 103–4

Kerferd, G. B., 8
Kerkhof, R., 30
Kinesias, 136, 138, 140
Kloss, G., 94n
Konstan, D., 16n
Kreitton Logos; see *Hetton Logos* and *Kreitton Logos*

Laches, 100, 105
laleō, 117–18, 175, 177
language: and age, 81–82, 94–96; analysis of, 9, 14, 37, 41; in *Clouds,* 20; comic criticism of, 40–42, 51, 81–82, 113; and cultural decadence, 113; and deliberation, 2, 82; distortion of, 42–43, 69, 80; education concerning, 82–83, 92; Eupolis' treatment of, 119–20; of Euripides, 150, 153, 171, 172, 174, 176, 177;

in Sicilian comedy, 26–30; as threat to the Demos, 21–22; unorthodox, 14, 40–41, 50–51, 81–82, 113; see also *logoi; Hetton Logos* and *Kreitton Logos*
Leontini, Athens' alliance with, 2–5
liturgies, in the restored democracy, 147–48
logoi: binary, 86; in *Clouds,* 85–91; Dikaios and Adikos, 86; metaphors concerning, 87; and *pragmata,* 88; in Protagoras, 20, 86, 88–91, 113; sophistic, 88; see also *Hetton Logos* and *Kreitton Logos*
Lysistratus, 6; language of, 41–42

MacDowell, D. M., 12
Macedon, and Euripides, 160–61
Marathon, 76–77, 80
Markantonatos, A., 148n
Mastronarde, D. J., 58n
McClain, T. D., 151
McGlew, J. F., 17, 47n, 109n, 135–36
Megarian decree, 110
Menander, rhetoric in, 182
metaphors: for protectors of the Demos, 70–71; for speech and oratory, 14–15, 40–41, 46, 48, 50, 62–63, 104, 119; transformation by, 87–88, 92
Mitscherling, J., 84n
Müller, D., 14
Murphy, C., 12, 56–59, 105–6, 107–8, 128, 137n, 143n, 168n
mythology, in Epicharmus' comedies, 26–27
Mytilene, debate over, 3–4

Naiden, F., 159
neologism, in comedy, 14, 40, 50; *see also* language, unorthodox
Newiger, H.-J., 87
Nicomachus, 166–67
nostalgia, Athenian, 69, 74, 76–77, 94, 109, 124, 175, 177, 180; *see also* empire

Ober, J., 2n, 17, 175, 180, 181–82
ochlos, 175; definition of, 165
Odysseus, as manipulative speaker, 149, 157
Old Comedy, 36–50; Athenian institutions in, 43–44, 49; formal rhetoric absent from, 39
oligarchy: aftermath of, 146–47; Athenian subjugation to, 123, 133–34, 135, 146, 168–69, 175; conspiracies for, 21, 149, 166; and limits on democracy, 21, 136–37
Olson, S. D., 33n, 53–54n
orality, 10–11, 60
oratory. *See* rhetoric; speeches
O'Sullivan, N., 12, 13, 14–15

Palamedes, 157–58; Euripides as, 176
Papageorgiou, N., 89n, 91n, 102n
parabasis: of *Acharnians,* 61–64, 75; of *Frogs,* 168–70; of *Knights,* 74, 76; *Lysistrata*'s lack of, 138
parrhēsia, 73, 183
Peace of Nicias, 115, 133
Peisetaerus, 20, 126–30; as *tyrannos,* 131
performance, of comedy, 17–18
Pericles: in A., 63–64, 110, 120–21; and Aspasia, 49; comic portrayals of, 19–20, 37, 40, 44–45, 50, 63, 75, 103–4, 110, 121; Eupolis' treatment of, 120, 121–22; as hero, 121–22; as Olympian god, 45–46; as orator, 40, 45–48, 122; redemption of, 120–22; in Thucydides, 47, 63; as tyrant, 46–47, 48
Persia, 141, 142, 144–45
persuasion, 1, 3, 9–10; in comedy, 16; as undemocratic, 20; *see also* deliberation; rhetoric; speeches
Pheidippides, 85, 87–92, 94–96
Pherecrates, 38

Philocleon, 31, 35, 100, 102, 104, 105, 107–10
Phrontisterion, 83, 92, 113
Phrynichus, 38, 182–83
pisteis, 57, 59, 106
Plato Comicus, 116, 165, 168
Plato: on change, 31–32; on rhetoric, 10–11, 24–25, 47; *Phaedrus*, 34; *Protagoras*, 83, 118; on the Sophists, 7–8, 84
plēthos, 103–4, 170; Cleon's use of, 73
Plutarch: on Pericles, 45–48, 120; on rhetoric, 45–46
Pnyx, 52, 53, 55, 56, 60, 76, 79; *see also* Assembly; translocation
Pope, M., 63n
probability, arguments from, 34, 38
Probouloi: authority of, 21, 135; in *Lysistrata*, 135–37, 139
Prodicus, 89n
prooimia, 13–14, 57, 61–62, 80–81, 106–7, 128
prosecutors, youth of, 20, 63–64, 94–95, 97–98, 105, 109
prostatēs tou dēmou, 78–79, 100, 111; meaning of, 70–71; *see also* Cleon; Demos
Protagoras: on *logoi*, 20, 88–91, 113; in Plato, 118
prothesis, 57, 59
Prytaneis: in *Acharnians*, 53–54; criticisms of, 73; in *Knights*, 75; in *Peace*, 112
Pythagoreanism, and Epicharmus, 28

Raaflaub, K., 67n
Race, W. H., 54–55n
Reinders, P., 61n, 78–79n
Revermann, M., 18
rhētores: in *Acharnians*, 97; and Cleon, 70–71; defined, 42–43, 97–98; in Eupolis, 122; female, 180; as manipulators, 111; production of, 77; and the Sicilian expedition, 134; and spectators, 63–64; and *synēgoroi*, 64, 97–98; and youth, 97

rhetoric: Aristotle on, 1, 10, 44; anxiety concerning, 9, 18, 20, 91–92, 182; and education, 2, 6; and ethics, 91–92; formal systems of, 7, 10–16, 18, 30, 34, 43, 49–50, 56–59, 105–8, 112–13, 117–18, 123, 128, 143, 168, 181–82; history and development of, 2, 6–10, 15–16, 18–20, 26, 34–35, 37, 83, 182; Plato on, 10, 47; Plutarch on, 45–46; in Sicily, 19, 24–25; of the Sophists, 8–11, 88, 92; terminology of, 12–14, 37–38, 49–50; and tyranny, 46–47; *see also* Gorgias; *Hetton Logos* and *Kreitton Logos*; speeches
rhētorikē, 38, 83
Rhodes, P. J., 76n, 147n
Roberts, W. R., 25n
Robson, J., 17n
Romer, F. E., 130n
Roselli, D. K., 94n
Rosenbloom, D., 17
Rothfield, T., 16–17n
Rothwell, K. S., 31, 180

Sansone, D., 58n
Sausage-Seller, 66–74; *agon* with Cleon, 69–74
Scharffenberger, E. W., 151, 153, 155
Schiappa, E., 10, 11, 12, 13n, 25, 26, 34, 59n, 88, 89
Scullion, S., 160–61
Seasons, A., 123
Sfyroeras, P., 163
Shear, J. L., 53n
shouting: associated with Cleon, 69, 75, 101, 111, 173; and demagoguery, 173
Sicilian expedition, 5, 18, 115–16, 131–32, 133; and *Birds*, 125–27; in *Lysistrata*, 137
Sicily: comedy in, 25–35; as influence on Athens, 2–3, 5, 9, 19, 23–35; rhetoric in, 24–25
Sidwell, K., 17n, 53n, 170n, 177n
Slater, N. W., 132n

General Index   **231**

Socrates, 8, 83, 90; A.'s depiction of, 8, 83–84, 89–91, 96, 124, 129; Eupolis' depiction of, 117–18; Plato's depiction of, 28
Sommerstein, A. H., 17n, 72n, 116, 166, 168, 170, 181
sophistēs, meaning of, 38, 117
Sophists: in *Birds*, 129; in *Clouds*, 20, 84–86, 88, 91; definition of, 8n; and education, 91; in Epicharmus, 30; *logoi* of, 88; modern views on, 12; as morally destructive, 20, 84, 88–89, 91–92; in *Philoctetes*, 149; Plato on, 8; reputation of, 8–9; rhetoric of, 8–11, 88, 92
Sophocles: compared to Euripides, 163, 171; in *Frogs*, 151, 163, 170, 171; *Oedipus at Colonus*, 148, 154; *Philoctetes*, 148–49; as Proboulos, 148
Sousa e Silva, M. de F., 12, 106, 143n, 168n
spectators: A.'s faith in, 175; Assembly as, 1, 3–4, 56, 57; Chorus as, 56; Cleon as, 75–76; contrasted with participants, 1, 3–4, 53–54, 55, 60, 72, 75–76, 80; Demos as, 175; and *rhētores*, 63–64; in the theater, 1–2; *see also* deliberation
speeches: composition of, 19–20, 30, 33, 39, 52, 60, 72–73, 143; divisions of, 9–10, 18, 34, 57, 59–60, 105–8; *see also* deliberation; metaphors, for speech and oratory; rhetoric
Spievogel, J., 17n
spondai, 87
Storey, I., 42, 118n, 119n, 124
storms, as metaphors for speech, 42, 48, 104, 119, 122; *see also* metaphors
Strauss, B., 17
Strepsiades, 84–86, 90–91, 94–97, 109
success, of the Demos: defined, 65–66; as result of deliberation, 77, 79, 82, 100, 109, 112–13, 129, 138, 139, 144, 145, 156, 159–60, 184; *see also* deliberation; empire; nostalgia
Suter, A. C., 153

Sutton, D. F., 89n
symposia: in A., 30–31; in Epicharmus, 29–30; as influence on comedy, 31; language of, 39, 41
synēgoroi, defined, 97–98
Syracuse, 24

tekmērion, 14
Tell, H., 38n
Tereus, 127, 129
terminology, rhetorical, 13–15, 37–39, 49–50; *see also* rhetoric, formal systems of
theater, as site of deliberation, 53, 61; *see also* Assembly; deliberation; translocation
Themistocles, posthumous reputation of, 77, 120–21
Theoria, in *Peace*, 112
theory, rhetorical. *See* rhetoric, formal systems of
Theramenes, 166, 169, 174–75
Thirty, reign of, 147, 149, 167, 179
Thrasybulus, 147–48
Thrasymachus, 5, 14, 42
Thucydides, 2, 4–5, 54, 56, 115–16, 131, 133–34, 153; and *Birds*, 126; on Cleon, 3–4, 56, 62–63; on Pericles, 47, 110, 121
Thucydides (son of Milesias), 64
Timaeus of Tauromenium, 2, 5
Timmerman, D., 11, 59n
Tindale, C., 11
Tisias, 9, 19, 24–25; and comedy, 33
tongue, as metaphor for troublesome speech, 40, 48, 73, 75, 94, 125, 150, 177; *see also* metaphors
tragedy: and civic identity, 147–48, 152, 161, 172, 176–77; comic parody of, 56, 108
translocation, of debate in A., 52, 58, 66, 76, 78, 82, 94, 104–5, 112, 118, 126, 135, 137–39, 140, 145; *see also* Assembly; deliberation
Trygaeus, 111–12
tyranny: A.'s opposition to, 170; Athe-

nian anxieties about, 67, 71, 101–2, 123–24, 130–31, 142, 148; of the Demos, 80, 101–2; Euripides on, 154–55, 156–57, 158–59, 161; and Pericles, 46–48; and rhetoric, 46–47

Usher, S., 57n, 59n

Westlake, H. D., 135–36
Whitehorne, J., 84n
Willi, A., 15

Wilson, N. G., 69n, 95n
Wilson, P., 60n, 147–48
women: as administrators, 21; included in deliberation, 137–40; *see also* inclusion

youth, as prosecutors of elders, 20, 63–64, 94–95, 97–98, 99, 105, 109
Yunis, H., 63n

Zimmermann, B., 17n
Zimmerman, C., 153

www.ingramcontent.com/pod-product-compliance
Lightning Source LLC
Chambersburg PA
CBHW021756230426
43669CB00006B/97